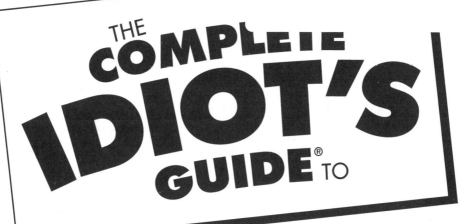

THE
COMPLETE IDIOT'S GUIDE® TO

MP3: Music on the Internet

Rod Underhill
Nat Gertler

201 West 103rd Street, Indianapolis, Indiana 46290

The Complete Idiot's Guide to MP3: Music on the Internet

International Standard Book Number: 0-7897-2036-1

Library of Congress Catalog Card Number: 99-61223

Printed in the United States of America

First Printing: September 1999

02   01   00   99   4   3   2   1

Trademarks

Warning and Disclaimer

Associate Publisher
Greg Wiegand

Acquisitions Editor
Angelina Ward

Development Editor
Gregory Harris

Managing Editor
Thomas F. Hayes

Project Editor
Dana Rhodes Lesh

Copy Editors
Ryan Walsh
Julie McNamee
Tonya Maddox

Indexers
Greg Pearson
Kevin Kent

Proofreader
Tricia A. Sterling

Technical Editor
Lorna Brown

Media Developer
Aaron Price

Team Coordinator
Sharry Gregory

Interior Designer
Nathan Clement

Cover Designer
Michael Freeland

Copy Writer
Eric Borgert

Layout Technician
Louis Porter, Jr.

Contents at a Glance

Contents

vii

8 Sound Squishing 117

9 Spreading Your Sound Around: Distributing Your MP3s 133

Foreword by Roger McGuinn

To begin with, if you're interested in MP3, you're not an idiot; you're on the cutting edge!

My first introduction to MP3 began back in 1996, when a college student came to our home for Thanksgiving dinner. He was aware of my involvement with computer recorded music from having seen my Web page, `http://folkden.com`. On this site, in an effort to preserve traditional folk songs, I place a new audio file each month in several different formats. The visiting college student gave me an MP3 encoder and suggested that I begin encoding my Folk Den songs in MP3. At that time, I didn't see the urgency of doing this, but gradually, as people bought faster computers and as the MP3 format became more popular, I decided that encoding my songs in MP3 would be a good idea.

I now see MP3 to be a silent revolution that will shake the traditional music business to its foundations. The future of music distribution is clearly going away from "brick and mortar," to online sales.

In February of 1999, MP3.com invited me to create a digital automatic music CD on its site. Since doing that, my CD has sold very well, and free MP3 tracks from *McGuinn's Folk Den Vol. 1* have been in MP3.com's Weekly Top 40 for many consecutive months.

I'm extremely excited about this new avenue of artistic expression!

I receive email from people who say, "I'd like to listen to your MP3 songs, but just don't know how to get started." Now fortunately, Rod Underhill and Nat Gertler have written this comprehensive guide, *The Complete Idiot's Guide to MP3: Music on the Internet*, for anyone from the complete novice to the most computer-literate person. I feel confident that this book will provide the answers to your MP3 music questions.

All the best,

Roger McGuinn
`http://mcguinn.com`

About the Authors

Rod Underhill is a musician, composer, songwriter, attorney, and director of music for MP3.com. He will keep singing songs and putting them on the Internet until somebody stops him.

The closest **Nat Gertler** has ever come to musical coolness was when the indescribable Canadian band Moxy Früvous seriously considered naming its second album after him. Nat is a computer-book-writing son-of-a-gun, having penned such popular tomes as *Easy PCs* and *The Complete Idiot's Guide to PowerPoint 2000*. He unleashes his personal creativity through comic books, having worked on well-known titles such as *The Flintstones* and *Blood Syndicate*, as well as on his own creations, *Mister U.S.* and *The Factor*. His ultimate goal is global domination, but he's taking his own sweet time getting around to it.

Dedications

To my mother, Edith Estelle Underhill.

—Rod Underhill

To Lara Hughes, and everyone else who keeps my world filled with music.

—Nat Gertler

Tell Us What You Think!

As the reader of this book, *you* are our most important critic and commentator. We value your opinion and want to know what we're doing right, what we could do better, what areas you'd like to see us publish in, and any other words of wisdom you're willing to pass our way.

As an associate publisher for Que Corporation, I welcome your comments. You can fax, email, or write me directly to let me know what you did or didn't like about this book—as well as what we can do to make our books stronger.

Please note that I cannot help you with technical problems related to the topic of this book, and that due to the high volume of mail I receive, I might not be able to reply to every message.

When you write, please be sure to include this book's title and authors as well as your name and phone or fax number. I will carefully review your comments and share them with the authors and editors who worked on the book.

Fax: (317)581-4666

Email: consumer@mcp.com

Mail: Greg Wiegand
          Associate Publisher
          Que Corporation
          201 West 103rd Street
          Indianapolis, IN 46290 USA

Introduction

The electronic music phenomenon known as *MP3* is stirring up a lot of interest...and not-a-little controversy. By making quality recorded music files small enough to download, MP3 has turned the Internet into a plentiful and practical source of music. This has created vast opportunities for the musician who wants to spread his music around. It has also created vast headaches for the musician (or record company) that doesn't want his music spread around without getting paid for it.

You might wonder just what the heck this MP3 phenomenon is and how it all works. You might be familiar with the technology and wonder where you can find some great music online. You might wonder what choices you have in terms of software or even portable players. You might be a musician wanting to record and distribute your music over the Internet.

Regardless of the origins of your interest in MP3 music, this book is your guide. It has information that will help you, history that will inform you, insights that will enlighten you, and cartoons that will amuse you. It also has a CD-ROM laden with software that will let you listen to and even make MP3s and MP3 files filled with hours of music and more.

Conventions Used in This Book

To get the most out of this book, we've used some standard methods of referring to the items you see onscreen and the things you should type. We've tried to put things together in such a way as to make reading the book both rewarding and fun. So, here's what to do when you see any of the following:

➤ Web page addresses (URLs) are presented in a `computer monospaced font`. When you're being told to click a link on a Web page, the link is presented in **bold**. Click the link (or enter the URL into your browser's address field) to proceed.

➤ Anything you need to type on your computer's keyboard is presented in a `computer monospaced font`. Key combinations are presented using a plus sign (+), such as **Shift+J**. For this combination, you hold down the **Shift** key and press **J**.

➤ New terms are presented in *italicized text*; pay close attention to these terms.

Extras

To pack as much information as possible into *The Complete Idiot's Guide to MP3: Music on the Internet*, we'll present a lot of additional tips and advice as you read the book. These elements enhance your knowledge or point out important pitfalls to avoid. Along the way, you'll find the following elements:

Jam on This

These boxes contain warnings, notes, and other information you'll find useful when using MP3.

Tune Talk

These boxes contain high-tech, in-depth information about the matter at hand. They'll define the sometimes-arcane terminology used by musicians and computer-savvy folk.

Rod Speaks

In these boxes, you'll see the personal opinions and insight from Rod, music director of MP3.com and primary writer of Chapters 9–14 (and Appendix A).

Nat Speaks

...while these boxes give you the skinny as seen by Nat, the cantankerous-yet-lovable author of Chapters 1–8.

Part 1

What the Heck Is MP3, Anyway?

MP3 is hot. It's happening. It's now; it's tomorrow; it's so incredibly next Thursday that I can't hardly believe it! It will cause world peace, bring an end to suffering, and drive the Banana Splits to reunite. It's technological; it's creative; it's digital! *It's the buzzword, the bomb, the real McCoy. Everybody who is anybody is talking about it, as are a few people who aren't anybody but want to be. It's going to be the biggest thing since the last big thing, and even bigger than the one two big things ago.*

But what the heck is it, and where did it come from? In this part of the book, we ask the musical question: Huh…?

Chapter 1

Compressed Music: What It Is and Why You Want It

In This Chapter

➤ What is digital music?

➤ What is compressed digital music?

➤ What is MP3 and what can it do for you?

The Internet is huge, but until recently, it hadn't really been rocking. It's been a great way to get text, and a pretty good way to get pictures, but because our ears are really amazing organs, it was horrible at sending recorded music. Our ears hear very precisely and pick up lots of subtleties in sound, and we can tell if those subtleties aren't right. In order to fool our ears into believing that they are really hearing a band perform, a recording needs to be very precise. The recording needs to hold a lot of information about the original sound.

Information, in computer terms, takes up space. A clearly recorded song takes up a lot of space on a computer's hard drive. Sending that much information over the Internet takes a lot of time. Sending an hour-long CD-quality music recording over the Internet using a fast modem generally takes about a day and a half. In addition, you could probably store only a few of those recordings on your hard disk, even after deleting your copy of *Space Bunny Blaster*, *WordMasher*, and all those romantic emails from that geek you used to date.

MP3 Saves the Day!

All these limitations of online recorded music were true until folks devised a way to use a lot less information to re-create the sound. People now use a format called *MP3* (I'll explain that weird name later) to keep that clear, crisp recording sound—a format that uses about one twelfth as much disk space! Now you have room to keep lots of music on your disk without eliminating the evidence of your geek-dating background (although you may want to do that anyway). Downloading a song takes mere minutes. The Internet is suddenly useful to music fans and music makers.

So What Does MP3 Let Me Do Now?

All this talk about the wonders of compression and sharing your music with the world makes it sound like something from the 1930 World's Fair, telling you how nuclear-powered flying cars will make life a breeze in 1965. Plenty of people are predicting that MP3 is the future, but it's easy to overlook all the wonderful things it can do in the present.

Free Music: Two of My Favorite Words, Together

There are already tens of thousands of songs legally available for download on the Internet, free of charge. More are being added all the time. These songs range from rock to classical, folk to rap. They aren't hard to find, either; there are a number of popular sites that offer large music catalogs.

Much of the free, legal music that's out there is from new and unknown bands, which means that much of it might be somewhat overpriced at "free." However, there are some high-quality discoveries to be made. In addition, more and more established artists are distributing free MP3s to drum up publicity and fan response.

Sink Some Shillings into Some Sounds

There are also sites that let you download popular songs by well-known musicians for a small fee. This fee is much lower than the cost of a CD-single, if that song were even available as a single at the time you went to buy it; the fee is also cheaper still than buying an entire CD for the one song you like. (It's cheaper yet than hiring the famous artist to hang around your house and perform the song whenever you want, although admittedly not nearly so cool.)

At this point, the number of songs available for commercial download is fairly small—at least when compared to the amount of songs available on CDs. However, it has been growing and will likely continue to do so as the music business works out ways to make selling downloadable songs profitable.

The Shu-Bop Heard 'Round the World

If you're a music maker, the MP3 revolution is your chance to get your music to the people. It used to be that to get your music heard, you either had to travel around and perform publicly or find a way to get your music on the radio. If you turn your song into an MP3 file, however, you can put it onto the Internet, where thousands of people a day can download and listen to it.

Turning your recordings into MP3s is easy. Once you've done that, you can upload it to major MP3 Web sites, where others can download it. Not only do the sites not charge for this service, some will also provide free Web space to promote your band, or even help you sell a CD of the recordings you've made.

Even if you're just looking to send the music to one person, emailing your MP3 files means that your music will arrive quickly and sound clear as a bell when received.

Make PC Stand for Polyphonic Collection

If your PC is equipped with the proper sort of CD-ROM drive (and most modern PCs are), you can take tracks from your favorite CDs, compress them into MP3 files, and store them on your hard drive along with all your downloaded MP3s. You'll be able to listen to those through your PC speakers.

"So what? If I wanted to hear the songs on that CD, I'd just play that CD," you mutter. The difference? When that CD is over, you have to go and put on another, and then another, and then another. You also have to suffer through the songs you don't like. Even if you have one of those big CD jukebox things with a randomize setting, you end up hearing all the wrong music at all the wrong times. It's good, but it's not ideal.

If you have all those songs on your hard disk, there's no need to switch CDs! Better yet, you can easily make and store separate *playlists* (lists of songs you want to hear) for different moods. You can have one playlist that tells your MP3-playing software to play only upbeat songs (to pull you out of a bad mood) and another playlist full of nasty and harsh songs (if you want to fully enjoy wallowing in a bad mood).

Portable Player Power

Those MP3 songs don't have to stay on your computer. There are portable MP3 players that let you bring the music with you, and they can do things for you that your CD player never could.

With an all-electronic MP3 player, you can download an hour or so of your favorite music from your PC and carry it with you. These players have no moving parts, which gives them three big advantages over portable CD and cassette players:

➤ They go through a lot fewer batteries. A good MP3 player will use one battery in the same time that a CD player uses four.

9

➤ They're lighter, which is important if you jog.

➤ They're immune to the problems caused by shaking and jostling. Shake a CD player and the music will skip. Shake a cassette player and the music will tend to screech. Shake an all-electronic MP3 player, and your arm eventually grows tired.

If your PC has a *CD-R* (CD recorder) drive, you're ready to take advantage of a different sort of MP3 player. A CD-based MP3 player looks like a standard portable CD player; in fact, it will play standard CDs. The player also can read MP3-compressed songs from CD-ROMs. Those CD-ROMs can store around 12 hours of music. (Standard CDs store about 74 minutes.) By making your own MP3 CD-ROMs, you can carry around your entire Beatles collection on a single disk, your entire Wu-Tang Clan collection on another. You can even make a disk with all of the Starland Vocal Band's greatest hits and still have 11 hours and 56 minutes worth of other music!

But I Heard MP3s Were Evil and Cause Warts!

There have been a lot of negative stories in the media lately about MP3. The record industry has come out attacking this format. If it's just a simple and high-quality way to compress music, what's all the fuss about?

The problem (as the record companies see it) is that it's *too* simple and *too* high-quality.

A lot of people have been purchasing CDs, making MP3s out of the songs, and illegally sharing those files online with people who have not paid for the music. The record industry fears that people who would otherwise have bought the CDs are instead listening to these illegal MP3 copies. Performers don't make any money from the illegal copies. Worse yet (in record industry eyes), the record companies don't make any money.

Of course, illegally duplicating music is nothing new. The record industry hasn't just been going after the illegal copiers, however. They've been going after MP3 altogether, through attacks in the media and in the courtroom.

Later in this book, we'll discuss the legal and ethical implications of MP3s and talk about how you can use them legally.

What Is Digitally Compressed Music, Anyway?

Music for Mathematicians

Deep inside, computers only really deal with numbers. If you want to find a way for a computer to deal with a word, a picture, or anything else, you have to find a way to convert that thing into a series of numbers. For example, when a computer is dealing with words, it's using a special code, in which the letter *a* is 32, the letter *b* is 33, and so on.

Sound is not naturally made up of numbers. Sound is actually a very small vibrating motion (called a *sound wave*) that is carried through the air. That vibrating motion shakes your eardrum, and that's how you pick up sound. A microphone is just a device that turns that air bounce into an electrical vibration that heads down the microphone cord. Speakers work the other way, turning vibrating electricity into vibrating air.

This is a drawing of a sound wave. How quickly does sound bounce? This sound lasts about 1/200th of a second.

Turning sound into numbers is called *digitizing*. A computer keeps checking that sound, repeatedly measuring how high the bounce is. By stringing together these measurements (called *samples*), the computer records the path of that bounce. How exact the re-creation of the vibration is depends on how precise each measurement is and how frequently the measurement is taken. For example, sound measurement on a CD (which was the first popular form of digitally recorded sound) takes over 44 thousand samples per second—each sample can be any of 65,536 different heights. As if that isn't enough, it's doing that all twice, to record separate sounds for the left and right ears and thus make *stereo*. Sure is a good thing we have computers to do the work because it would take a long time to figure that all out by hand!

When the recording is stored on a CD or as an uncompressed computer recording (called a *WAV*—pronounced *wave*—*file*), the file just has a list of the value of each sample. You can easily understand how all those thousands of samples add up to a lot of information very quickly.

The same sound, digitized. Each column is a single sample, measuring the height of the wave at a single moment.

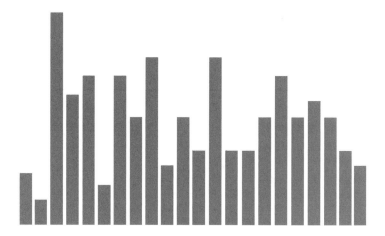

Sound Squishing

Your ears are amazing things. In addition to helping keep your sunglasses from falling into your soup, they can also hear precisely enough that they don't get fooled easily. Thousands of sound samples per second are needed to fool the ear. At least, that's true for part of the sound.

For other parts of the sound, though, the ear is not so precise. It doesn't recognize all of the information that's in an uncompressed file. If that information isn't being used, why bother saving it? That's where a lot of the compression takes place: getting rid of sound information you can't hear.

Another aspect of MP3 compression is that the vibration of sound goes up and down in certain shapes. Just as you can't step down 100 feet with one step and then up 100 feet with the next (unless you have pogo shoes!), a series of samples can't bounce quickly between the highest and lowest possible measurement. Instead, the sound moves smoothly from level to level. The compression can record the shape of the sound more efficiently than recording the height of every single point along the curve.

Stereo offers another place to use less information. An uncompressed digital recording stores separate full recordings for each ear. The two recordings are very similar. MP3 uses less information space by keeping one main recording, and then keeping track of how the sound differs from ear to ear.

Finally, MP3 saves space by keeping track of repeating information. If the same number is repeated 10,000 times in a row in an uncompressed file, all that information is stored on the disk. It's kind of like telling someone to get to the store by saying "walk one block north, then another block north, then another block north, then another block north…." When the MP3 compressor sees repeated information, it counts the repetitions and stores the information, as well as how many times it repeats ("walk 10 blocks north").

Tune Talk

Lawsy Me, It's Lossy!

Because the MP3 format doesn't store all of the information that's in the uncompressed sound file, it's considered a *lossy* format. In the rate of compression usually used with MP3, that loss makes no difference in what you can hear. Once you have an MP3 file, you can copy and recopy it, and the sound never gets any worse, which makes it much better than a cassette tape. Every time you copy one cassette to another you end up losing sound quality, but MP3 copies *losslessly*.

Tune Talk

High Fidelity Details

My description of MP3 compression is obviously not very detailed. It's actually more than you'll ever need to know, unless you're going to design your own MP3 recorder or player. If you're an audio-theory buff and not afraid of advanced math and a lot of technobabble, however, you can find more detailed descriptions of the compression scheme at www.iocon.com/mp3/coding.html on the Web.

Squishing Sound to Death

When we say that compressed MP3 music sounds are as good as uncompressed music, we're talking about the best qualities of MP3 compression. You can use MP3 to compress different amounts. Even if you have a complex sound specifically chosen so that the ear could detect any loss in sound quality, you can compress that sound to one-sixth of its original size and still have a re-creation so perfect that your ears can't tell the difference. With standard music, you can compress down to one-tenth the space and it will sound like CD-quality to most people (although they might be able to tell the difference if they carefully compare the compressed version to the uncompressed version).

Things get a little trickier if you want to compress a sound even further than that. Compressing it that much will lose some of the information, and there will be an audible difference in quality. It's kind of like how they take coffee and turn it into instant coffee—when you turn it back into coffee, it still looks and tastes and smells like coffee. It just doesn't look and taste and smell like good coffee.

You see, in order to save space, the compressing program starts throwing away some of the vital information of the sound. The notes just won't sound as crisp or as clear. It will sound less like a CD and more like listening to the same music over an FM radio. Compress it more, and it sounds like an AM radio. Compress it even more, and it sounds like it's coming out of an old See 'n Say toy. Still, highly compressed sound can be good for things that don't need high-quality recording, such as books on tape or audio letters from Aunt Martha.

The Least You Need to Know

➤ *Digital* music is music that is stored as a series of numbers. Computers can only handle digital music.

➤ *Compressed digital music* is digital music that has been stored in a way that takes up a lot less space, without compromising sound quality. *MP3* is a popular format for compressed digital music.

➤ There is plenty of music available for free on the Internet in the MP3 format. You can also take music from CDs you own and convert it into the MP3 format.

➤ You can play MP3 format music on your computer and on special portable MP3 players.

Chapter 2

MP3: A Compressed History

In This Chapter

➤ What does *MP3* mean?

➤ Where did MP3 come from?

➤ How did MP3 become so big?

The MP3 file format didn't just spring up out of nowhere. All that compression, that controversy, that potential—it all came from somewhere. Even that cryptic name—*MP3*—doesn't give away any clues. Perhaps you will better understand where MP3 came from if you know what the *MP* stands for.

Well, the MP stands for *moving pictures*.

No, that doesn't help. It doesn't even make sense.

MPEG: Many Professional Engineers Gather

Most file formats come from companies. A company coming out with a word processor creates a file format to store word processing documents, or a company (say, MicroCat) with a cat-folding program comes up with a document to store cat-folding designs. If another company (DataCat) wants to put out its own cat-folding program, it comes up with its own file format. You may not be able to move a cat-folding design easily from one program to another, but it's not often that you'd need to.

If you need to be able to use the same file with various programs, there are two ways to go. One is to pick the format already used by a popular program and have everyone design their programs to use that format. The problem with this option is that MicroCat's format, while well-designed for MicroCat's programs, may not be able to hold the information that other programs need. Plus, anytime MicroCat puts out a new program, it can change how the file format works and mess everyone up.

The other way is for everyone to work together, teaming up a bunch of engineers from various companies and from academia, and have them work on the format. By doing it that way, you make a format that is useful for everyone and that isn't owned by any one company. *Standards organizations* exist not only to design file formats, but to design all sorts of standards for physical and electronic items, so that light bulbs by one manufacturer fit into sockets made by another, and important things like that.

ISO: Is Surely Official

The big boy of standards organizations is the *International Standards Organization*, better known as the *ISO*. The folks at the ISO saw that digital TV was on the way and that in order to save information space, they would need a standard method of compression to handle digital video. In January of 1988, they gathered together 25 experts in the field and called them the *Moving Pictures Expert Group*, or *MPEG*.

MPEG set about inventing a *codec* (short for *compressor/decompressor*) standard for video. Its first standard, MPEG-1, came out in July of 1989. MPEG-1 was designed for video stored and played on computers. When you buy a video CD, you don't just have a very shiny coaster, you also have MPEG-1!

Three Layers, No Frosting

Early moving pictures (or *movies*, as the young folk call them) had no sound, and people liked it that way. Then again, some of them also liked playing mumblety-peg. Nowadays, we can't even pronounce *mumblety-peg*, and we expect sound with our movies. We want to hear every nuance of Charlie Brown's teacher's speech. Because of this, it was important that MPEG-1 have a format for compressed sound to mix with the compressed video.

Those wacky MPEGeniuses didn't come up with a way by themselves. They basically got the German company Fraunhofer-IIS to come up with a way. Actually, they came up with three ways, calling them *layers*:

➤ *Layer I* only uses a few of the compression tricks. The downside of this is that it doesn't compress very well. The upside is that decompression doesn't take a very powerful computer.

➤ *Layer II* uses more of the compression tricks. It compresses okay, but needs a more powerful computer to decompress it.

➤ *Layer III* uses the whole bag of tricks, but it needs a very powerful personal computer to decompress it. Very powerful, that is, by 1989 standards. A decade later, and just about any computer you can get will be more than adequate.

Is This How KRS-1 Got His Name?

Now there's this great method of compressing sound in a video file and some smart engineer says, "If I want just music in the file, why don't I just use this method?" Thus, the format is separated from the video usage. The engineer needs to create a file extension for this format. A *file extension* is a period followed by up to three characters that come at the end of a filename; the extension identifies what type of file it is. Four characters are often used outside the Windows world, but you have to stick with three if you want Windows to understand it.

Other M-pressive MPEGgings

The efforts of the Moving Picture Experts Group did not end with MPEG-1. The group not only continued to work, but also grew, going from 25 experts to 350. They followed up MPEG-1 with MPEG-2, which was a standard for full-digital television compression. The future of TV is very much tied to MPEG-2, with its usage in HDTV. In fact, it's a growing part of the present, as DVDs use MPEG-2 video.

MPEG-2 also included some improvements for Layer III audio, including the capability to handle all the channels of sound needed for today's home theater systems. Oddly enough, North American DVDs don't use MPEG audio compression. Instead, they include another form of compression developed by Dolby, building that into the MPEG-2 compressed video. The group later added a standard for somewhat improved sound compression to MPEG-2. This standard is *Advanced Audio Compression (AAC)*, but some folks just refer to it as MP4.

The MPEG-4 standard goes beyond defining just a single stream of sounds and pictures in a fixed order. Instead, it's designed around setting up an audio–video scene, which can be used for interactive purposes. Expect to be running into MPEG-4 in ATMs, interactive advertising, and video Whack-a-Mole games.

Work is zooming along on MPEG-7, a standardized manner for describing multimedia content. Eventually, MPEG-7 will make it easier for you to search the Web for national anthems sung by house pets, for example.

To learn more about the Moving Pictures Expert Group, surf on over to `http://drogo.cselt.stet.it/mpeg/` on the Web.

To fit this short description area, *MPEG-1 Audio Layer III* gets compressed to the *.mp3* file extension. People saw this and simply began referring to them as *MP3 files*. Thus, a name was born.

MP3 Goes to School

Once you have a compressed music standard in place and software available to compress and play this music, it's all ready to take off. All you need are the right conditions to get it started. You need some place with a lot of people who are into music, people with computers, people with a good understanding of those computers, lots of data storage, and some high-speed data connections to make it all quick and easy.

In other words, you need a college—a wonderful place for playing with computers, listening to music, and all sorts of things that let you avoid starting that report on the economics of southeast West Virginia that isn't due for a whole three hours yet.

Repositories of thousands of songs have begun popping up on college hard disks. Students from various schools exchange songs via the Internet. Leaving your computer running in the background playing the latest tunes is now common. The students are quite happy, even those dressed in black.

The record companies aren't so happy, though. They love it when a student shells out $16.99 for a copy of Depressed Students In Black's latest release, *Sophisticated Pouting*. When that student converts all the songs on the album into MP3s and puts them on a network where everyone can get them, the record companies are less than happy. Suddenly, it is not only cheaper but actually easier for thousands of students to get the album over the Internet rather than buying the album or having a friend tape it. This illegal distribution worries the record companies because it looks like the wave of the future.

Little Bit Legal

Not all MP3s were illegal, even in the early days. Techno-savvy music composers started distributing their creations in MIDI format via computer long before there were MP3s; those composers quickly expanded to show off their work via MP3s. Bands only needed one computer nerd—er, I mean *enthusiast*—among their members or fans to get themselves compressed.

These weren't generally bands anyone had heard of, and MP3 seemed like a good way to spread their sound around. Since it was their own music, it was perfectly legal for the bands to spread it around in that format. In terms of showing off the band at its best, this high-quality electronic reproduction worked a lot better than encouraging fans to make tapes for their friends, with each generation of tapes sounding worse than the last.

What's This MIDI Stuff?

MIDI stands for *Musical Instrument Digital Interface*. If an MP3 file is the computer version of a CD, then a MIDI file is the computer equivalent of sheet music. The MIDI file contains a list of what instruments are supposed to be heard and what notes each instrument is supposed to play. MIDI files are often used to control electronic instruments. People downloading them from the Internet can listen to the music on their PC, which synthesizes the sound of the instruments. When your PC synthesizes a glockenspiel, for example, it may sound very different than when the composer's PC synthesizes a glockenspiel. What you're hearing may not be what he intended, and the file has no efficient way to include vocal recordings.

The MOD file is a cousin of the MIDI file. It too can include a digital sample of one note from each instrument. The PC playing the MOD file can use this sample to create the same sound as the composer intended—but there's still no way to include vocals.

One advantage to MIDI files is their small size. They're typically less than 20KB, compared to several megabytes for an MP3 file.

Most of these legal MP3s were overlooked in the past, however, in the vast stream of illegal tracks from well-known names. When you're trying to find Public Enemy or Sheryl Crow, it's easy to ignore Bouncing Joe and His Almost All-Girl Band.

Dotcomming the Format

At first, the MP3 craze was largely an invisible movement. You could look around the World Wide Web and see no mention of it if you weren't looking specifically for it—but people were looking for it. They had heard about this stuff. Some were searching for large sites full of illegal MP3 tracks, or for the software needed to make and play MP3s.

The folks in the Web business noticed and began setting up sites for the MP3 fans. Consider Michael Robertson. Here's a guy who wasn't a particularly fervent music buff. He didn't even know what MP3 was. But Michael had a Web site called filez.com, which was a popular search engine for finding downloadable files. As a good businessman, he kept an eye on what it was that people were searching for, and he noticed that two words kept popping up: *sex* and *MP3*.

Michael knew what sex was. In fact, he'd heard good things about it. He also knew that there were already plenty of Web sites offering sex (or at least as close to sex as anyone can put out on the Internet).

Master of His Domain

A little research told Michael not only what MP3 was, but also that there really wasn't a major Web site feeding this lust for MP3 files. Someone had already bought the rights to the Web site name MP3.com, paying $100 for the name. Michael offered a full $1,000 for the site name—a 900% markup.

In November 1997, Michael took that name and opened a Web site that offered thousands of free downloadable MP3 files. You could also download from MP3.com all the necessary MP3 software and instructions on how to use it. MP3.com is currently worth more than 10 million dollars.

It took more than just the name to get there. Michael didn't just discover the MP3 format, he fell in love with it. He quickly grew to be one of its most visible champions, speaking out for and defending MP3 at all opportunities, and employing other MP3 enthusiasts such as my co-author, Rod Underhill.

Legal and Legitimate

The folks at MP3.com worked to make sure that the MP3 files on their site were legal. Some of them are from well-known acts, but the vast majority are from those who are struggling to succeed or those who have no particular designs toward big-time record contracts.

Because the people who find sites like MP3.com aren't finding a lot of pirated music, they're eagerly downloading what they do find. Someone downloads a song by an unknown band millions of times per month. It's really the free and legal sites that are spearheading MP3 as a way for fresh young bands (and refreshing old ones) to reach a new audience.

MP3 Without PC for Me, You See

The time is March, 1998. The location is an electronics trade show in Hannover, Germany. The event is the unveiling of the very first portable MP3 player. The MPMan F10, manufactured by the Korean company Saehan Information Systems, Inc., grabs a lot of acclaim at the show.

The mainstream media doesn't pay much attention to MP3 until the release of a competing product. Diamond Multimedia, best known for its powerful PC video cards, tries to compete with the MPMan with its own unit, the Rio. The product gets good reviews, but it also gets negative reaction from some very powerful folks: the Recording Industry Association of America (RIAA). RIAA exists to represent the needs and desires of the big CD publishers.

R-I-A-A Versus R-I-O

The RIAA is against MP3, having seen how it can be used to pirate millions of dollars worth of music. The Rio, with its capability to carry MP3 music beyond the constraints of the PC, seems to scare them. They raised a legal fuss over the Rio, trying to prevent its release.

Do they stop it from coming out? No. In fact, it backfires on them. They draw press attention to the product. This publicity generates a large demand for the Rio. (For more on the details of this lawsuit, see Chapter 12, "Pirates, Legal Troubles, and Big Business.")

Meanwhile, the recording industry has formed the *Secured Digital Music Initiative* (*SDMI*), its attempt to provide a piracy-proof alternative to MP3. The SDMI works with various manufacturers trying to come up with a format that would let the recording industry sell music online while preventing people from distributing the files. (Of course, they could sell MP3 files, but then one buyer could distribute the file to all her friends or post them on her Web page.) Several different formats exist, but so far there is little consumer interest in them. They rely on *encryption*, electronic scrambling of the music. Only the purchaser can decode and play the song clip.

And here we are today: a popular yet controversial file format, Web sites with thousands of legal songs, portable players, one riled recording industry, and millions of MP3 fans.

The Least You Need to Know

➤ The Moving Pictures Expert Group came up with the MPEG audio/video compression format.

➤ The format known as MP3 is actually Audio Layer III of the MPEG-1 standard.

➤ MP3 first gained popularity as a separate audio format on highly computer-connected college campuses.

➤ MP3 has generated controversy due to the ease with which music can be pirated and recording industry attempts to suppress MP3 products.

Part 2

Getting and Playing MP3s

So far, we've talked mainly about the compressed *part of compressed music. If that's the part you're most interested in, you're probably a science geek. (Although as a reformed science geek myself, I can tell you that even geeks like a good tune—although our favorites tend to be things like Tom Lehrer singing "The Elements" or that Flanders and Swann song that explains the first and second laws of thermodynamics.)*

In this part of the book, we talk about the music. Specifically, we tell you where you can download music from the Web as well as how to set up software to play MP3s. We even take a look at the new and upcoming MP3-playing hardware, so you can listen to your tunes on the go.

Chapter 3

Installing and Using MP3 Player Software

In This Chapter

➤ How do you install MP3 software from the CD-ROM?

➤ How do you play music?

➤ How do you set up your Web browser to work with your MP3 player?

As far as your computer is concerned, an *MP3 file* is just a string of ones and zeros. It's not much fun unless you have a way to convert it back into sound. To do that, you'll need a computer with speakers, and you'll need an *MP3 player*, a program that reads the file and sends the sound to the speakers.

The Windows Media Player

If you have a recent copy of Windows 98, you may already have an MP3 player. Windows 95 and 98 comes with the Windows Media Player, a program that can interpret a number of sound and video formats. Although earlier versions of this program don't play MP3s, newer versions do. Microsoft got hassled by the recording industry for including MP3 compatibility. Between that and the fact that Microsoft is now promoting its own alternative to MP3, don't be surprised if future versions of Windows don't include that feature. (Finding out whether your version of Media Player supports MP3s is easy: Try following the instructions here for playing MP3s. If they don't work, you don't have a compatible version!)

If you use the Web-based Windows Update feature in Windows 98 (click the **Start** button, choose **Settings**, and then choose **Windows Update**), your system can automatically check to see if you have the latest version, and recommend that you download the new one if you don't. If you're using Windows 95, you can just point your Web browser to `http://www.microsoft.com/windows/mediaplayer/` and download the current version.

Playing Songs with the Windows Media Player

You can start Windows Media Player and select a song in several ways. If you haven't installed any other MP3 players, Windows knows that the Media Player will work with your MP3 files. Find an icon for an MP3 file (using Windows Explorer, or by double-clicking the **My Computer** icon on your desktop and finding it there). Double-click the **MP3** file icon, and the Windows Media Player starts up and starts playing that song.

Finding the Song Files on the CD-ROM

To locate the free music tracks included on the CD-ROM that came with this book, put the CD-ROM into your CD-ROM drive. Double-click the **My Computer** icon on your desktop. In the resulting window, double-click the icon for your CD-ROM drive. The contents of the CD-ROM will appear. Double-click the folder marked **Music**, and you will see folders containing all the song files, broken down by musical genre. Double-click the folder of your choice and double-click one of the songs to begin playing it.

You can also start the Windows Media Player by clicking the **Start** button and selecting **Programs**, **Accessories**, **Entertainment**, **Windows Media Player**. This sequence starts the program, but it doesn't begin playing a song. You can play a song by choosing **File**, **Open**, clicking the **Browse** button, selecting a song file by navigating to it in the Open dialog box, and then clicking **OK**.

Controlling Windows Media Player

The Windows Media Player interface for MP3 files is fairly simple. That's because it really can't do much, just load up one song and play it. The following are the controls:

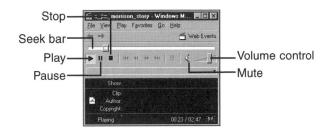

Stop

Seek bar

Play

Pause

Volume control

Mute

The Windows Media Player appears like this when playing audio formats. It may appear different when first opened because it's set up a bit differently when it expects to play a video file.

➤ The *Play button* starts a song playing after it has been stopped or paused.

➤ The *Pause button* stops the song. After pausing, the Play button restarts the song right where it left off.

➤ The *Stop button* stops the song. After stopping, the Play button restarts the song at the beginning.

➤ Dragging the slider box across the *Seek bar* changes what section of the song is playing. The left end of the bar represents the beginning of the song; the right end represents the tune's end.

➤ Dragging the *Volume control* bar left decreases the volume; going right increases it. (You'll likely find it easier to leave this control on high, and use your speaker's volume control to adjust.)

➤ Click the *Mute button* to silence the song quickly. The song keeps on playing, you just can't hear it. Yes, this is kind of stupid. It makes a lot more sense if you're using the Windows Media Player to view a video. Click it a second time to resume hearing the song.

Drag and Drop Is Not a Drag at All

Most MP3 players support *drag and drop*. This means that after you've started the program, you can drag the icon for an MP3 file from a Windows Explorer window, from the desktop, or from any other file icon display, into the program window to play the song. Drag and drop is an easy way to handle things; just leave a window open displaying your song files.

Better yet, if the player program puts an icon on the desktop (and most do), you don't even have to start the program first. Instead, just drag the song's icon over the program icon and release the mouse button.

Other Media Player Features

The Media Player is a basic, no-frills viewer for a wide range of audio and video formats. It can play CD audio tracks, MIDI files, WAV files, and videos in MPEG, QuickTime, and AVI formats, among others. You can open those files in the same way that you open MP3 files.

Virtuosa Gold for Windows

Virtuosa Gold, created by AudioSoft (`www.audiosoft.com/virtuosa/`), is more than just an MP3 player. It also plays CD tracks, WAV files, and MIDI files, among other formats. It can convert songs from your CDs into MP3s, and (if you have a CD-R) help you make CDs.

The full version of Virtuosa Gold will cost you about $30. The version on the CD-ROM is an evaluation version. It works fine as a player forever, at no charge to you. Unless you pay for it, the convert-to-MP3 functions only work on the first track of a CD, and the conversion and CD-burner functions stop working after 15 days.

Virtuosa Requirements

The Virtuosa program requires Windows 95 or higher (including Windows NT), running on a Pentium or faster processor. You will, of course, need a sound card and a CD-ROM drive. The CD-burning program supports a long list of CD-R drives, although it's missing some of the earliest ones.

Installing Virtuosa Gold

To install Virtuosa Gold, first insert the CD-ROM that accompanies this book. Close any running programs. Next, double-click the **My Computer** icon on your Windows desktop. In the resulting window, double-click the icon for your CD-ROM drive to view its contents. Double-click the **Programs** folder, and when that opens, double-click the **VirtuosaGold** icon.

The program spends some time unpacking files it needs from the compressed file on the CD-ROM and placing them on your hard disk, like some unexpected guest unpacking its suitcase and using up your closet space. It throws its logo on the screen for a few seconds, and then opens an installation program.

The first screen that appears is the Welcome screen. Click **Next** to move on to the licensing agreement. Read this, and if you agree to it, click **Yes**.

The next screen is marked Choose Destination Location. By default, the program is installed in a new AudioSoft folder in your main program folder. This is a good place for it, so click **Next**. (If you want to put it somewhere else besides your main disk, or just want to change the folder it goes in because you have nothing better to do, click **Browse** to invoke a file navigator that will let you choose the location.)

Next is the Select Components screen. Click **Next** again. (Yes, that's a popular button.) Doing so brings you to Select Program Folder. You can select an existing program folder from the list, type a name for a new folder, or just accept the default, a new program folder named AudioSoft (which is a good choice only if you love to memorize the name of the manufacturer of every program you use;

otherwise, type in a recognizable name, such as Virtuosa MP3). Guess what you click next? That's right, **Next**!

The next screen gives you a serial number and tells you to write it down somewhere. This serial number is used to create and identify MP3s that can only be played on your machine. Using this number, music sites can sell you files that will only work on your PC, so they don't have to worry about you emailing the song to all your friends. Copy it down somewhere handy (my monitor case is covered with sticky notes containing information like this, many of which I will never use again), and then click **Next**.

A form with spaces for your name, country, and email address appears. You have to provide at least your name and country, or the installation will not continue. Then click (drum roll, please) **Next**. The Start Copying Files screen now appears, and it's time for you to exercise your **Next**-clicker for the last time. The program starts copying all the files onto your hard drive. When it's done, the Setup Complete screen appears. Click **Finish**, and the installation program closes. A window appears telling you when your trial period runs out. Click **OK**, and the program starts.

License Agreeee...snnnnnore

Yes, license agreements are long, boring, often badly written legal documents. A lot of people just skip reading them. But it is something you're agreeing to legally, so you really may want to look it over. After you've read a few of them, you'll find they tend to look the same.

Automatic Launch Can Fail

Sometimes the Virtuosa program doesn't start properly the first time, due to problems with the launcher. If this happens, the program closes itself automatically. Restart it using the **Start** menu.

Playing Songs with Virtuosa

The Virtuosa window opens with a number of smaller windows inside it. Initially, you see a Music Data Base window, a Now Playing window, a CD Player window, and a Volume window.

Virtuosa Gold has so many windows that it's practically a greenhouse.

Music Data Base window

Now Playing window   CD Player window   Volume control

Double-Think the Double-Click

Unlike many Windows MP3 players, Virtuosa cannot be set up as your default player for MP3 files. Finding an MP3 with Windows Explorer or My Computer and then double-clicking the icon won't start up Virtuosa.

The Music Data Base is where Virtuosa keeps track of all the songs on your hard disk. When you first start using Virtuosa, you're going to want to add all your songs to the data base. The easiest way to do so is to right-click the window and choose **Add Tracks**. A file browser opens. Navigate to the directory where you have MP3 files stored, press **Ctrl+A** to select all the music files in that directory, and then click **Open**. All of those files are added to the Music Data Base. (You can also use drag-and-drop to drag file icons out of a file browser window into the Music Data Base window.) To play any song in the data base, just click it. If you don't see the data base window, press **F2** and it appears.

Managing the Data Base

Some song files have the name of the artist and the track built into them, and Virtuosa uses this information to make them easier to keep track of. For other songs, all Virtuosa knows is the filename, which isn't the best thing to use when finding a single song out of the hundreds you'll have on your hard disk. Right-click a song and choose **Properties** from the pop-up menu; a form appears with spaces for the artist name, the album name, and the song name. Fill these out and then press **Enter**, and Virtuosa will know and display this information.

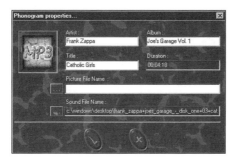

Virtuosa refers to your file as a phonogram. *Try using that word without being laughed at!*

If you want to add information on a bunch of songs from the same album, hold down the **Ctrl** key, and click each song from the album. When you have them all selected, release the **Ctrl** key. Right-click any selected song and choose **Properties**. The Properties form appears, but with check boxes above the fields for performer and album name. Put a check in those check boxes, and then fill in the performer and album name. Virtuosa adds that information to all the selected tracks.

Virtuosa can sort the songs by artist, album, file date, or song title. The name of what it's currently sorted on is shown on the window's title bar. Click the **Sort** button in the Music Data Base window to cycle through the different methods of sorting.

Creating Virtuosa Playlist

You don't want to keep interrupting whatever you're doing every time a song ends. If you're playing a track from the data base, Virtuosa automatically follows it up by playing the next track on the list. Remember, songs are arranged alphabetically by default. So if you have a favorite Barenaked Ladies song you've been listening to, after it's done, you're likely to be hearing your four-year-old son's favorite Barney the Dinosaur ditty. Or your favorite Raffi song might be followed by your three-year-old daughter's favorite Rage Against the Machine tune.

Does the Program Recognize Voices, or What?

Many players can automatically identify the musician and the title of songs. This recognition isn't some magic trick; it's due to *ID3*, a standard for embedding track information into an MP3 file. It's up to the person who encodes the file to include this information, and many people don't remember to do it, so there's a lot of MP3s out there without this information.

To avoid this problem, Virtuosa lets you create *compilations*, lists of songs that you want to play together. (Most MP3 players refer to such lists as *playlists*.) That way, you can create a playlist with all the songs from the same album, or all your jazz tracks, or a list of songs about Warren G. Harding.

To create a compilation, press **F3** to open the compilation list window. This window shows all the compilations you've made. Click **New Compilation** to create a new one. A form appears for you to enter the name of the compilation. Type something descriptive and press **Enter**.

A new window appears, with the compilation name in the title. To add songs to the compilation, just drag them from the data base window into the compilation window. When you do this, the song stays on the data base list as well as on the compilation list. If you want to, you can put the song "I'm Allergic to the Sight of You" by Whinemaster Mark into every compilation you make.

Sequence your songs by dragging and dropping!

To start playing from a compilation, just click any song in the window. Virtuosa plays the list of songs starting with that song. If you want to rearrange the order of the songs on the compilation, just drag any song from where it is on the list to a new position.

Don't Play Out of Control!

To control the playing of the song, use the Now Playing window. (Pressing **F4** opens this window, if it isn't already open.) Across the top of the window are a series of VCR-style buttons:

➤ *Previous Track* starts playing the previous song on the list.

➤ *Play* restarts playing the song after it has been stopped or paused.

➤ *Pause* stops playing the track, but remembers just where it left off.

➤ *Stop* stops playing the track, and resets to the beginning of the track.

➤ *Next Track* skips ahead to the next song.

At the bottom of the window is a slider, showing what portion of the song you're hearing. Drag it left to hear earlier in the song or right to hear later in the song.

The Virtuosa song-playing controls.

The Volume window, of course, controls the volume of the playback. Drag the oval up to make it louder, or down to make it quieter. Dragging it left or right adjusts the balance between the stereo speakers.

Using Other Virtuosa Features

Using Virtuosa to convert CD tracks to MP3 is covered in Chapter 8, "Sound Squishing." To learn more about using Virtuosa to play CDs, burn CD-ROMs, or purchase and download copy-controlled songs, use Virtuosa's help system. Press **F1** to access Help. If you explore this system, you'll find that Virtuosa has many subtleties and options that you can take advantage of.

Newer Versions Can Be Had!

The various programs that come on the CD–ROM were the newest version we could put out with the book. However, MP3 is a rapidly growing field, and newer versions of these programs are being released frequently. When you decide which program you like, check out the company's Web site. You'll probably find a more recent version of the program on there, with new features, improved old features, and old bugs replaced with new ones.

Winamp for Windows

Winamp is an MP3 player program manufactured by Nullsoft (www.winamp.com), a small company which has been bought out by online megacorporation AOL. The program is a player only; it can't encode MP3s, burn CD-ROMs, or juggle tubas. It will play MP3 files, CD tracks, and a number of other formats. It's a colorful and feature-laden player, and a lot of people are creating cool customizations for it.

Winamp Requirements

Winamp requires Windows 95 or 98, or Windows NT 4 or higher. It will run on a very fast 486, but you're better off if you have a processor of Pentium-or-better power.

Installing Winamp

To install Winamp, first insert the CD-ROM that accompanies this book. Close any running programs. Next, double-click the **My Computer** icon on your Windows desktop. In the resulting window, double-click the icon for your CD-ROM drive to view its contents. Double-click the **Programs** folder, and when it opens, double-click the **winamp223** icon. A dialog box opens suggesting a folder to store the program files in. Click **Next**.

Jam on This

Winamp Is Shareware

Shareware is a system where sharing your software files with others is encouraged (as opposed to software you buy in a store, where sharing it is generally illegal). Anyone can try out a copy of Winamp for 14 days at no cost. If you like the software and want to keep using it on your machine, then you pay for it. The price is just $10 for personal use, $25 for commercial use. If you have a credit card, you can pay for it at Nullsoft's Web site (www.winamp.com). Otherwise, just mail your payment to: Nullsoft Inc., 60 Palisades Drive North, Sedona, Arizona 86336, USA.

A dialog box appears with a checklist of options:

➤ **Autoplay Audio CDs**   Whenever you put a CD into your CD-ROM drive, Winamp launches and starts playing the CD.

➤ **Make Winamp the Default Audio Player**   Whenever you double-click an icon for an MP3 or other sound file, Winamp automatically starts. If you don't select this option, you can still use Winamp to play your sound files. You'll just have to start Winamp first, and then tell it to play the file.

➤ **Add Group to Start Menu**   Creates a new Winamp group in the Programs section of your Start menu.

➤ **Add Icon to Desktop**   Puts a Winamp icon on your desktop.

➤ **Add Icon to Quick Launch Bar**   Puts a Winamp icon on your quick launch bar, which most Windows 98 or Windows NT users will find just to the right of the Start button.

➤ **An Internet connection-style drop-down list**   Choose the type of Internet connection you use.

➤ **Check for New Versions of Winamp**   Checks over the Internet from time to time, and tells you when a new version of Winamp is available.

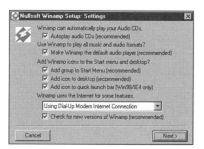

You can choose to let Winamp practically take over your system!

Make your selections and click **Next** again. A window opens displaying the contents of the new Winamp program group. You may have to close this window to see the dialog box that asks you for personal information. If you don't want to bother with this step, you can click **Later**. Otherwise, fill it out and click **Next**. (They do ask some personal information, like age and gender, but they swear that it's just for statistical purposes. Be sure to keep the **Please send me Winamp announcements** check box clear if you worry about getting too much email.) After you fill in the information, Winamp connects to the Internet. (You may need to click the **Connect** button on your Dial-Up Connection dialog box for the connection to go through.)

After you're done, a dialog box offers you a link to run a *Winamp Flash Walkthrough*, a quick tutorial session. You'll need the Macromedia Flash plug-in for your browser for this tutorial to work. Click the link to do that, or just click the **Run Winamp** button to get started.

Starting Winamp Playing

There are a lot of ways to start Winamp playing an individual song. If Winamp isn't already playing, you can double-click the icon for any song file (if you chose to set up Winamp as your default audio file player) or drag and drop the icon onto the Winamp logo on your desktop.

*The Winamp window has four sections, each of which can be separated or closed by clicking on its own small Close (**X**) button.*

After you've started Winamp running (either by one of the methods I just mentioned, by using the Start menu, by double-clicking the Winamp icon, or by clicking on the Winamp button on the quick launch bar), you'll see that the Winamp display has four sections:

➤ Player

➤ Equalizer

➤ Playlist

➤ Browser

You can start a song by dragging and dropping a song icon onto the player section. You can open up a file browser to choose a song file to play by using one of several methods:

> ➤ Clicking the **Eject** button on the player
> ➤ Pressing **L**
> ➤ Clicking the upper-left corner of the player portion and selecting **Play File**
> ➤ Right-clicking an unmarked area of the player portion and selecting **Play File**

In other words, there are few things you can do in this world that *won't* start Winamp playing a song. I think it starts playing music if you slurp your soup, or if the Phillies win the pennant.

Winamp Playing Controls

The player display has the standard VCR-style controls to skip ahead or back a track, and to start, pause, or stop the song. It has a slider to adjust where within the track is playing, another slider to adjust the volume, and a third to adjust the balance between the left and right speakers.

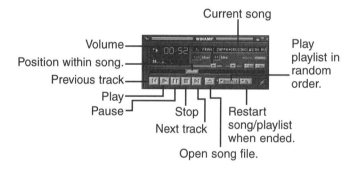

The Winamp song-playing controls.

The equalizer window lets you adjust the way the music sounds. You can crank up the bass to set the whole room a shakin' (or, if you have typical underpowered computer speakers, set a couple sticky notes a tremblin').

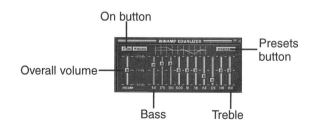

The Winamp equalizer doesn't make your music equal, it makes it better!

To take advantage of the equalizer, you first have to turn it on by clicking the **On** button. You can see that it's on by the little green light that appears on the button. The slider on the far left adjusts the preamp level, adjusting the overall volume; slide it up for more volume, down for less. The rest of the sliders adjust the level of individual portions of the sound. The leftmost sliders adjust the lowest (*bass*) sounds, while the rightmost adjust the highest (*treble*) sounds.

Tune Talk

Stuttering Sounds?

If your music starts sounding choppy or has little stutters in it, it means that your player is having problems keeping up with the music. Usually, this happens if you're running some other program that is using up processor and hard disk time, or if you're using a computer that's too slow. However, Windows performance tends to decay after it has been running a while, so if it starts happening later in the day, your best bet may be to close all your programs and reboot your system. To reboot, click **Start** and select **Shut Down**. In the dialog box that appears, choose the **Restart** option, and then click **OK**.

Different music sounds good with different equalizer settings. After you find a combination that you like, you can save it by clicking the **Presets** button, selecting **Save**, **Preset** from the resulting menu, and then entering a name for the combination. You can load an equalizer setting by clicking the **Preset** button, selecting **Load**, **Preset** from the menu, and then double-clicking the name of the setting you want.

Playing with Winamp's Playlist

Winamp's playlist window may look too small for viewing and working with a large list, but you can enlarge it by dragging the lower-right corner.

To add a song to the current playlist, you can just drag the song's icon into the playlist window. You can also click the **Add File** button and select the file using a file browser. Right-clicking the **Add File** button gives you a menu that lets you add an entire directory of song files (shortcut: **Shift+L**) or, for those of you lucky enough to have high-speed connections, the URL of a file on the Web (shortcut: **Ctrl+L**).

The Winamp playlist controls.

Playlist

Add File button
Delete File button
Select All button
Options button

Load List button

Song-playing controls

To work with the songs already on the playlist, you need to be able to select the songs to work with. Click any one song to select it. To select a range of songs, click the first song in the range, then hold down **Shift**, and click the last song. To select a bunch of songs that aren't in a row, hold down **Ctrl** while clicking the songs. Select all the songs by clicking the **Select All** button.

After you have the songs selected, you can drag them to a new position on the list. You can also delete them by right-clicking the selection and choosing **Delete** from the pop-up menu.

To save the playlist, right-click the **Load List** button and select **Save Playlist** from the pop-up menu. Use the file navigator to select a name and directory for the playlist, and

Don't Add CD-ROM Tracks to the Playlist!

I'm not saying the great MP3 music on this book's CD-ROM isn't worth putting on playlists. Instead, when you find songs you like, copy them from the CD-ROM to your hard disk. Otherwise, you'll have to have that CD-ROM in the drive each time you play that playlist.

then click **Save**. To open a saved playlist, click the **Load List** button, find the playlist with the file navigator, and double-click it.

*To view or edit the information on a song in the playlist, right-click it and select **File Info** (shortcut: **Alt+3**).*

Nifty Winamp Features

The Winamp minibrowser is a simple little Web browser. This may not seem to be important (after all, you probably already have a far better Web browser), but if all you're using your computer for is playing MP3s, it's a quick and handy way to get MP3s off the Web. (If you've closed the minibrowser, press **Alt+T** to make it reappear.)

The minibrowser is also good if you want to pick up SHOUTcast broadcasts. *SHOUTcast* is a system developed by the Winamp people to enable someone to broadcast a continuous stream of audio over the Internet. To view a list of SHOUTcast channels, click the up-arrow button on the bottom of the minibrowser and select **Shoutcast Top 50** from the menu that appears.

Winamp also supports *skins* and *plug-ins*. A *skin* is just a different visual design for Winamp, making it look like a car radio, a space design, or any of literally thousands of other appearances. A *plug-in* is an add-on program that expands Winamp's capabilities. Some plug-ins allow Winamp to play additional music formats, ranging from old Commodore 64 formats to next-generation compressed music formats. Others add special effects to the sound output. Most of them, however, just add nifty-looking moving visual effects to accompany the music, ranging from psychedelic patterns to dancing-stick figures that look suspiciously like former surgeon general C. Everett Koop.

Head on over to www.winamp.com to find a selection of over 100 plug-ins and more than 3,000 skins to pep up your Winamp experience.

MusicMatch Jukebox for Windows

MusicMatch is another all-in-one audio file player, encoder, CD player, and cat scratcher. (Okay, you can scratch the cat with the CD-ROM.) The free version included on the CD-ROM has almost all the features you're likely to want. About all that's missing from the free version is the capability to encode MP3s at the highest-quality rates, but if you upgrade the software for $29.99 at MusicMatch's Web site (www.MusicMatch.com), you can quickly give it the capability to do even that.

MusicMatch Requirements

MusicMatch requires a multimedia PC with Windows 95 or newer, and 30MB of hard disk space. Theoretically, it will run in 16MB of RAM, but things will go smoother if you have at least 32MB, as well as a 166MHz or faster processor.

Installing MusicMatch Jukebox

To install the Jukebox, first insert the CD-ROM that accompanies this book. Close any running programs and double-click the **My Computer** icon on your Windows desktop. In the resulting window, double-click the icon for your CD-ROM drive to view its contents. Double-click the **Programs** folder, and then double-click the **mmjb4161** icon. An onscreen meter shows the progress of the installation program. After everything is in place, the installation program begins.

On the Welcome screen, click **Next**. The license agreement appears. (It's a long one, but it includes some guidelines on what is legal to convert to MP3s.) If you agree to the license agreement, click **Yes**. (If you disagree with it, click **No** and then go do something else, because you're not going to get the software installed until you choose Yes.)

The installation program suggests a folder to install the software in. Click **Next** to accept the default. This is followed with a suggestion of a folder to store the music you encode; again, click **Next** to accept this suggestion. It then suggests a new Start menu folder for the software. You can accept that suggestion, or you can click on one from a list of your existing Start menu folders. Click **Next** after you've made your selection, and the installation takes place.

A dialog box asks you if you want MusicMatch Jukebox to be your default CD player. Choose **Yes** or **No**. After you make that decision, the installation is complete. Click **Finish**.

Put a Dime in the Jukebox and Start It Playing

Before the first time you start MusicMatch, put a standard audio CD into each of your CD-ROM drives. MusicMatch is going to need those there because it will run a test on your CD-ROM drives. This test gives it information it will need when you start encoding MP3s (as described in Chapter 8).

Because MusicMatch Jukebox makes itself your default MP3 player, you can start it up by double-clicking any MP3 file icon. Additionally, you can start it using the Start menu, by double-clicking the **MusicMatch** icon on your desktop, or by dragging and dropping an MP3 file icon onto the MusicMatch icon. MusicMatch opens two windows: a window with the song-playing controls and a playlist, and a help window.

After you have the program going, you can play a song by dragging and dropping the program file onto the player window. When you do so, the song title or filename appears in the playlist window at the right end of the MusicMatch panel. What MusicMatch really wants you to do, however, is to enter your songs into its music library. That way, it knows where all your songs are, and all you have to do is click the song name on the library list to hear it.

MusicMatch Jukebox has different visual themes. On some themes, the buttons may be in slightly different places.

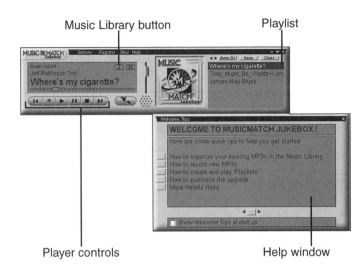

Music Library button   Playlist

Player controls   Help window

So Where's This Music Library, Already?

To see the Music Library, click the tiny button with the picture of a musical note. The Music Library window opens, with a list of all the songs in the library. The surprising thing is that there actually is a song there the first time you open it up. Jukebox comes with a song (actually, a short song segment), that is handy for testing it out if you don't have any MP3 files yet.

MusicMatch Jukebox has a Music Library system, and you don't even need a library card to use it.

To add songs to the library, click **Add**. A file navigator opens that looks different than the standard file navigator you see in many Open dialog boxes. Icons for your drives and your desktop appear in the left panel. Click the plus sign next to **Drives** to see a list of all your drives, each with a plus sign next to them. Click the plus sign next to any drive to see a list of folders in that drive, and on the plus sign next to any folder to see the folders in that folder.

Click on any folder icon, and the right panel displays a list of all the MP3 files in that folder. When you find the song you want to add, click that song to select it. If you want to add all the songs in that folder, click the **Select All** button. After you select the songs you want to add, click **OK**, and they are added to the music library.

If no songs are playing, you can start any song in the music library by clicking the song title, and then clicking the > that appears next to the song.

MusicMatch Jukebox Playlist Funtime!

At any time, you can add any song to the current playlist by double-clicking the song title in the music library, or by dragging and dropping it (either from the song's icon or from its entry in the music library) into the playlist.

To save a playlist, click the **Save** button. A dialog box appears, explaining saving and loading playlists. Click **OK**, and another dialog box appears. Type a name for the playlist, and press **Enter**.

To load a playlist, click the right-arrow button next to the AutoDJ button. The playlist area expands to include a list of saved playlists. Double-click any playlist name to load that playlist. You can shrink the playlist area back to its usual size by clicking the left-arrow button.

Controlling the Play

The player portion of the window contains the standard VCR-style controls, with buttons for Previous Song, Play, Pause, Stop, and Next Song. There is one control that most of the other players don't have: a Record button, which you'll use when converting audio CD tracks to MP3. (You'll learn more about that process in Chapter 8.) It also has a left-right slider to control where in the track you're playing, and an up-down slider for the volume.

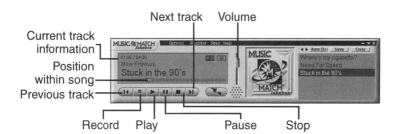

Like other players, MusicMatch uses VCR-style controls. Considering how many people have trouble using their VCRs, this may not be wise...

AutoDJ: Not to Be Confused with Auto-da-fé

Click the **AutoDJ** button above the playlist, and you can take advantage of a feature that automatically plays songs out of your music library, based on criteria you select. You can listen to songs by specific artists, or specific tempos, genres, moods, or other criteria. There's one major problem: MusicMatch can't really tell by itself the tempo, mood, and so on, of each song. It relies on that information being embedded in the song itself, and many of the songs you download won't have that info.

The dialog box that appears when you click the button has everything you need to set your criteria. First, enter the number of hours you want the AutoDJ to play. Next, select the category of criteria from the first criteria option button list. After you select the category (for example, **by Artist**), a list of all the possible entries within that category appears next to it (Sound Victims, Juan Word & The Echoes, The Beatless). Click the check boxes for all the entries that are acceptable to you.

The AutoDJ feature lets you select just to listen to your favorite types of music, or just your least favorites, if you want.

First, select the number of criteria.

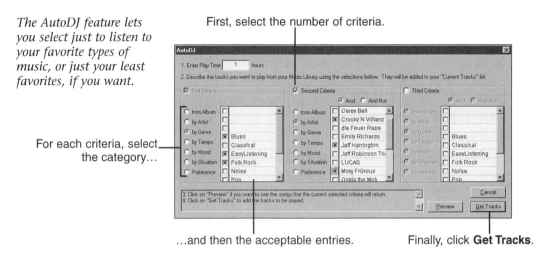

For each criteria, select the category...

...and then the acceptable entries.

Finally, click **Get Tracks**.

If you want to set more than one criteria (if, for example, you want to listen to only upbeat songs by the Doom 'n Gloom Quintet), click the **Second Criteria** check box before setting up your first criteria. Doing so reveals a second list of option buttons, and a list of possible entries for whatever you select. If you want a third criterion, click the **Third Criteria** check box right after clicking the **Second Criteria** button. Three's the limit. The second and third criteria also have an **And Not** option; click this to *exclude* songs based on a criterion.

After you've set all your criteria, click **Get Tracks**. The program searches the music data base, and reports how many songs meet your criteria, as well as their total play time. Click **OK** to let it know that you've seen the information (or that you didn't see it and just don't care.) The songs it found are added to the playlist.

As I noted, this only works if the song files have the information in them. Luckily, this chapter does have a section on how to add song information using MusicMatch, which we call:

How to Add Song Information Using MusicMatch

Adding information is easy. Right-click the song in the music library list, and select **Edit Track Tag** from the pop-up menu. A dialog box appears, with fields for the track title, the lead artist, and the album name. Just type in that information.

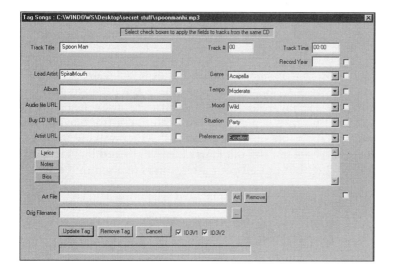

MusicMatch can read and even change tags—information about the song hidden in the MP3 file itself.

Then, it's time to *describe* the music. Use the Genre drop-down list to choose any music style ranging from *polka* to *punk*. The Tempo drop-down list lets you indicate the speed of the song's rhythm. The Mood drop-down list lets you define the song as anything from *wild* to *comatose*. The Situation drop-down list lets you align the song with situations ranging from romance music to rave music. And using the Preference drop-down list, you can keep track of whether the music is darned fine or just plain stinky. With any of these settings except Genre, you can also type your own description into the field instead of using the drop-down list. That way, if you want to mark certain songs as being appropriate when you're in a *cat-licking* kind of mood, you can!

After adding all this information, click **Update Tag**, and the information is added directly into the music file.

What Are All the Rest of Those Fields for, Then?

The Tag dialog box has a number of fields that you're not likely to use when adding information to a single file. Some of the fields are more for when you're encoding an entire CD, and others are for when you're encoding your own song for distribution to others. As such, those fields are covered in more appropriate chapters of this book.

Closing and Shrinking Windows

The MusicMatch windows may not look like standard Windows windows, but they do still have Close (x) buttons in the upper-right corner of each window. You can use these to close the help window or the Music Library window. If you click the one on the player/playlist window, it closes the whole program, stopping your music from playing.

To the left of the Close (x) button on the player/playlist window is a down-arrow button. Click this one, and the window shrinks. All you'll have is a little window with the VCR-style controls and a small readout about the current track. After you have your playlist going, this minimized panel is all you need to control playing your songs. Plus, it's small enough that the boss may not notice it when walking by. (Of course, the fact that your speakers are blaring out Laura Loveland's autobiographical album *Strait Two L* might be a clue that not all your attention is focused on your work.)

When you reduce MusicMatch, it shrinks enough that it won't get in the way of your important solitaire game.

 ─Enlarge button

Next to the Close (x) button on this window is a small up-arrow; click this to get the full-sized window again.

Giving MusicMatch a Second, Third, or Fourth Look

You can choose from different visual *themes* for your MusicMatch windows. Themes are different designs for different appearances. To choose a theme, click the **Options** button on the player window and choose **View**, **Change Theme**. A dialog box appears listing the different visual themes. Double-click any theme name to apply the theme. After finding one you like, click **OK**.

MusicMatch's Other Tricks

MusicMatch has a number of other capabilities beyond playing MP3s. It also encodes MP3s, which is covered in Chapter 8. It also plays audio CDs, encodes into RealAudio format, and cures boogie fever.

Sonique for Windows

Sonique is an MP3 player program put out by Mediascience (www.sonique.com). The program is a player only; it can't encode MP3s, burn CD-ROMs, or make your clothes whiter and brighter. It will play MP3 files, CD tracks, and a number of other audio formats. It's yours to use, free.

Sonique has a number of nifty built-in special effects, both audio and visual. Because it's such a unique-looking program, getting used to its controls can take a little time, but it's definitely a fun player to try.

Soniquirements

To run Sonique, you'll need to be running Windows 95 or newer on a computer with a Pentium 100 or faster processor. You will also need at least 16MB of RAM, and a sound card, of course. Oh, and speakers. And ears to listen with.

Installing Sonique

To install Sonique, insert the CD-ROM that accompanies this book. Close any running programs. Next, double-click the **My Computer** icon on your Windows desktop. In the resulting window, double-click the icon for your CD-ROM drive to view its contents. Double-click the **Programs** folder, and when that opens, double-click the **s100wma** icon. A dialog box tells you that you are about to install Sonique, and asks if you want to continue. Click **Yes**. An onscreen meter shows the progress of the installation program. After everything is in place, the installation program begins.

A Welcome dialog box appears. Click **Next**. The licensing agreement for the software appears. If you agree to this agreement, click **Yes**. (If you don't agree to it, then it's not really a licensing agreement, is it? More of a licensing *disagreement*. But if you disagree, you don't get to use the software.)

The program gives its expectation of a proper destination location for program installation. There's no need for an exclamation in this situation! For installation continuation, click **Next**.

Then the installer will suggest creating a new program folder called Sonique on your Start menu. You can accept this folder by clicking **Next**, or you can select one of the existing folders from a list, and then click **Next**. You are then shown all the settings you accepted during this installation. Click **Next** again. (I bet you're feeling like a next-clicking expert by this point, eh?)

A dialog box appears, listing different audio file types you can put Sonique in charge of:

➤ MPEG files (including not only MP3, but the lower compression schemes *MP1* and *MP2*, short for *MPEG-1 Layer I* and *MPEG-1 Layer 2*, respectively)

➤ *Modules*, which are various formats of sheet music–style song files

➤ *Waveform audio files*, which are uncompressed digital audio files such as WAV

➤ Audio CDs

Select the check boxes for the audio types for which you want Sonique to be your main player, and then click (of course) **Next**. Another dialog box asks you what sort of Internet connection you use. Select the appropriate option button, click **Next**, and the actual installation takes place. Finally, the installer tells you that the setup is complete and that you have to restart Windows before you can use Sonique. Close all other programs you have open, and then click **Finish**. Windows will close down, restart, and Sonique will be ready to rock 'n roll!

Getting Musique Out of Sonique

You can start Sonique using the Start menu, or by double-clicking the **Sonique** icon on your desktop. You can also drag and drop music files onto that desktop icon.

The first time you start Sonique, it pops up a dialog box asking for your name and email address so that your free copy can be registered. (It also has a check box for putting you on Sonique's emailing list, and that defaults as checked, so you might want to clear it if you don't like getting corporate email.) Click **Register Now**, and your information will be sent via the Internet (or just click **Register Later** to skip the whole thing).

Sonique's Unique Displays

Sonique doesn't just have the full-sized player and the miniaturized player that other players have. Instead, it has four different sizes, each of which looks very different, and each of which has different uses.

The large Sonique display is needed if you want to edit playlists or set options.

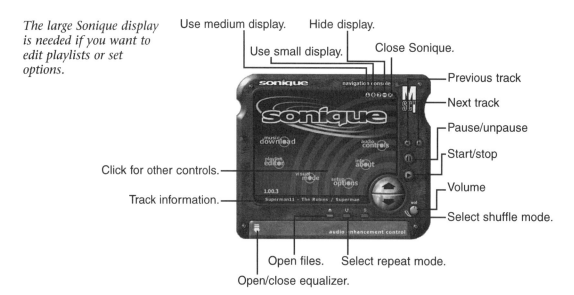

The Sonique buttons work a little differently than the buttons on other players. If you click **Pause**, for example, you have to click the same button again to restart, rather than clicking the Play button. In fact, there isn't a dedicated Play button; when you click it to start the track playing, it turns into the Stop button. And when you click **Stop** to halt the music, it turns into the Play button. To open a song, you can either drag and drop the song's icon onto the player, or click the **Open Files** button and select the file using the file navigator. (This navigator also has a place for a URL, for playing songs directly from a high-speed Web connection.)

Click **Visual Mode** to see the main display area replaced with full track information and a *vis*, a nifty little light show that accompanies the music. You can use the big gray up-arrow and down-arrow buttons to choose from several different vis styles. The name of the vis appears above the vis display. To the right of the vis name are two little buttons. Click the second one, and the Sonique goes into *full-screen vis mode*, Sonique's largest mode.

Full-screen vis mode turns your entire display into a psychedelic light show. While Sonique is in this mode, there are no onscreen controls. You'll have to use Sonique's keyboard controls:

➤ Press **X** to start or stop playing a song.

➤ Press the right-arrow key to move through your playlist.

➤ Use the up- and down-arrow keys to change the volume.

➤ Press **.** (period) to change which vis is playing, **[** (left bracket) or **]** (right bracket) to change the colors of the vis, or **+** (plus) or **-** (minus) on the number pad to change the screen resolution.

➤ Press **Esc** to return to the large display mode.

Clicking the down-arrow button in the upper-right corner of the large display replaces it with the medium display. This is a curvy little number that looks more like a futuristic handheld player.

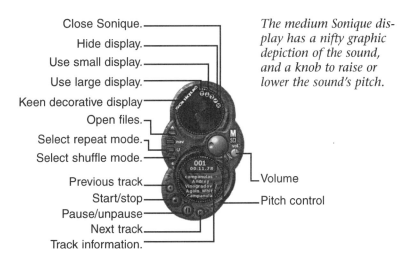

Close Sonique.
Hide display.
Use small display.
Use large display.
Keen decorative display
Open files.
Select repeat mode.
Select shuffle mode.
Previous track
Start/stop
Pause/unpause
Next track
Track information.
Volume
Pitch control

The medium Sonique display has a nifty graphic depiction of the sound, and a knob to raise or lower the sound's pitch.

This medium display has most of the same controls that are around the edges of the larger version. It also has a control knob that lets you raise the pitch of the music, letting you turn even the most deep-toned singer into one of the Chipmunks. There's also an area for vis display. Point to this area, and arrows appear that let you cycle through the various vis styles.

Where Are the *Normal* Players?

All the tricky buttons and fancy fonts are fun to look at, but when I'm using a music player, I want to enjoy the music. There should be some full-featured player/ encoder out there that just looks like a normal computer program. What would be so hard about having a play button that's actually marked *Play*, or a playlist that displays in the standard system font, or that uses the standard system colors? These features would make the player easier to work with and easier to understand. I don't want *all* the players to be straightforward and bland; I just need one that I can easily teach my mother to use.

Click the down-arrow button here, and the display shrinks down to the smallest size possible. All this display shows is the track number currently playing and the time within that track. Point to this display, however, and you see a minimal set of control buttons.

Sonique's small display has the least you need, and it only shows that when you point directly at it.

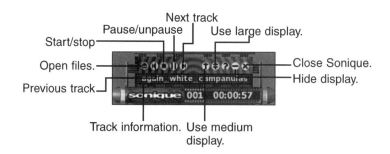

Playlists in Sonique

To work on your playlist, you need to be using the large display. Click **Playlist Editor**. (If you don't see that option, right-click the display area, and it will appear.) The interior of the display switches to display the playlist, and playlist-related controls.

You can't drag and drop songs to add them to your playlist (if you try, it replaces the whole playlist with that one song). To add songs to the playlist, click **Add**. A file navigator appears. Use this navigator to select the song to add to the playlist. (When you're navigating a directory, you can add all the songs by clicking one song, pressing **Ctrl+A** and then clicking **Open**.)

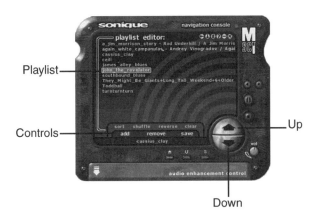

Playlist ─

Controls ─

Up ─

Down

Sonique's playlist editor appears in the large display's central area.

To delete a song from the playlist, click the song name, and then click **Remove**. You can rearrange the list randomly by clicking **Shuffle**, put it in alphabetical order by clicking **Sort**, or reverse the current order by clicking **Reverse**. To move any one song through the playlist, click the song, and then use the up and down buttons to move it to the new location.

You can save the playlist by clicking **Save**. You can open a playlist in any display mood by clicking the **Open File** button and selecting the list from the file navigator, or by dragging and dropping the playlist file icon onto the display.

To leave the playlist editing mode and return to the main large display mode, just right-click the central display area.

Soniqualizer

Sonique has an equalizer function, with a handful of preset arrangements designed to bring out the best in certain sorts of music. To use it, click **Audio Controls** on the large display's main screen. To use one of the preset equalizer layouts, put a check in the **Equalizer Enabled** check box, and then click the left or right buttons to cycle through the choices (Classical, Dance, Pop, Rock, and Jazz).

If you want to design your own settings, click the down arrow along the bottom of the large display. A "drawer" opens, displaying 20 equalizer sliders, ranging from the deepest tones (at left) to the highest (at right). Push a slider up the screen to increase the mix of that tone, or down the screen to decrease it. Remember, this only works if the **Equalizer Enabled** check box is checked. If you put a check in the **Spline Tension** check box, then dragging one slider also repositions the ones beside it, keeping a smooth distribution of the sound. You can return all the sliders to the center by clicking **Reset**.

Sonique's playlist editor appears in the large display's central area.

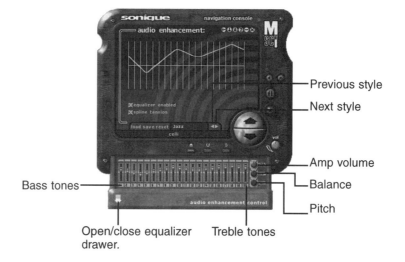

Previous style

Next style

Amp volume

Balance

Pitch

Bass tones

Open/close equalizer drawer.

Treble tones

When you have an equalizer arrangement that you like, you can save it to reuse at any time. Click **Save**, and a list of 10 preset locations appears. Click any one of those 10, and your settings are stored. To return to that setting, click **Load**, and the list of presets appears again. Click the setting you want.

To the right side of the equalizer sliders are three knobs. The top one adjusts the amplifier volume, the second one the side-to-side balance, and the third the pitch of the sound. To use one of these knobs, point to it, hold down the mouse button, and move the mouse forward or back. On the Amp knob, pushing forward makes the music louder. On the Pitch knob, pushing forward raises the pitch. And on the Balance knob, pushing forward moves the sound to the right. You and I would probably design it so that dragging the mouse *right* shifts the sound to the right, but that's why we aren't making millions in the software design business.

To close the equalizer drawer, click the down arrow on its lower edge. To return the large display area to the main window, right-click it.

Expansionique

Various plug-in expansions are available for Sonique. Some provide support for additional audio file formats, while others add different vis styles. Both can be found at www.sonique.com/plugs.html. Don't try installing them before you've installed Sonique, used Sonique, and then exited the program.

Sonique also supports *skins*, which can make your player look like anything from a portable CD player to a British flag. Skip on over to http://skins.sonique.com to find the latest and greatest skins to download.

Changing Your Default MP3 Player

Most of the MP3 players automatically configure themselves as Windows' default MP3 player when you install them. That way, when you double-click a song file icon, that program automatically starts playing the song. But what if you install the latest version of MegamaxiPlayer3, and decide that you don't like it that much, and you would rather go back to using that version of Jane's Music Thingy you downloaded? Assuming that you haven't uninstalled Jane's Music Thingy, it's pretty easy.

First, find a song file icon, using either My Computer or Windows Explorer. While holding down the **Shift** key, click once on the icon to select it, and then right-click the icon. Release the Shift key, and choose **Open With** from the pop-up menu. A dialog box appears, listing programs on your system. Click the MP3 player you want to use. (If it isn't on the list, click the **Other** button and use the file navigator to find the program file.) Put a check in the **Always Use This Program to Open This Type of File** check box, then click **OK**. Voilá! That's easier than memorizing the lyrics to the Batman TV theme!

Players for Non-Windows Machines

There aren't nearly as many players available for the Macintosh as you might expect, considering how much of an artsy/college machine it is. If you want a player, check out the one available for download at www.macamp.com.

If your machine runs some other operating system, the best place for you to check is MP3.com's software section. They have a growing number of players for operating systems like Linux and BeOS, and I suspect innovative programs will soon be offering an MP3 player that will run on your abacus.

Web Browser Power!

You can set up your Web browser to automatically start your MP3 player to play any MP3 song when you click its Web link. This arrangement can work out well if you have a high-speed connection to the Web (or to an intranet where MP3s are stored). It's really not that useful if you have a standard modem connection because you'll end up slowly redownloading the song every time you want to hear it.

Internet Explorer for Windows

For Internet Explorer 4 or higher for Windows, you first have to set the player to be your default system player, as described earlier. Next, click the **Start** button and choose **Programs**, **Windows Explorer**. When Windows Explorer opens, choose **View**, **Folder Options**. In the Folder Options dialog box, click the **File Types** tab.

Now comes the tricky part: On an alphabetic list of file types, you have to find MP3. That sounds pretty easy, if you have most of the alphabet memorized. However, some

Tune Talk

Musical Mimes?

The term *MIME* in computer jargon stands for *Multipurpose Internet Mail Extensions*. Basically, it's a standard description of a file type that your computer can use to recognize the type of file that it is receiving via email or the Web.

programs change the name of file type to something like MusicMonster Audio File, putting the name of their player into the file type. So if you don't find it listed as MP3, look for the name of your browser on the alphabetic list. After you find the right file type, click it. In the File Type Details area below the list, it should say Extension: MP3. If it doesn't, you haven't found the right file type yet.

Next, click the **Edit** button, and the Edit File Type dialog box appears. In the **Content Type (MIME)** field, type audio/mpeg and then click **OK**.

Netscape and Other Browsers

For other browsers (including earlier versions of Internet Explorer), you have to set up the player within the browser's options. The browsers associate different programs with different file types. You want to tell it to associate your player with files with the extension .MP3 and the MIME type audio/mpeg. To do this, use your browser's **Options** or **Preferences** command.

The Least You Need to Know

➤ Current versions of the Windows Media Player will play MP3s.

➤ Virtuosa Gold is an MP3 player/encoder, which handles a number of other audio formats as well. The version on the CD-ROM is a 15-day free trial version.

➤ Winamp is a popular music player that supports a range of interesting and useful plug-ins. Winamp is shareware, and must be registered if you want to continue using it.

➤ MusicMatch Jukebox is a full-featured music player/encoder. The version on the CD-ROM is fully usable, except for some limitations on encoding.

➤ Sonique is a graphically impressive player-only program. The version on the CD-ROM is free for your use.

➤ Macintosh users don't have as many options when it comes to players. The most popular one is probably MacAMP, available at www.macamp.com.

Chapter 4

Where to Get 'Em and How to Download 'Em

In This Chapter

➤ How do you find MP3 sites?

➤ How do you find the tunes you want?

➤ How do you store the tunes on your hard disk?

So far, you've heard *about* MP3 files. Now you want to just *hear* MP3 files. And the first step is to get some MP3 files.

The CD-ROM that comes with this book has hours of MP3 files on it. That sounds like an awful lot, but it's nowhere near enough to satisfy a real music fan. Luckily, there's plenty more music out there. How much? You could listen to MP3 music from dusk to dawn every day and never hear it all, because all the time you're listening, more new songs are being uploaded than you have time to listen to.

So now let's hunt down some of the most music-filled sites and see what they have to offer. (We're assuming that you know how to use the World Wide Web; if you don't, maybe you should head on over to the store where you bought this book and see if they have a copy of *The Complete Idiot's Guide to the Internet*.)

MP3.com: Digital Compressed Music's Central Core

The Web site MP3.com is the best known and the most active of the free 'n' legal music sites. It boasts thousands of artists offering tens of thousands of tracks, causing hundreds of thousands of downloads every day. It's popular because it has a lot of music, and people keep putting more music there because it's popular.

Finding a Track on MP3.com

There are many different ways you can select music on MP3.com. For example, from the opening page you can

➤ Click the **Song of the Day** link to get one new song selected each day by my co-author, Rod. This should be a good song, although it may not be in your favorite style of music.

➤ Click one of the songs featured in the Hot New MP3s list. Each one is listed with its genre. This is a good place to find quality new tracks and tracks by big-name recording artists. (If you see an interesting track by a big name, grab it quickly! Sometimes the artist's label gets mad that the artist has uploaded it, and moves quickly to get the song removed.)

➤ Click the **Music** link at the very top of the page to go to another page with links for many new artists and new tracks. It also has the Top 40 list, with links for the most popular songs currently on MP3.com. Some are popular because they are very good; others are popular merely because they have a cool title or have been well promoted. There's also a search field, in which you can enter a word to search for, and then click **Search** to see a listing of all songs and artists with that word in the name.

➤ Click a musical genre on the **Songs by Genre** list to go to a list of subgenres, see a listing of the top 40 MP3s in that genre, and view a list of popular artists in that genre.

The only one of these techniques that immediately starts a download is clicking the title of the Song Of The Day. Click any other song link and you'll be taken to a page on MP3.com focusing on that artist. It lists all the artist's available MP3 tracks. It also has a lot of information about the performer or group, such as a list of CDs available (many of which are available directly from MP3.com), the artist history, description, and comments.

The Three Beavers and Their DAM CD

A lot of artists on MP3.com offer Digital Automatic Music (DAM) CDs on their page. These CDs are usually made up of a mixture of tracks available for download and tracks that can only be had on the CD. What makes them different from standard CDs is that they also have all tracks on them in MP3 format, so you can put the disk in your CD-ROM drive and quickly copy the compressed tracks onto your computer.

Downloading or Playing a Track

For each song on the artists page, there are three links. The Play link is designed for people with high-speed Internet connections, such as a cable modem, a permanent network connection, or a direct line link at a university. Clicking this link launches your MP3 player and plays the song as it downloads, *if* you have your Web browser set up so that it knows where your MP3 player is (as described toward the end of Chapter 3, "Installing and Using MP3 Player Software"). This process won't work if you're using a phone modem, because these modems are too slow. The player would have to keep stopping and waiting for the rest of the song to download before it can play.

Clicking the Save link is supposed to just save the file to your hard disk. Note that I said "supposed to." Depending on how folks have used your PC and Web browser in the past, clicking this link may just save the file somewhere on your disk. Or it may open a dialog box that asks if you want to save the file or *open* it (start playing it with your MP3 player when the download is done), or it may just open it without asking. Opening sounds good, right?

Well, it really isn't. When your Web browser thinks you want to open a file, it assumes you want to treat it like a typical Web page: look at it now, and when you're done, you don't care what happens to it. So either after you close your MP3 player or after you've surfed the Web for a while longer, the song file is automatically deleted from your hard disk. If you want to hear that song again, you'll have to download it again, and with a long slow download, that's a pain in the neck.

Unless you're using an old or strange Web browser, the browser has a command to save the file a link goes to. For example, Windows users should right-click the **Save** link. On the resulting pop-up menu, there is a command named something like **Save**

Target As or **Save Link Document As** (the exact wording depends on your Web browser). Choose this command, and a file navigator appears letting you choose where to put the file.

Instant Play

The song's Instant Play link provides a way to start listening to a song almost immediately, even if you're just using a phone modem. However, it doesn't use MP3 technology. Instead, it uses a format called *RealAudio*. To be able to use the Instant Play feature, you'll either need to have the current version of the Windows Media Player or you'll need to install a piece of software called the RealPlayer, available for free from www.real.com. After you have RealPlayer installed, all you have to do is click the **Instant Play** link, wait a few seconds, and you'll start hearing the song a few seconds later.

The quality of the sound is not as good as with MP3. Instant Play is best for trying out a song quickly before you decide whether it's worth downloading. Instead of tying up your modem for 15 minutes getting a song that's pretty weak, you can listen to the song's first 30 seconds and save yourself the time.

Tune Talk

Streaming Versus Downloading

You may wonder why MP3 addicts like the folks at MP3.com are using RealAudio instead of MP3 for their instant play features. Have they gone goofy? Well, yes, some of them, but that's not why. The RealAudio format and the RealPlayer were designed for *streaming* audio, listening to audio at the same time as it is coming across the Internet, without storing it on your hard disk. The MP3 file format was really designed around *downloading*, getting the entire file onto your hard disk and then listening to it.

The dividing line between the two types of audio format are blurring. As the Play link on MP3.com shows, MP3 files can be used in a streaming manner on high-speed lines (or with low bit-rate MP3s). And some of the MP3 encoders and players can also create and play back RealAudio tracks.

Other MP3.com Features

At the top of each MP3.com Web page is a series of links leading to different sections of the site:

➤ The News link takes you to probably the best-maintained site for news and opinions about MP3 and other compressed digital music formats. You'll find all sorts of information here on who's announcing what, who's suing whom, and so on.

➤ The Software link takes you to pages where you can download a wide array of MP3 players, encoders, and other MP3-related software.

➤ The Hardware link takes you to a page where you can find listings of various hardware-based MP3 players. Some of the listings are a bit too indiscriminate; you can't always tell quickly whether the item listed is something you can buy today at your local electronics shop, or whether it's just something that a student somewhere bets that he and his pals and some hired experts could come up with if they just had the money.

MP3.com also has what they call *radio stations*. These use the RealAudio streaming format to play music continuously. This is a nice way to listen to a lot of new music while you work, although it uses up some of your Internet bandwidth and thus slows down anything else you're doing on the Internet at the same time. Plus, the radio station often pauses while you do other things on the Net.

Most MP3.com artists have their own radio stations, which will loop through all the artist's available-for-download songs. There are also radio stations available for each genre of music on that genre's main page.

Non-Musical News, Non-Musical MP3s

Also on the front page of MP3.com is a Listen to the New York Times link. It can be a little hard to find, so if you can't find it easily, just go right to `http://www.mp3.com/audible/` to find the New York Times entry. That's right, headlines and articles from the New York Times, fresh every weekday, read out loud and stored in the MP3 format. Maybe they should change their ad-line to "All the news that fits your Rio!"

Why All the Legal Sites?

You may wonder why the sites I'm listing in this section are all ones that carry only *legal* MP3s, distributed with the permission of the creators. Don't I know about sites out there that have all the latest CDs, ripped and compressed and ready for download? You bet I know about them. And I'm against them.

Pirating music may seem like a victimless crime. It's not like shoplifting, where you're walking out with a physical object, right? So who loses out?

The musicians and the people they work with lose out. Recording artists make most of their money off *royalties*—their cut of that $16 you shell out for a CD. It isn't a big cut, but it's how they make their money, how they pay for the recording and all the people that helped them. As a writer, I make my money off book royalties, so I understand the position they're in.

There are some standard arguments in favor of music piracy. Let's take a look at them:

"Well, I wouldn't buy the album anyway, so they're not really losing anything." Except all that music your stealing is filling your need for music, and thus may be leading you to buy less legal music in general, hurting everyone in the business. And the recording artist is losing something: control over his music. Besides, if the recording isn't worth buying, is it really worth stealing?

"They should really be giving out samples for free anyway, to convince me to buy the CD." But because it's their music, isn't that their choice? If you believe in free samples, you should be supporting the artists who give out free samples, which is what all those songs on the free 'n' legal sites are.

"But I could listen to this song for free on the radio, and there's no difference between that and listening on my computer." Actually, there is a difference: the radio station is paying for playing the music.

"Information wants to be free!" Funny how the recording studio time doesn't want to be free, the cups of coffee don't want to be free, the braces for the mixing engineer's daughter's overbite don't want to be free...

EMusic: Music Worth Paying For

EMusic, located at www.EMusic.com, is the leading *commercial* MP3 download site. That's right, you have to pay for most of the songs on EMusic. But for the price (generally, 99 cents per song, charged to your credit card), you're not getting the same would-be up-and-comers that make up most of the tracks on the free sites.

Instead, you get commercial recordings from some medium-to-big name folks. Some of the biggest names are actually big-but-dead names, ranging from Leadbelly to Frank Zappa. And these folks aren't offering entire albums, but a song or two from one CD and a song or two from another, so you're really buying more of a sampler than a full album. If you're really into these artists, you probably won't be satisfied with what you get here.

But they do have other, living, breathing recording artists. Many are folks who are seemingly past the peak of their career, generally people who have left their major label and are moving on. This doesn't mean that their music isn't better than ever, it's just not what the kids are buying these days. If you're into what The Pixies were doing, you can check out front man Frank Black's new recordings with his band The Catholics. If you like Gene Loves Jezebel, their new music is here as well. And with these folks, you aren't just getting individual tracks, you are getting entire albums.

You can buy an entire album for $8.99, or you can buy any individual track off most albums for 99 cents. There's even one free track on many albums, something you can download and listen to and then decide if you want the whole thing.

Look for EMusic to grow into carrying not only a larger selection but more impressive work as time goes on. They've announced a new album by respected off-beat pop charmers They Might Be Giants, an album that will *not* be released on CD but will *only* be available in MP3 format.

Getting MP3s from EMusic

On the EMusic front page, click the **Artist Index** link, and you are taken to a list of the performers they currently carry, which number in the hundreds rather than the thousands you'll find at a good CD store. Click the name of an artist to be shown a list of albums and non-album tracks he or she has available. Click on an album name to see a list of tracks on that album.

Is Buying an Album Online Worth It?

Whether shelling out the bucks to download an album is worth it depends on how you're listening to your music. Let's consider, for example, Gene Loves Jezebel's album *VII*. If you want to buy the album in a store, the list price is $16.97. Of course, most stores discount some from the list price, but you may have a tough time finding this album in a store because it's not by a currently hot band. If you order the album from online discounter CD-NOW (www.cdnow.com), it'll run you $11.88, plus shipping, and then you have to wait days for it to arrive. But then, you actually have a physical CD. If you're not totally converted to MP3, you can still play it in your car CD player, on your Discman, and so on. And when you're tired of it, you can probably sell it for a couple bucks to your local used CD shop.

Still, if you've built your previous musical life around CDs, you probably already have enough CDs to serve your car and Discman needs...and you can store up the money you save towards buying that portable MP3 player that will let you take it on the road.

An example of an EMusic page for an artist who offers just individual songs, not an entire album.

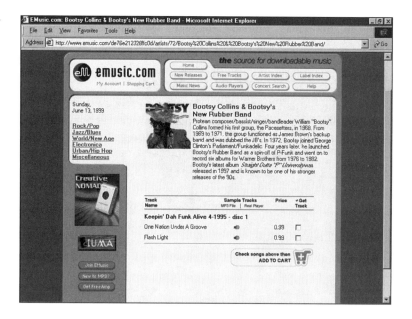

For each listed track, you can download a sample clip. Just right-click the icon in the MP3 column and select **Save Link As** or **Save Target As** or some similar command (depending on your browser), then use the file navigator that appears to navigate the file list. The same instructions go for the Free link on the free tracks. (Some tracks also have a RealAudio symbol that you can click to hear the track more quickly, but at lower quality, if you have a RealAudio player installed.)

Ordering Individual Tracks

Each track you can purchase has a check box next to it. Put a check in the box for each track you want to buy. After you've checked off all the tracks you want for the page, click the **Add to Cart** button. Doing so adds these tracks to your online *shopping cart*, a list of the things you plan to buy. When you add items to your cart, you will be shown a list of everything in your cart. This list also has controls that allow you to remove items from your cart. One of the nice things about a virtual shopping cart is that, unlike a real shopping cart, when you remove something from it, you don't have to look both ways to make sure that nobody notices you sticking the item back on the wrong shelf.

Ordering an Album

When you've found an album on the artist's page that you want to order, click the **Download Album** link under the album's cover image. If you don't have an account, you are taken to the Log In screen; go through the steps described in the following section, "Getting an EMusic Account," to create your account. If you do have an account but told the system not to remember you, you must enter your account name and password now. After you do so, the album is added to your shopping cart.

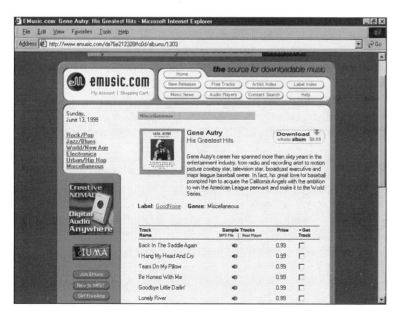

You can select any individual song from this album. The link to buy the whole album is at the top of the page.

Getting an EMusic Account

"They'll Sell My Email to the Devil!"

If you're worried about what EMusic will do with your name and email address, check www. emusic.com/help/privacy for their privacy policy.

Before you can pay for and download all those phat tracks you've put in your shopping cart, you're going to have an EMusic account. Otherwise, they'll think of you as a no-account kind of person, and won't deal with you.

To set up your EMusic account, click the **My Account** link toward the upper left of any EMusic page. You are taken to a Log In screen, where the system wants to know your name and password. You don't have a password? No surprise, because this is your first time here!

Click the **Create New Account** link to set yourself up. A form appears asking for your name, email address, and your choice for a password. Fill out this form, and then click **Update Our Records**. Now you have an account! You also have a screen listing various mailing lists you can join. If you join a mailing list, you will get occasional emails about EMusic, their partners, or specific musicians, depending on the topic of the list.

Getting the Music You've Ordered

After you've got all the songs you want in your shopping cart, it's time to check out. Click **Shopping Cart** at the top of any page to view the contents of your shopping cart. You'll see a list of the items you've put in the cart, as well as the price of each. If you've changed your mind about some item ("Wait, that's not *Disco Inferno*, that's *Discount Inferno!*"), click its **Remove** check box, and then click **Update Cart**.

When you're happy with the list, click **Check Out**. If you haven't logged in this session, you'll need to enter your email address and password, so EMusic knows that it's you. The log-in form also has an option that instructs the system to always remember you, so when it's time to log in, you can just click the **Log In** button and skip entering your name and password. This option is a good idea for your computer at home because it saves you time each time you use EMusic. It's a bad idea for your computer at work because EMusic will think that anyone who uses your computer is you, even if they have a really funny-looking haircut.

An invoice of what you've ordered appears. At this point, they're going to want a bunch more information so that they can bill your purchases to your credit card. Click **Add a New Credit Card** to get a form of credit card information. Fill out the form, and then click **Add Credit Card**. On the next screen, click the **Continue** button. (You'll only have to go through this rigmarole the first time; after that, EMusic remembers your credit card information as part of your account info, and you can charge automatically to that card.)

After you've entered your credit card information, EMusic puts the purchase order through, so your credit card is billed. A list of songs you've ordered appears. Each of these songs has a download link. Use these links to download the songs, as described earlier.

Yes, it does take quite awhile to download entire albums. Don't worry about something going wrong in the midst of a download; after you've purchased a song, you're allowed to download it up to three times.

Conquering Credit Card Crime!

If you're worried about someone stealing your credit card number when you send it over the Internet to a site like EMusic, you're causing yourself unneeded stress. Modern major browsers all support *secured* mode, a communications mode where everything you send via a Web form is encoded so that people using Internet snooping tools can't read it. You can tell your browser is in secured mode by looking at the bottom bar of the browser window; if you see an unbroken key or a closed padlock, the security is in force.

Remember that you don't have to wait for one file to finish downloading before you start the next. Your Web browser can usually handle several files at a time. That way, you can start the various files downloading just before going to bed, or before heading off on a trip to the Himalayas. Those of you with high-speed links shouldn't have much problem getting the music you bought, but those of us still using the same phone modems our grandparents used when they were kids will find getting that album a bit more trying.

Other EMusic Features

EMusic doesn't just support music by selling MP3s; it offers a number of useful informational links. Other features of the EMusic site include

➤ A page of downloadable MP3 players (not nearly so many as MP3.com, but with more description)

➤ A concert search (you can find out the next time that The Wascally Weasels are coming to your town)

➤ A general music news page (so you can find out that The Wascally Weasels have broken up because the lead Weasel got elected to Congress)

AMP3: Music, and Just a Little More

AMP3 seems to have taken a cue from commercial radio. At `AMP3.com`, you can download free music from hundreds of bands. And that's not all! In addition to the free music, there's something else you get for free:

Advertising

That's right, attached to each song is a short little ad clip, just a few seconds long. Every time you play the MP3, you'll hear a little jingle for some sponsor.

So why would you download from here when you can be downloading ad-free music from other places? After all, if you're a fan of music, you don't really want to have to sit through even a few seconds of ads, and if you're a fan of ads, you really don't want to have to sit through several minutes of music to hear each one.

The answer is that AMP3.com hopes to provide you with *better music* because of the ads. Every time someone downloads a song with an ad in it, the advertiser pays AMP3.com money. When that happens, AMP3.com passes half of the money along to the performer. By doing this, they hope to attract musicians whose music is worth paying for. The deal for the musicians is actually quite attractive because the amount they get paid per download (ranging from 5 to 25 cents) is around the same rate they would get paid for the song if it were on a CD. In the long run, you may see folks building careers from this sort of distribution, rather than getting some attention with a few free tracks and then hopping off the MP3 bandwagon onto the CD bandwagon.

Getting this arrangement fully working and profitable is a long-term goal for AMP3; they don't have everything going quite as well as they probably hope to. At this point, the ad jingles they run are jingles for the one advertiser they can most easily land: AMP3.com itself. And they give themselves a discount on the ads, only paying the performer 2 cents.

Finding Music on AMP3.com

The front page of the site has a list of their recent Pick Hit Of The Day picks. This is a spot that their artists really desire; not only does it mean a lot of visibility and more downloads, but they get a $50 bonus for being the Pick Hit. Better still, if the same song is a Pick Hit for two days, they get $1,000, and for three days, $10,000.

Running down the left edge of the page is a list of musical genres, ranging from Alternative to Zydeco. Click any of these links, and you'll see the most popular downloads in each category. When I visited, their genre list was a bit overzealous, as I found at least one genre for which they had no music. That's another sign that their goals are set well beyond what they've achieved.

Every Web Site Aims to Grow

In my coverage of AMP3.com, you'll see a few comments noting that they clearly aren't yet at the level of success that they are aiming for. Does this mean they're failures? Heck no! Few of even the most popular Web sites have achieved their goals. Even those sites whose stocks are skyrocketing are losing money by the bucketful, and aren't that worried about it. They know that if they can get their Web site established now, there will be plenty of opportunities to make money when the Web has even more users and a much larger bandwidth.

For each song listed, you can use the link for the name of the song to download it, or click the performer's name to see an information sheet on that performer and a list of all their songs available to download, each with a download link.

Other AMP3.com Features

At the time of this writing, there isn't much more there. They have an introductory MP3 guide, some hardware reviews, and some links to a handful of MP3 software providers. Again, expect this site to grow.

RioPORT

RioPORT is a site run by Diamond, manufacturers of the Rio portable MP3 players and other multimedia gadgets. As such, there is a visible emphasis on providing music for people with Rios, and convincing people who come looking for music that they should get a Rio to play it on.

Head on over to www.rioport.com and you'll see what I mean: some large ads for the Rio and Rio-related stuff, plus an alphabetically ordered list of links to various musical genres. Click one of those links, and you'll get a handful of tracks in that genre displayed, each with an illustration. The download link for the track is the track's title. There's another link for each track with the name of a Web site that includes the artist; click that link to see the Web site.

When you select a genre, you also get a list at the left of the screen of Web sites that provide authorized MP3s of that sort of music. You can click any one of these links to visit that site.

The RioPORT opening page provides music and news links.

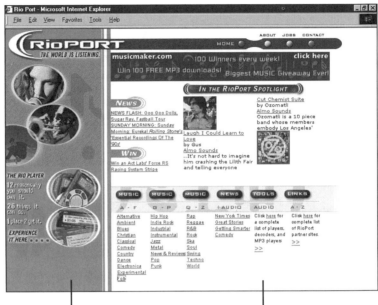

Diamond Rio information   Available music genres

RioPORT has folk music for musical folk.

Sources for other tracks in this genre

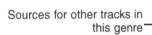

Genre name   Tracks available from RioPORT

All in all, there aren't that many songs on the RioPORT site (although they are hand-picked ones and thus tend to be good quality). What the site does best is help you find other MP3 sites that have music in a given genre.

Other RioPORT Features

In addition to musical genres, RioPORT has a list of spoken word genres (news, comedy, and so on). These categories all link to the Audible.com site, which I'll discuss in a little bit. The news is the same *New York Times* news that MP3.com carries. (Oddly enough, although clicking the link on RioPORT pulls up the Audible.com page with the *Times* news, a similar link on one of Audible's pages pulls up the MP3.com page!)

Audible: Lots o' Words, No Music

New Jersey-based Audible, Inc., is an interesting company. Years before the first portable MP3 players were available, Audible had their own portable electronic compressed audio player, the Audible MobilePlayer. This little handheld device doesn't have as much memory as the MP3 players (even the newer MobilePlayer-PLUS has only half as much memory as the earliest Rio), but they've been able to get hours of playtime out of the memory by using higher compression rates. The sound isn't as high quality as a good MP3, but that didn't matter so much for its intended use. Audible wasn't trying to replace CD players with their device; their target was the books-on-tape market.

Books on cassette tape are a huge market in the United States. I know that when I was driving from Minnesota to Alaska, my spirits were kept up by listening to such things as Richard Feynman's lectures on physics. Of course, that subject isn't to everyone's taste. (Some people I know would drive from Minnesota to Alaska just to avoid six hours of physics lectures.) But the good news is that all sorts of books, from the utterly vapid to the completely inscrutable, are available on tape.

One of the problems with books on cassette tape, however, is that they aren't cheap. Even an abridged edition will often take up four or six cassettes. Get a nice thick book like Stephen King's *Four Past Midnight*, and you'll find that the cassette edition is four volumes totaling 20 cassettes. That version will cost you about $100 more than buying the printed book in paperback, which runs about $8. The folks at Audible realized that if you didn't actually have to manufacture the cassettes, the costs come way down. If all they had to do was to have you download the electronic files, they could offer a lower price and still make a good profit. For example, King's *Bag Of Bones*—clocking in at more than 21 hours—costs about $60 on cassette, and $80 on CD, but if you download it for your MobilePlayer, it costs just $18. That's less than the hardback ($20), although still well more than the $8 paperback.

Sure, the MobilePlayer costs something (starting at about $80), but it doesn't take a lot of Stephen King audio recordings to save you money. Plus, the ability to make a recording available quickly online means that they can offer things that would be impractical to offer on a cassette, such as fresh National Public Radio news and interviews.

Enough About Not-MP3! Get to the MP3!

Audible realized that the Diamond Rio was a hot seller. Suddenly, tons of people were getting this player that worked a lot like their own. If they could just sell the files in the MP3 format as well, they could open up a large market of people who might not cough up $80 for a non-music player. And so they began converting the books that they offer to the MP3 format, and cozied up with Diamond so that they could help each other. (They may be delayed by the people who license them the rights to the recordings. After all, an MP3 of a book faces the same copying concern as an MP3 of a song.)

Despite being close to Diamond, Audible will tell you that their own player is actually better for books than the Rio. After all, if you pause the Rio in the middle of a chapter and don't start playing again soon, Rio resets to the beginning of the chapter, and when you want to listen again, you'll have to fast-forward to find your place. The Audible player doesn't lose its place. Because they're friendly with Diamond, however, they don't tell you that some of the *other* MP3 players (such as the MPMan) also don't lose their place.

Because of the higher level of compression (using a non-MP3 format) they use, the MobilePlayer-Plus can actually store more audio than the standard Rio.

So Where Do I Get These MP3 Books?

Surf on over to www.audible.com/mp3/ to get to their MP3-oriented site. After you get there, you'll see that they really want you to sign up with them. They'll want your name, phone number, and email address.

At Audible.com's MP3 site, you'll find links for a number of types of spoken information and entertainment. They have news, literature, humor, and more. They even have some alternative rock and jazz. Click one of these links, and you'll see a list of available items for download. Click one to get a fuller description, with a download link.

At the time I'm writing this, most of the downloads are shorter items (20 to 80 minutes), which are available for free, as samples. Soon (perhaps by the time you buy this book), you can expect to see more material available for sale.

They Want Your Number

It really gets my goat when someone wants more personal information than they legitimately need before you can access their site. The Audible MP3 site asking for my phone number is a clear example of that. How do I know they won't give my number to the fine folks at Evil Jack's Phone Company, who will call me at 3 a.m. to offer me their new phone plan ("Buy 10 minutes of long distance for $50, and your next 10 seconds are free!") Some sites at least offer you a privacy policy letting you know what they might do with your information before you give it to them; no such luck at Audible. And some sites don't give a fuss if you leave out some information; again, no such luck here. So consider these facts before you decide to give any site your information.

Mac Maniacs, Beware

To make longer works easier to handle, some of them are broken down into separate MP3 files for each chapter. In some cases, you can download a book chapter by chapter, which is fine. In other cases, however, they have combined the book's files into a single file that has a built-in program to split its component files back apart. This program is for Windows; it won't run on the Mac. If you see that the file you're downloading from Audible ends in .exe instead of .mp3, it isn't Mac friendly.

MP3now: An MP3-Less MP3 Site

The site at www.MP3now.com is supposed to be a central site for the MP3 fan. You might think they would have a lot of MP3s, some MP3 software, all the latest MP3 news articles, perhaps a search engine that lets you find the MP3s you want (legal or, alas, otherwise) and so on.

Actually, they don't have any of that stuff.

Links, Links, and (ummm, Let's See) More Links

What they *do* have is *links* to all that stuff. You can click a link on the site to pull up MP3.com's top 100 list from their site, another link to pull up the list of download-able music from an online rap label, and so on. They have reviews of software, and they have a download link, but that link starts the download from someone else's server, not their own. Click one of the MP3-related news headlines, and it'll pull up the page from someone else's site, not from MP3now.com itself.

And whenever you do link to a page on another site, MP3now.com opens that page either in a new window or in a frame on the existing window, making sure that you still have their site open.

The site does offer some music and a top 100 list that it *says* is part of MP3now.com, but if you look at the URL in your browser window, you'll discover that it really comes from another Web site, www.nordicdms.com. If you surf on over to that site, you'll see that they offer all those songs themselves.

Do They Have Anything of Their Own?

They do have some original content, material that talks *about* MP3 in some way. They have information on how to make and play MP3s, reviews of MP3 software, things like that.

They also own Findsongs.com, a site designed to help you search for MP3s. But in the MP3now.com tradition, this site doesn't actually have a search engine of its own. Instead, it lets you enter the information your searching for and select from a long list of other people's search engines. The results get displayed in a frame, so you're always kept at the Findsongs site.

A Disposable Web Site

So if MP3now doesn't have original material, does that mean that it's useless? Not really. It's useful like a disposable tissue is useful: use it once.

MP3now.com can be a good place to find out about other MP3 Web sites. Go there once, see if any of the sites that they link to are interesting, and add them to your Web browser's bookmarks. You don't need to keep going back to MP3now.com every time you want to get back to a site that they link to because doing so will just slow you down.

The Least You Need to Know

➤ Go to www.MP3.com for tens of thousands of free, legal recordings to download.

➤ www.EMusic.com offers downloadable tracks by known musicians for sale.

➤ AMP3.com offers free downloadable songs with a short ad jingle attached to the beginning of each one.

➤ Diamond has a Web site at www.RioPORT.com which offers free music as well as information on the Rio portable players.

➤ The company Audible, set up at www.audible/mp3/, sells mostly spoken word recordings, but it now offers plenty of free samples, including complete stories.

➤ At www.MP3now.com you'll find links to content on other MP3-related sites.

Chapter 5

Portable MP3 Devices and Other Hardware

In This Chapter

➤ Portable MP3 for your headsets

➤ MP3 for your stereo system

➤ MP3 for your car

MP3 music on your computer is great, but it's only useful as long as you're sitting in front of your computer. Now, if you spend all day in front of your computer, that should be good enough. But if you do spend all day in front of the computer, you should get out more. There's a lot of exciting things happening out there, a whole life to lead. Your mother and I have been worried about you.

And we're not the only ones. A whole industry has popped up to create other sorts of MP3 players, so don't feel you have to stay stuck in front of your PC in order to hear your favorite tunes.

Diamond Rio PMP300

The best known MP3 player is the portable Rio PMP300, manufactured by Diamond Multimedia, previously best known for their high-quality PC video cards. The Rio is about the same size (and flavor) as a deck of playing cards.

The Rio stores music in *flash memory*, a type of computer memory. Flash memory is different than the standard memory in your PC, because flash memory remembers even when the power is turned off. The basic PMP300 (which lists for around $200, but can easily be found for less) comes with 32 megabytes of flash memory, about enough to store half an hour of songs in CD-quality compression, or more if you use a lower grade of compression. (You can keep a fairly sharp sound and get a full hour of music in it.) The PMP300 Special Edition, for about $50 more, comes with twice as much memory.

There is also an expansion slot, so you can add another 16 or 32 megabytes using a standard SmartMedia flash memory card. These cards run from about $60 to $100 apiece.

Forgettable Uses of Memory

More and more folks are using SmartMedia flash memory cards in their digital cameras and other digital appliances. If you've got some of these and want to use them in your Rio, *be careful!* First off, flash memory cards come with different voltage ratings; some of the flash memory cards out there are 5v, and the Rio needs 3.3v.

More importantly, once you use a flash memory card in the Rio, you *can't* use it any more in your camera or in other products! The Rio changes the internal for-matting of the memory, so that other devices can't understand it. (This is Diamond's way of addressing a US law that requires that the Rio not be able to transfer files to other devices.)

Installing the Rio's Battery

The Rio takes a single AA battery. It's a little tricky to install. The plastic battery door is on a metal hinge on the bottom of the Rio, but in addition to pivoting on that hinge, the door can slide along the hinge.

To open the battery door, use your thumb to push it toward the side of the Rio, sliding it along the hinge beneath. Once you have it pushed out, the hinge will flip open easily. The battery goes in positive end first. (That's the end with the little bump sticking out of it.) Closing the battery door is the tricky part—you have to make sure that the door is slid all the way out along the hinge, then close the hinge, and then push the door in along the hinge. It's easy to make the mistake of first trying to slide the door in and then trying to force the door inward. At best you'll be frustrated. At worst, you'll damage the little door and you'll have to hold together this nifty cutting-edge electronic device using a piece of duct tape, and that ain't cool! (Then again, if you own a pager, you're probably used to this awkward little battery dance.)

If you're not going to use your Rio for days at a time, take the battery out. Even when you're not using it, the Rio will slowly use up the battery that's in it. If the battery isn't in it, it can't get run down. Perhaps more importantly, you eliminate the chance that an aging battery will start leaking battery acid all over the inside of your player, turning the electronic marvel into a low-quality paperweight. The good news is that because the Rio uses *flash memory* (a special sort of computer memory that doesn't forget everything when the power is turned off), you don't lose the music when the battery is removed.

Nat Speaks

Save Money *and* the Planet

If you find yourself going through a fair number of AA batteries in your player (and in other uses), consider switching to rechargeable batteries. They cost more up front (particularly since you have to buy a battery recharger), but can save you in the long run. Plus, it's more ecologically sound.

Hooking the Little Box to Your PC

In order to make use of the Rio, you're going to need a PC that runs Windows. (Sorry, Macintosh folk, they're not ready for you yet.) But don't worry, you don't have to carry the PC with you everywhere you go. You'll need the PC when you want to add or change the songs in your Rio.

The Rio comes with two sets of software on CD-ROM. It comes with a copy of MusicMatch Jukebox software, as seen in Chapter 3, "Installing and Using MP3 Player Software." This is not a fully registered copy of MusicMatch; it can handle all your encoding needs for a while, but it will stop encoding after you've encoded 50 songs, while the rest of the functions will continue working. (The evaluation unit I tested had a somewhat older version of MusicMatch, but I expect that by the time you read this, they'll be offering a more recent version.) You will use MusicMatch to turn tracks from your favorite CD-ROM into MP3s, so you can put them on the Rio.

The other set of software is special Rio software. While it can be used to play MP3s, its main usage is to send files to the Rio and to remove older files to make space. Before you can do any of this, however, you'll have to hook your Rio to your PC. To do this, complete these steps:

1. Power down your PC.
2. Unplug your printer cable from the back of the PC.
3. Plug the Rio adapter into the printer port.
4. Plug your printer cable into the adapter.

5. Plug the Rio cable into the special slot in the adapter. The side of the cable marked UP goes away from the printer connector.

6. Plug the other end of the Rio cable into the Rio. The side of the cable marked UP goes toward the face of the Rio.

7. Power up your PC.

Printer Confusion

These days, there are a lot of nonprinter devices that use the printer port. For example, I have a scanner that plugs into the printer port, and then I plug the printer into a port on the scanner. The problem is that devices like that or like the Rio adapter assume that they're the only device using the port besides the printer. With the adapter plugged into the PC, the scanner plugged into the adapter, and the printer plugged into the scanner, my printer started acting crazy the moment I turned the PC on. If I plugged the scanner into the PC and the adapter into the scanner, the PC couldn't communicate with the Rio.

How can you get around this problem? Well, you can get rid of any nonprinter items hooked up to your printer port, but that's probably not practical. Some PCs have multiple printer ports, in which case you can just plug the Rio connector into a different one than your other nonprinter devices. Or you could unplug your other devices when you want to use the Rio.

If you're going to be using the Rio and the other devices fairly regularly, however, you'll probably want to avoid the difficulty and wear-and-tear on the parts of constantly unplugging and replugging. What you'll need to do is purchase an *A/B switch*, which is a box that plugs into your printer port. It will have two different out ports, one which you can connect the Rio to, the other for your other device. Then you just turn a knob or push a button on the A/B switch whenever you want to change which device is connected. When you buy your A/B switch, be sure that the package says that it *passes through* (connects) all 25 leads from the printer port; cheaper A/B switches only pass through the few leads that printers use, and won't attach the leads that other devices use.

Installing Rio Software

To install the Rio management software, stick the Rio's software CD-ROM into your CD-ROM drive. On most people's PC, the installation program will start automatically after a few seconds. If it doesn't start for you, double-click **My Computer**, double-click the icon for your CD-ROM drive, and then double-click the icon marked **Setup.exe** or just **Setup**.

The installation program suggests a folder to store the program in. Click **Next** to accept this folder. Then a list of suggested installation options appears, with the most appropriate choices already checked off. (If you already have a current, registered version of MusicMatch running on your system, you'll probably want to clear the check box to install the new one.) Click **Next** again. On the next screen, click **Next** again. The installation takes place, and you'll be informed when it's done. Click **Finish** to acknowledge that it's done.

But wait! It may not be done! If you chose to install MusicMatch, the MusicMatch installation program will automatically start. Just follow its instructions to complete that installation.

Sending Music to Rio

To copy MP3 songs from your PC to the Rio, first start the Rio software by clicking the **Start** button and choosing **Programs**, **Rio**, **Rio Manager**.

The window that opens up is a basic Windows MP3 player. As a player, it's kind of lame. If you just want to play MP3s on your PC, you'd be better off using the MusicMatch software. About the only reason you'd really want to start this player is so that you can click the **Mem** button.

—The Mem button

When you start the Rio manager, you get a lame MP3 player with a vital button marked Mem.

When you click that button, a Rio Internal Memory window opens up. The program communicates with your Rio, and displays a list of all the songs stored in the Rio's *internal memory* (the memory that's built in to the Rio, as opposed to any add-in memory card you have installed, which would be considered *external memory*). The first time you run it, there won't be any music there, of course, unless the ghost musicians who haunt the Rio plant have secretly stored their cover of the Chiquita Banana song on your machine.

The easiest way to add a song to the list is to drag and drop the song's icon onto the song list. You can also add a song by clicking **Open** and finding the song using the file navigator that appears.

The Rio memory manager manages Rio memory in a memorable, manageable fashion!

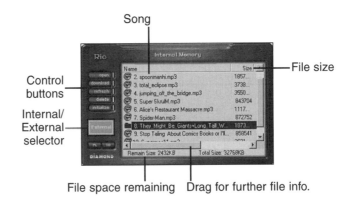

Song

Control buttons

Internal/ External selector

File size

File space remaining   Drag for further file info.

If the song file is bigger than the remaining space in your Rio, you'll get a dialog box telling you so in nice, non-insulting terms. Which is kind of a shame, because if programs treated us as sarcastically as our friends do when we mess up, we might not trust them so much, and would thus be ready to stop the joint computer/robot attempt at world domination that's scheduled for June 3rd, 2003 (unless my toaster oven is lying to me). You can make room for the song by deleting other tracks. To delete a track, just click on it and then click **Delete**.

Once you have the right set of songs on the list, click **Download**, and any new files you added to the list will be downloaded to the Rio. This may take a few minutes. (A standard, unexpanded Rio without any files on it takes about six minutes to fill up.)

If you do have a memory card inserted into the Rio, you have to set up a separate list of music that will be stored on it. Click **External**, and the manager switches to managing the memory on the card. To return to managing the internal song list, click **Internal**.

Once your done downloading, unplug the connector cable from the Rio. You can leave the other end plugged into adapter, so that you don't have to reconnect it every time you want to download to the Rio, and so that your cat will have a nice dangling cord to play with. (Cats are considered accessories and are not included with the basic Rio models.)

Using the Rio

Plug a set of headphones into the Rio, and you're ready to start high-quality digital listening. You can use the headphones the Rio came with or any other headphones with a standard Walkman-style jack.

To start playing the downloaded songs, just press the **Play/Pause** button. The Rio will automatically turn on and quickly display the amount of memory the system has, and then a second later, you'll be hearing pure digital sound, assuming you remembered to stick the headphones in your ears.

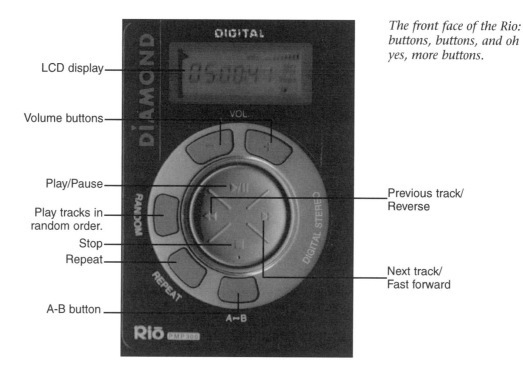

LCD display—

Volume buttons—

Play/Pause—

Play tracks in
random order.

Stop—

Repeat—

A-B button

Previous track/
Reverse

Next track/
Fast forward

*The front face of the Rio:
buttons, buttons, and oh
yes, more buttons.*

The main controls are on the front face of the Rio:

➤ Press the **Play/Pause** button to start playing music. Press it again to pause the playing and then again to restart it. (After you paused a track for about half a minute, the Rio will lose its place in the track; press **Play** after that, and you're back at the start of the song.)

➤ Quickly press and release the **Next track/Fast forward** button to skip to the next song. If you hold down the button, you'll fast forward through the current song.

➤ Quickly press and release the **Previous track/Reverse** button to skip back to the previous song. If you hold down the button, you'll zoom backwards through the current song. (You won't actually hear the music while fast forwarding or reversing. You can only tell where you are in the song by looking at the display.)

➤ Press **Stop** once to stop the music playing. Pressing it a second time turns off the Rio. (The Rio will turn off automatically after about 15 seconds if there isn't any music playing and you're not doing anything, unless you're in Pause mode.)

➤ Use the + and - volume buttons to increase and decrease the volume. The Rio has 20 different volume levels, which is enough that you should be able to find a level that is audible but comfortable in most situations.

➤ Press **Random** to hear the songs play in random order. (Even in this mode, you will hear songs stored on the internal memory first, and only once you've heard all of those will you hear songs from the memory card.)

➤ Pressing **Repeat** cycles between repeating one song, repeating all the songs (automatically restarting the first track when the last song is done), and just playing through the songs once and then stopping. If you're in one of the repeat modes, the display will show an arrow turned back on itself in the lower-right corner, followed by either 1 or All, depending on the repeat mode.

➤ The **A-B** button is used to repeat a short segment of a song. For example, if the singer is singing, "You're a simple pleasure like hot dogs, like discovering new songs," you can press the button once after the word *hot* to set the start of the repeating segment. Press the button again in the middle of the word *discovering* to set the end of the repeating portion. Suddenly, your Rio will start repeating the phrase "dogs like disco" time and time again. Press the button for a third time to resume normal play.

The Rio also has three buttons across the top:

➤ The **Menu** button is one you won't be using often. It only works when the music is stopped. Press it once to go into menu mode. The letters tI will be displayed, followed by the number of total internal memory megabytes. Press the **Next track/Fast forward** button repeatedly to see the total external memory (tE), the amount of unused internal memory (RI), the amount of unused external memory (RE), and the version number of the software built into the unit (V). Press **Menu** again to return to music playing mode.

➤ Press the **EQ** button to cycle between the four different sets of equalizer settings, optimized for different types of music. There are settings for Normal, Classic (misspelled *clasic*), Jazz, and Rock.

➤ Press **Intro** to hear the first 10 seconds of each song. This makes it easy to find an individual song when you don't remember what order the songs were stored in. When you find the song you like, press **Intro** again to return to normal playing mode.

The final control is on the side of the unit. It's a small, unmarked switch. Slide this switch up, and none of the buttons will work anymore. Why would you want this? Well, if you're going to stick the Rio in your pocket, or somewhere else where it's going to get banged against things, having this Hold button on will keep your music from starting, stopping, or being otherwise abused by accidental button pushes. Just slide it back down when you're ready to take control again.

Rio's Display: Information in Formation

The Rio has a convenient display on the front. Convenient, that is, unless you're using the belt clip on the back of the unit to hold it to your pants. Then you have to bend yourself in half to see the display, and even then it will appear upside-down. Either that, or you can just briefly unclip it from your pants and lift it to your eyes.

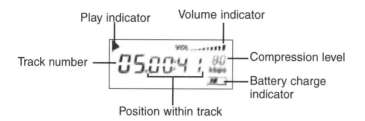

The Rio display is actually clear to read, just hard to photograph.

The Play indicator in the upper-right corner displays an arrow when playing, or two parallel lines when the song is paused.

The Volume display indicates the sound level as a series of line segments of increasing size. The more segments displayed, the louder the play is. It's not a precise display (it only shows 10 different volume levels, when there are actually 20), but it's close enough.

The battery charge indicator gives you a sense of how much energy is left in your battery. The more black showing in the image of the battery, the more power remains. When you get down to just a small segment of black remaining, carry a spare battery with you.

Tune Talk

Maybe the Writer Was on LSD?

The Rio manual repeatedly refers to the display as an *LED display*. Problem is, it's not true. *LED* stands for *Light Emitting Diode*. LED displays are ones with glowing figures, like on the fronts of many VCRs. The Rio display is neither light–emitting nor made of diodes. It's properly called an *LCD display*, the same sort of display that most digital watches have. *LCD* stands for *Liquid Crystal Display* (which means that *LCD display* stands for *Liquid Crystal Display display*, but that's just normal technical silliness).

83

Thanks for the Memory Card

To add additional memory to the Rio, insert the memory card into the slot at the bottom of the unit. (A diagram on the back of the unit shows you how to orient the card for proper connection.) When you push the card in, the large slider on the back of the Rio will slide up. Once the card is in place, push the smaller slider to the left to lock it into place.

To remove the card, push the small slider to the right, and then push the large slider down.

Rio Is for Me-o!

After spending a month with the Rio, I think it's a rather sharp gadget. The sound quality coming from songs compressed at 128Kbps is amazing. The unit is rugged, making it great for use while you're jogging (or sitting in the park laughing at the joggers). It's small size means that one can carry it in a large pocket so you have it when you want it...just try that with a portable cassette player or a CD player. And if you try it with your record player, you'll rip your pocket right off!

However, the 32 megabytes that the basic unit has stores only half an hour of that high-quality compression. If you're going for a longer jog than that, you'll have to either settle for repeating the same music, or using higher compression, lower-quality audio. Even if you throw in money for additional memory, you top out at a couple hours of music.

And just as headphones can point up the strengths of high-quality audio, they also accent the weaknesses of lesser quality. If you use files compressed down to 80Kbps or even 64Kbps, you'll hear a metallic echo to the music, as if your fave band was playing in a culvert. The higher the compression rate, the deeper into the culvert they get.

At first, this echo was irritating, but after a while I grew accustomed to it. While listening to this high-compression material never got as enjoyable as listening to the better-quality material, soon the echo was no more annoying than the hiss of a cassette player or the light static of AM radio.

Filling the Rio with music was a bit of a pain in the neck at first, but that was because whenever I wanted a new song, I'd have to get the CD and convert the song to MP3. Once you have your music collection on your hard disk, things get a lot easier.

This Rio is clearly a member of the first generation of MP3 players. Assuming that memory prices continue to fall, you'll be able to carry several hours of high-quality audio with you at all times. With that much, I'd be able to keep a lot of good stuff with me, rather than re-downloading my half hour or hour of music each time I plan to go out. But then, with technology changing so fast, you can count on something better coming out in a few months no matter when you buy.

The MPMan F10: First Ain't Best

I'm not going to fully cover the Eiger Labs MPMan F10, the US version of the first MP3 hardware player release. Suffice it to say that if you're considering buying one, think again. You may be able to get a bargain price on it, but that's because it's been quickly outdated by newer releases, including its own sequel, the MPMan F20.

The Eiger Labs MPMan F10—the first, and no longer the best.

There is no real problem with the sound quality; it is still the same crisp digitized sound that you'd get from any of the players, and it even has a nice two-lever bass boost system. It's the little things that make the difference. For example, there's no memory card slot. If you want more than the 32 megabytes that the unit comes with, you'll have to send it back to Eiger Labs and plunk down about $75 to get the memory doubled.

There's no belt clip either. You'll have keep it in a pocket (or buy the carrying case, which has a belt loop). It does come with rechargeable batteries, which is a plus, but they aren't the same size as standard batteries, so you can't easily carry a spare around with you for when the battery runs out.

The F10 comes with a *docking station*, a holder that you place the unit in to recharge the batteries as well as to download your tunes. The docking station plugs into your printer port, with no pass-through, so if you only have one printer port, you'll have to unplug the printer every time you want to change your tunes.

Don't get me wrong. The F10 was a big step, much bigger than any of the little steps that have taken place since. But those little steps make things much nicer, so if you have a choice, go with a more recent MP3 player.

Got an F10?

Most MPMan F10s shipped with downloading software that fails to recognize some MP3s. Surf on over to `http://eigerlabs.com/MPMan/f10/downloads.htm` for the latest version.

MPMan F20: Now That's More Like It!

At a glance the second version of the MPMan, the F20, looks a lot like the original, only in black instead of gray. That itself is not exactly a technological advance, as the color black has long been found in nature in the night sky, the sheen of coal, and the clothing of art students. If you look a little closer, however, you'll quickly find that the worst aspects of the F10 have been erased.

Gone are the special rechargeable batteries, replaced instead by a single AA battery which will play for up to 12 hours. And with the need to charge the batteries eliminated, gone too is the bulky docking station, replaced by a direct cable connection to the PC's parallel port. A slot has appeared for external flash memory, letting you quickly expand the F20's capacity. Basically, if you cross the workings and color of the Rio with the look of an F10, you have an F20.

F-Plusses and F-Minuses

The F20 has certain advantages over the Rio, as well as certain disadvantages. Unlike the Rio, you can use the F20 to transfer non-MP3 files from one PC to another. Just download the file to the F20, and then carry the F20, cable, adapter, and software disk to another PC, install them there, and upload the files. This may seem a little awkward, but if you're trying to move a 20MB file and don't have a compatible large-size disk drive, it's a way that will work.

As with the Rio, the F20 will take 3.3 volt SmartMedia flash memory cards and reformat them, rendering them unusable for any other purpose. However, the reformatted card can be moved from F20 to F20, data intact. That way, you can load your latest recording (your original opera based on the book *Is Sex Necessary?*) onto a memory card and pass it on to a friend, who can put it into her F20 and listen to it. This trick won't work with Rios.

The F20 also has a bass-boosting switch that lets you turn up those driving beats. If you're one for bopping to a dance beat as you walk, this may suit you better than the Rio's equalizer feature.

On the downside, the F20 (which fits nicely into a shirt pocket) still lacks a clip; if you want to hang this on anything, you will have to spring for an additional carrying case, which includes a belt loop. The Rio's clip may not be perfect, but it generally gets the job done. The F20's small controls are good for subtle discreet movements, but awkward for the jogger or the person carrying something, where again the Rio will shine.

All in all, the two players are definitely in the same league. If you're deciding between the two, it's likely to come down to a question of personal taste and of price. At the moment, the Rio is about $30 cheaper than the F20, but that number is likely to change as competition heats up between the two manufacturers and the newer entrants into the fray.

Money is an issue for me, so if I was making my decision now, I'd certainly lean toward the Rio. If money isn't an issue for you, however, feel free to buy me whatever player you choose!

The Other Players in the Players Game

The Rio and the MPMan set up the market for portable all-electronic music players. Once they proved the market was there, others rushed to jump in. Here are just some of the players hitting the shelves in 1999.

Nomad Ain't so Bad

Creative Labs, the company that set the standard in PC sound cards with their Sound Blaster line, offers the Nomad line of players (visible at www.nomadworld.com). These little units have the two features that seem to define the second generation of MP3 players: FM radio reception and voice recording. Voice recording lets you use it instead of one of those little portable cassette recorders for taking notes; you can upload the recording to your PC later.

There are two models, differing only in the amount of memory they include. One has 32 megabytes, the other 64. (Really, it's the same product; one just includes a 32 megabyte flashcard to plug into the flashcard slot.) The Nomad uses rechargeable AAA batteries. A docking station is used both for recharging the batteries and for transferring MP3 files from your PC. It also comes with MP3 encoding software. List price is about $170 for the 32 megabyte version, $250 for the 64 megabyte version.

The Nomad, in its docking station.

Yup, It's Called Yepp

International electronics giant Samsung weighed in with the Yepp, which can be seen at http://yepp.co.kr/eng/ or at various electronics stores. The Series E model comes equipped with 32 megabytes of built-in memory (expandable using SmartMedia flash memory cards) and supports voice recording as well as an address book function. The Series B adds a battery-recharging docking station and a 16-character LCD display to show song title information. And the top-of-the-line Series D adds an FM tuner to the feature mix, as well as an included SmartMedia card to expand the memory.

That's right, their models are E, B, and D, in that order. Clearly, Samsung is not a strong believer in alphabetical order.

Samsung also came up with a recording station for the Yepp. This is an accessory that you can hook up to a CD player, a cassette deck, or just about any sort of sound output device, and have their sound output converted into MP3s and stored on your Yepp. That way, they can sell you a Yepp even if you don't own a PC!

RCA's Lyra: Memory Free!

The Lyra, from RCA and Thomas Multimedia, has no flash memory built in. That's right, none. If you want to use any flash memory, though, just plug in the 32 megabyte card that's included with this $200 unit.

Why is there no memory built in to the device? Because you won't be connecting the Lyra to your PC to download. Instead, you have a separate memory writer connected to your PC. Plug your memory card into this device, download your songs into the memory, and then plug the memory card into the Lyra. With the PC connector and the memory writing capability built in to a separate device, there's that much less hardware that needs to be built in to the portable device, keeping it smaller and lighter.

However, the Lyra (the name rhymes with animated superheroine She-Ra) offers another possibility. You can buy a *microdrive* (an extremely tiny hard drive manufactured by IBM) and plug that in. Suddenly, instead of having 32 megabytes, you have up to 340, enough to store about five hours of top-quality MP3s, or a heck of a lot of lower quality, higher compression recordings.

That's the good news. The bad news is that a microdrive will set you back hundreds of dollars.

Another advantage to the Lyra is that it carries two AA batteries, which weighs it down a bit but lets it run for up to 20 hours without a battery change.

I-Jam, U-Jam, We All Jam for I-Jam

The IJ-100 player from I-Jam (www.ijamworld.com) uses the same space-saving trick as the Lyra, using a separate memory writing device that you connect to your PC. It also uses the SanDisc memory card, which is smaller than SmartMedia-type cards and again saves space.

The selling point that the manufacturer stresses isn't the size (overall, it's only a little smaller and a little lighter than the Rio) but the shape and color. Instead of being a box, it's a curvy shape, kind of like a slice of bread from a squished loaf. And it's available in a range of vibrant colors. And for those who think that Windows is too boxy, it also supports Macintosh.

For Those Who Jog for 12 Hours Straight: Portable MP3 CD Players

As attractive as the all-electronic players are, the limits caused by limited memory size really mean that they can't hold much. Oh, you can buy external flash memory cards for most of them, and carry multiple cards with you to switch songs in and out, but the flash memory to hold half the music from a CD will run you several times the cost of the CD.

As an alternative, manufacturers like Synos Tech (www.synostech.com) are developing portable CD players which can read CD-ROMs filled with MP3s. These are aimed mostly at people who have CD-R or CD-RW drives on their computers, so they can make their own CD-ROMs filled with MP3s. You can store about 12 hours of music at typical compression rates on one CD-ROM, or about 50 hours of reasonably good voice-grade recording. The players, a little larger than a typical portable CD player, can read the MP3 files and playlists from the CD-ROM. They can also play standard audio CDs.

The downside to these players (in addition to requiring the user to have a CD-R or CD-RW drive, which start at around $250) is that they still have a lot of moving parts. As such, they don't replace the all-electronic player. However, they do a fine job of replacing the standard portable CD player. You can carry an assortment of discs with you and quickly change what you're playing. After you've spent awhile with a portable MP3 player planning and downloading the day's music in advance, this becomes a very desirable feature.

AudioReQuest: Because Music Is for Stereos, Not PCs

Let's face it, your PC is not the ideal place for playing music. Even the high-grade PC speakers are designed for playing to someone seated at the PC, not the crowd at your party. If you want to hear a song now, waiting several minutes for your PC to start up is a pain in the neck. You've got a nice home entertainment center in the living room, and you'd really rather hear your music through that.

A new breed of MP3 players is arising, designed to be part of your stereo system. These fall into the category of *tethered systems*, because they are designed to be connected (tethered) to your PC, but to be their own devices. The AudioReQuest by ReQuest, Inc. (www.audiorequest.com), shipping in the later half of 1999, is at the forefront of these devices. For a price of about $600, you can bring MP3s to your stereo system.

Two Drives, No Waiting

The AudioReQuest looks a lot like a standard component CD player, and it wires up to your amplifier in the same way. However, in addition to having a CD drive, it also has a hard drive built in, and a parallel port that can connect to your PC's printer port. Using these features, the AudioReQuest can:

➤ Play standard audio CDs. (That's no big deal. These days, just about every appliance can play audio CDs. I'm listening to the Barenaked Ladies on my toaster oven at the moment.)

➤ Take an inserted audio CD, encode the tracks, and store them on the hard drive, for playing at any time.

➤ Copy MP3s from your PC to the system's hard disk, for playing at any time.

➤ Play MP3s encoded on CD-ROMs.

➤ Copy MP3s from CD-ROMs to the hard disk, for playing at any time.

➤ Connect other audio devices (record players, cassette players, and so on) to the AudioReQuest's line in port, so you can digitize, encode, and store music from other sources.

The main goal is to get your favorite music onto the hard drive, which holds about 150 hours of music. (That's about 2,000 songs, or 3,000 ditties, or one really overindulgent drum solo. ReQuest does plan to offer units with larger hard disks, if one solid week's worth of music just isn't enough for you.) Once the music is there, you have a high-quality, high-capacity jukebox. You can set up playlists to have your favorite music for different moods.

Look at All the Pretty Music

AudioReQuest includes a video-out connector, which you can use to hook it to your TV. If you do so, you can watch all sorts of mesmerizing displays that accompany your music. Bouncy colored blobs which mesmerize you and create an inexplicable fascination...oh, wait, you still have the TV tuned to TeleTubbies. Switch it over to watching the patterns generated by AudioReQuest, and you still get pretty, mesmerizing colors, but these are in time to the music.

You can even create your own visuals for music. AudioReQuest lets you transfer scanned photos and other images for display while playing your music.

That's not all the TV hookup is for, however. It also allows you to control your AudioReQuest through onscreen menus. This isn't needed for simple things like playing an individual song, but it comes in handy when you're doing more complex things, like building a playlist. (AudioReQuest can read song ID information that's encoded into the MP3s. If you're digitizing your music by putting your CDs into AudioReQuest, however, you should consider throwing down the extra money for the optional wireless keyboard, which makes entering data a lot easier.)

What It Won't Do

You can't copy an MP3 file from the AudioReQuest's hard drive to your PC, or to any other device for that matter. This was a careful design decision built into the device, so that it won't violate the U.S. Audio Home Recording Act, which sets strict limitations on digital audio copying machines.

FutuReQuest

With all of the competition in the compressed audio field, it's clear that MP3 won't be the only popular format in the long run. AudioReQuest is designed so that you can upgrade its software to play whatever new standard takes hold. (Of course, you're gambling on the company still being around and supporting the product at the time.)

ReQuest Inc. is looking at a number of other functions for future upgrades and new versions. Most notable among these is some form of Internet connection (possibly through your PC) which would let the AudioReQuest look up the album name, performer, and track titles for any CD you insert, thus saving you the effort of entering all that information yourself. They are also considering adding support for some sort of removable recordable drive (such as a Jaz drive or a Zip drive), to allow you to effectively expand the unit's capacity.

MP3 Your Model T: A Player for Your Car

We all love listening to music in our cars. Not only does it make those long commutes cheerier, but it also helps us deal with that annoying little grinding noise that would cost about $2,000 to properly repair, but can be drowned out with a twist of the volume control.

Getting MP3s into your car is many people's dream. In fact, if you surf on over to www.mp3.com/hardware/ you will find a healthy list of sites describing various devices for playing MP3s in your car. Follow most of these links, however, and you'll discover that it's some hobbyist who decided to build an entire PC into their trunk, and then hook that up to their car's stereo with a remote control. These homebrew projects sound like a wild idea, but they aren't what I'd recommend to, well, sane people. (There are even commercial versions of these, but they still seem like cool kludges rather than real long-term solutions.)

However, there are now starting to be genuine MP3 players for your car, items that aren't homebrew kits or awkward kludges, but which let you have at your fingertips far more music than any car CD changer will ever give you. At the forefront of this is Empeg.

Empeg: A Hard Drive to Make Your Drive Easier

The Empeg player, manufactured by Empeg Limited (www.empeg.com), fits into a standard European dashboard slot (or, with a common adapter, a US dashboard slot). Behind a fancy glowing display is a hard drive that holds your MP3s and playlists. The base model, which will run you about $1,100, has a 4 gigabyte drive, which stores about 35 hours of music. Expanded models are available with up to a 28 gigabyte drive, storing over 400 hours of music.

MP3 for Your Car—Quick, Easy, and Cheap!

Most of the designs for car-based MP3 players assume that your goal is to store dozens of hours of audio in your car, for playing any time. A laudable goal, that. However, if your goal is simply to listen to a given MP3 while you're on the road (for example, if you've downloaded an audio book and want to listen to it on your way to work), you can do it a lot more cheaply. In fact, you may already have everything you need!

You will need a portable MP3 player—a Rio, an MPMan, a Yepp, or anything like that will do fine. (Obviously, if you don't have one of these anyway, this is a major expense.) You'll also need a CD-to-car cassette adapter; this looks like a cassette tape with a cable coming out of it. If you don't have one lying around (they come with many portable CD players), you can buy one for about $20 at most stores that carry portable CD players. And you'll need a cassette player built into your car.

First, turn the volume on your MP3 player all the way down. (This is important; if you set the volume too loud, there's a slight chance you will do damage to your car stereo.) Unplug the headphones from the player, and plug the cable from the cassette adapter into the headphone jack. Turn on your car radio, and set the radio's volume to a level you like. Push the cassette adapter into your car's cassette player. Press the **Play** button on your MP3 player and then slowly turn the volume on the MP3 player up. You will start hearing the sound from the MP3 player coming out of your car stereo. Keep turning the MP3 player volume up until it matches the volume you heard coming from the radio before.

Whatever you do, don't just wear your MP3 player headphones and listen to your MP3 player as you drive! Driving with headphones on is dangerous (it can block out vital road sounds) and may cause you trouble with the police (and I don't mean Sting's old band!).

The Empeg is removable. This not only makes it easy for thieves to steal it (alerted to the unit's presence by the bumper sticker and window decal that come with each unit, letting everyone know you have this expensive unit in your car), but it also makes it easy for you to take it with you so that thieves can't get at it. Even if crime weren't an issue, the removability is important because it lets you take the Empeg inside and hook it up to your PC, so you can transfer all your MP3s onto it. Otherwise, you've just paid a thousand bucks for a fancy blue digital display. It supports both serial connections (mostly used to hook up to older PCs) and USB connections (which transfer data much more quickly and are supported by most modern PCs).

In order to use the Empeg, you'll need to have an amplifier of some sort already in your car. It does have standard audio-out connectors, which you can connect to the audio-in jacks on many car stereos, or to a dedicated amp. There simply wasn't enough room in the Empeg to build an amp in. (In fact, to fit everything into the unit, they had to use the smaller hard drives made for laptop computers...which is just as well, because those drives are made for the sort of shaking and battering that driving along bumpy roads will provide.)

The unit also has a radio tuner built in. Alas, it's FM only, since the unit's internal circuitry would wreak havoc with an AM signal.

A small remote control gives you access to the full range of the player's functions. The included home power supply can be used to run the unit as part of your home stereo system.

All in all, it's one powerful box.

Tune Talk

Repeg Your Empeg

The Empeg runs on the *Linux* operating system, an operating system popular with the hardcore computer users. The dazzling user interface is written in *Python*, a computer language popular with Web designers because of its relative ease. If you're a computer programming nut, you can redesign the user interface to meet your needs.

The Least You Need to Know

➤ All-electronic portable MP3 players like the Rio let you download music from your PC and carry it with you anywhere.

➤ Portable MP3 CD players will read MP3s off of CDs you make yourself, enabling you to carry around 12 hours of music on each CD.

➤ Tethered systems are stereo system components that connect to your computer, letting you build a library of MP3s that play on your stereo.

➤ You can connect your all-electronic MP3 player to your car stereo.

➤ The Empeg is an example of an MP3 player designed for a car. It's removable, so you can take the player to your PC and download your MP3s from the PC to the car player.

Part 3

Making MP3s

Making your own MP3s is easy. Soon you'll be taking every CD, LP, and cassette that you own and transferring it to MP3 format—well, except for, perhaps, that tape you made of you and your college roommates trying to sing "Total Eclipse of the Heart" at 4 a.m. on the night of the fraternity rush parties. Some things don't need to be saved for future generations.

However, if you make your own music, you can make it an MP3. If you want to send an audio letter to your mom, you can record it, "MP3 it," and ship it to her via email. If you want to bake some cookies, convert them into an MP3, and ship them to your daughter via email, you might have to wait a few years. The technology for cookie compression is pretty crumby at this point.

Chapter 6

Rippin' Good Music

In This Chapter

➤ Copying audio CD tracks onto your hard disk

➤ Ripping with Virtuosa Gold

➤ Ripping with MusicMatch Jukebox

My friend Kevin came up to me a while back and said, "Hey, it's Saturday night! Let's go out and get *ripped*!"

I didn't understand what he was talking about, so I pulled out the nearest dictionary, which happened to be *The Guide to Geek Jargon*. I found this definition there:

> **rip** (verb): to copy the digital audio recording from a CD to an uncompressed file on a computer's hard disk.

I need to get some friends who make more sense, or at least who don't want to be converted into a file, compressed or otherwise.

Why People Used to Rip Songs

In the old days (and by old days, I mean 1998; days get old pretty fast in the MP3 world), if you wanted to encode an MP3 track from a CD, it took two steps. First, you would use a *ripper* program to *rip* the song, copying the digital-format audio from the

CD to an uncompressed WAV-format file. Then you would run your *encoder* to turn the WAV file into an MP3 file.

However, these modern all-in-one MP3 programs can skip the middleman. They can read the song from the CD and encode it directly, basically ripping and encoding in one, without ever writing a WAV file. So if you're using MusicMatch or Virtuosa Gold and want to start turning your CDs into MP3s, head on down to Chapter 8, "Sound Squishing," to see how it's done.

Why People Rip Songs Still

Ripping has not disappeared, for a number of reasons. Many people aren't using all-in-one products, they are still ripping and encoding. But even if you're using the all-in-one products, there are times that you might want to just rip.

For example, let's say that you have a recording of Evil Nasty Demons' medley of Anne Murray tunes. You don't like the whole medley, you just like their cover of "Just Another Woman in Love." If you convert the medley into a WAV file, you can load it up into any standard audio editor (such as the Sound Recorder program that comes with Windows) and remove the rest of the medley, leaving only the part you like.

Or if you're like me, and used to really enjoy putting the record player on the wrong speed, you can use better sound editing software to speed up "When Doves Cry" (by The Artist Back Then Known As Prince But Now Known As a Talented Guy Who Has Trivialized Himself by Playing Silly Name Games) by about a third. (It turns into a wicked dance track at that speed.) Take your favorite Chipmunks CD and slow it way down, and you'll hear what the guys singing really sound like!

Getting Ready to Rip

In order to rip, you're going to need a computer with a CD-ROM drive. That doesn't sound very tricky, but there is one problem: it won't work with all CD-ROM drives.

You see, when they started making CD-ROM drives, they figured you'd be using them for one of two purposes. Either you'd be using them to read data off of a CD-ROM, or you'd be playing audio from an audio CD and sending it to your sound card. They didn't realize that people might want to read data off of an audio CD, so they didn't set up the CD-ROM drives to do so.

As time went on, they figured out that we crazy folks were wanting to do things with their CD-ROM drives that they have never intended, so they started making drives that support Digital Audio Extraction (DAE). However, there are still drives made today that do not support this feature.

Some CD-ROM Drives Are Better Than Others

While CD-ROM drives are extremely careful in making sure they've read programs correctly, they are not so careful in checking data from CD audio tracks. If they misread something, they may not go back and double-check it. Because of this, the ripped file may not be an exact copy of the original audio track, even on the best of CD-ROM drives. Generally speaking, drives connected using the SCSI standard will read more cleanly than drives using the ATAPI or IDE standard. Setting up a PC for SCSI does cost more, though. I know people who absolutely swear by the quality of Plextor CD-ROM drives for this purpose; again, they generally cost more than the bargain brands.

How Do You Tell If a CD-ROM Drive Can Rip?

Most of us don't have the high grade of x-ray vision needed to stare into our CD-ROM drives, look over the internal schematics, and see if it supports DAE. If you happen to know your drive manufacturer and model number, you can scootch on over to `www.mp3.com/cdrom.html` where you will find a well-maintained list of CD-ROM drives and whether they support ripping.

You can also just try to use ripping software and see what results you'll get. Not every piece of software supports every DAE-enabled CD-ROM drive, but the Windows version of Digital Audio Copy, available from `www.windac.de` on the Web, supports the vast majority of them, and the programs covered in this chapter support most you are likely to have.

If your CD-ROM drive doesn't support DAE, that fact doesn't mean that you can't convert your CDs to MP3s. What it does mean, however, is that you'll have to convert them by having your CD-ROM drive play the audio (converting the digital encoding into an analog audio signal). The audio will be picked up by your sound card, which will re-digitize it, converting the analog signal into a digital format. This sounds like more complex an effort than it really is; programs like MusicMatch will do it automatically. However, when you do this, you will lose some sound quality.

Ripping with Virtuosa Gold

You May Already Have a Ripper!

If you have a CD recorder (either a CD-R or CD-RW) that came with software to help you make an audio CD, that software probably has the ability to rip. (It may describe it as *pre-recording*.)

Don't Play That CD!

Windows is usually set up to automatically start playing an inserted audio CD. To get around this, press **Shift** while inserting the CD and hold it down for several seconds.

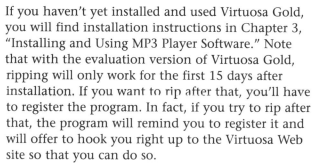

If you haven't yet installed and used Virtuosa Gold, you will find installation instructions in Chapter 3, "Installing and Using MP3 Player Software." Note that with the evaluation version of Virtuosa Gold, ripping will only work for the first 15 days after installation. If you want to rip after that, you'll have to register the program. In fact, if you try to rip after that, the program will remind you to register it and will offer to hook you right up to the Virtuosa Web site so that you can do so.

To rip with Virtuosa Gold, first start the program by clicking the **Start** button and selecting **Programs**, **Audiosoft**, **Virtuosa**. With the audio CD you want to rip from in your CD-ROM drive, use Virtuosa's **View**, **CD Player** command (shortcut: **F7**) to open up the CD player window.

Getting Track Titles

The CD player will list all the tracks on your CD. However, they will all have rather boring names: *Track01*, *Track02*, and so on. This isn't because your favorite group has very little imagination in song titles. It's simply because CDs don't have song names built in to the data. All they have is an identification number. Luckily, that's all you need.

Click the **Query CDDB** button, and Virtuosa will try to contact an Internet database of CDs. Using the CD identifier number, Virtuosa will find out the name of the album, the performer, and all the songs. If it finds it (and the database does have most common CDs, but certainly not everything) the CD player window will now list the artists and song titles for the tracks.

Be aware that Virtuosa will automatically start up the Internet connection if you are not already connected, but it will *not* automatically disconnect when it's done. You'll have to disconnect it yourself, if you're worried about your phone line being tied up or your Internet time being used up.

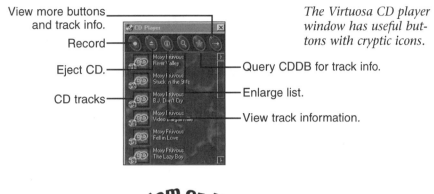

View more buttons and track info.

Record

Eject CD.

CD tracks

Query CDDB for track info.

Enlarge list.

View track information.

The Virtuosa CD player window has useful buttons with cryptic icons.

Got Clicks in Your Music?

If you hear a clicking noise or gaps in your music when played from the WAV file, there were probably problems with the ripping. To minimize the chance of repeating the problem, eject the disk, reinsert it, select the track you want to rip, and rip it again. *Don't* play the track before you rip it, and eject the disk between each track you rip. Doing so will clear the buffer and minimize the chances of the sort of reading error that causes this clicking.

Setting Recording Options

Select **Preference**, **Options** (shortcut: **Ctrl+O**) to get the Virtuosa options dialog box. Click the **CD Player** tab to see the options relevant to recording.

If you're planning to rip songs to uncompressed files, the most important option here is to select **Wav Sound File** from the Output file drop-down menu. If you have more than one CD-ROM drive, select the drive that you want to record from on the Drive drop-down menu. Click the **Digital** option button, so that Virtuosa knows to read the audio data directly from the audio CD, rather than playing and resampling it.

Record It, Already!

You have to tell Virtuosa which tracks you want to rip. Press **Ctrl+A** to select all the tracks on the CD, or hold down the **Ctrl** key while clicking on the name of the individual tracks you want to rip. Once you have the files selected, click the **Record** button.

*So many options to choose
from, so few right ones....*

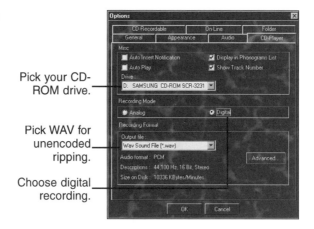

Pick your CD-
ROM drive.

Pick WAV for
unencoded
ripping.

Choose digital
recording.

The first thing that Virtuosa will do is check to make sure you have enough disk space to store this CD. A typical CD will take up more than half a gigabyte in WAV format...that's why they had to develop compressed formats, remember?

Then Virtuosa will rip the tracks. Each track ends up in its own file, in a subdirectory called Songs in the Virtuosa program directory. (If you want to change the directory your songs are stored in, choose **Preferences**, **Options** and click on the **Folder** tab. You'll find the setting there.) The track names will include the name of the artist and the name of the song.

Virtuosa also automatically adds the WAV file to its music data base, so that you can play the song as part of your playlists.

Ripping with MusicMatch Jukebox

In order to start ripping with MusicMatch Jukebox, you're going to need to install the program, as described in Chapter 3. You're also going to need to have an audio CD in *each* of the CD drives on your system the first time you run the program. (You probably have only one, but some people who have CD-R or CD-RW drives also have a standard CD-ROM drive.) This is because the first time you run MusicMatch, it tests all your CD drives to see which ones are capable of Digital Audio Extraction.

Start MusicMatch by double-clicking the MusicMatch icon on the Desktop. To get into the recording process, click the **Record** button (the one with the round dot) on the main MusicMatch display. A Recorder window opens up, and MusicMatch will test the CD-ROM drives. The test will only take a few seconds.

When the testing is done, right-click the top bar of the Recorder window and select **Recorder**, **Quality**, **WAV Format** from the pop-up menu. Right-click again and select **Recorder**, **Source**, and then choose the CD drive with the CD you want to record from on the submenu.

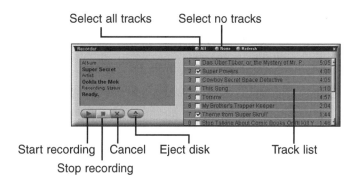

Select all tracks   Select no tracks

Start recording | Cancel   Eject disk   Track list

Stop recording

MusicMatch's Recorder window might look a bit different, depending on the theme you have selected.

Selecting and Recording

To select individual tracks, just check the box next to the track name. You can select all the tracks by clicking **All**, or clear the selections by clicking **None**. (If the track names aren't listed, either MusicMatch hasn't connected to the CDDB via the Internet, or the CDDB doesn't recognize your CD. There might be an Internet Connection dialog box in which you need to click **Connect** to complete your connection. Otherwise, just select each track name and type in the real name.)

To start ripping, click **Record**. MusicMatch will rip one track at a time, with a completion meter on the track listing showing you what percentage of the track is ripped at any one time. If you need to stop the ripping, click **Cancel**. (If you just click **Stop**, MusicMatch will think, "Yes, Master. I shall stop ripping this track right away!" And then it will abandon that track and start ripping the next selected track. This is kind of like when you tell your kid brother to stop teasing that cat, and he turns around and teases the other cat instead.)

Catching the WAV

To find out where your WAV file ended up, right-click the top bar recorder window and choose **Recorder**, **Settings** from the pop-up menu to get the Options dialog box. On the **Recorder** tab, click the button marked **Songs Directory**. The dialog box that appears will list the directory where the files are stored. It also lists a variety of other options in the creations of subdirectories for individual albums, as well as in how the files are named. You're more likely to be using these options when you're encoding MP3s, so we've covered them in Chapter 8.

Mac the Ripper

As noted elsewhere, there is a shortage of good Mac software for MP3 users. If you're encoding MP3s on your Mac, you're probably using Xing's AudioCatalyst (see www.xingtech.com for ordering). That program does have ripper capabilities built in.

The Least You Need to Know

➤ *Ripping* means digitally copying recordings from an audio CD onto your system into an uncompressed format.

➤ These days, most MP3 programs read the digital audio recording and encode it as a single step, eliminating the separate ripping step.

➤ Ripping without encoding is still used for getting tracks you want to edit.

➤ Some CD-ROM drives cannot be used for ripping.

➤ Two programs included with this book's CD-ROM, MusicMatch Jukebox and Virtuosa Gold, have ripping capabilities.

Chapter 7

Digitizing

In This Chapter

➤ Transfer cassettes and records onto your PC

➤ Record your voice with your PC

➤ Get your original music ready to be compressed

Not all music comes on CDs. Odds are good that you have a few cassettes in your music collection. If you're a little older, like me, you may have records. Older still, like my dad, and you may have 8-track tapes. Before that, there were cylinder recordings, and before that there were huge dinosaurs roaming the earth, leaving you little time to listen to music.

Just because you can't stick a record into your CD-ROM drive (not even if you fold it carefully!), don't think that you can't get the music from these non-digital sources onto your PC. All you really need to do is play the music from these sources into your PC, and use your PC to re-record it in digital mode. This is called *digitizing* the music. If you want to create MP3s of music that is not already digitized (including your own performances), you'll have to learn to digitize it yourself.

Digitizing Equipment

In order to digitize music, you're going to need whatever device plays the music you have to digitize. If you're like me and have a big pile of records but no record player, then you're just plain out of luck. It's time to go shopping for a player, or perhaps just marry someone who has one.

You're also going to need a computer with a sound card, which you probably already have. (The bad news is that many computers come with the *cheapest possible* sound card, and they won't do as nice a job digitizing as a better sound card will. If you're digitized recordings sound a lot worse than when you listen to the recording directly on the player, it may be time to buy a better sound card.)

Digitally Dupe It

If you're copying from a digital medium, such as *minidisc* or *digital audio tape* (*DAT*), you'll get the best quality results if you don't try to redigitize the music. Instead, you want to copy the digital information from the player to your computer. To do this, you'll need a sound card that supports digital input and output (*digital I/O*). For example, Creative Labs' SoundBlaster Live sound card (but not the SoundBlaster Live Value Edition) has the ability to connect to some types of digital I/O. (But to connect to optical digital I/O, as many minidisc and DAT systems use, you will need to buy an add-on card.) The software needed to copy tracks digitally will come with the card.

Finally, you'll need cables to connect the two items. That's tricky enough that I'll give it its own heading:

Confounding Cable Combinations

Standard sound cards are expecting to get sound in from a *miniplug* (also known as *a 3.5 mm plug*), the same sort of plug that you use when plugging headphones into a portable cassette or CD player. However, the device you're recording from may use one of three different sorts of jacks that you need to connect to.

➤ If you're recording from a portable player of some sort, you'll be connecting to the line out connector (if it has one; most cassette players don't, but many CD players do) or the headphone jack, which is the same sort of miniplug jack as the sound card has. You'll need a cable with miniplugs on both ends.

➤ If you're recording from a typical stereo component, it will have a pair of *RCA jacks*. These are generally marked *line out* or *audio out*, with one for the right channel and one for the left. You'll need a cable linking two RCA plugs to a single miniplug; these cables are often included with portable CD players. The red RCA plug goes into the jack for the right output, and the other RCA plug (either white or black) goes into the jack for the left output.

➤ If you have a cheap all-in-one system, it may not have RCA jacks. Instead, you'll have to connect to the headphone jack. You'll need an adapter for connecting miniplug headphones to full-size headphone jacks (these often come with the stereo, or with mini headphones), and a cable with miniplugs on both ends.

If you're hooking up a record turntable, there is an additional concern. The basic turntable setup doesn't put out a strong enough signal for your sound card to make much out of it. You're either going to need a turntable that has a built-in amplifier or get an external preamplifier to hook it up through (that'll run you $30 to $50), or simply plug your turntable into the turntable inputs of your stereo amp and hook the computer up to the amp's line out or headphone jacks.

A good audio electronics store should be able to supply you with any of these cables, preamps, or adapters.

Kwality Kabling

To get high-quality digital music, you want to make sure that the music doesn't get degraded on the way into your PC. To that end, the length of the cable can be very important. Instead of buying a long cable to run all the way from your cassette deck in the living room to your PC in the den, take your cassette deck and move it close to your PC, and use a shorter cable.

When you do run the cable, try to avoid running it against electric cords. The electrical current causes a field that will interfere with the audio signal. (This is, by the way, good advice for all your audio and video equipment.) You should also try to avoid running it by electrical appliances, particularly phones, speakers, and computers. Of course, you can't avoid bringing it to the computer entirely, but try not to have the length of the cord wrapping around the computer.

Tune Talk

Socket to Me

A *socket* (a connector with a hole for something to be inserted into it) may also be called a *jack* or a *female connector*. A *plug* (a connector which is designed to stick into a socket) may also be called a *male connector*.

Double-check to make sure that you are connecting to the right socket on your sound card! You want the Line In socket, not the Microphone In socket nor the Speaker socket, both of which also use miniplug sockets. Many sound cards have the sockets marked, although some of them have them marked with little pictures, much like cave drawings. This is very handy for cavemen who need to hook up their 8-track player to their Compaq, but not of much use to many modern humans. If you're not sure which sockets are which *check the manual*. Don't just guess; there is a potential for damaging some of your equipment (and a likelihood of making some ugly loud noises) if you cable up the wrong things.

Using Your Computer As a Stereo Base

You can check to make sure that your hook-up between your audio player and your computer is working before you try to digitize anything. That way, when something goes wrong (and it will), you'll find it a lot easier to isolate the problem.

Before trying to use your PC as an amp for an external audio device, play an MP3. Doing so will let you know that your PC sound system is working and is set to a reasonable volume, as well as getting you in a good boogying mood.

Nat Speaks

Mark It!

Once you figure out which port is which on your ill-marked sound card, use small pieces of masking tape next to the sound card to mark which socket is which. It'll save you time in the future!

Volume Controls in Volume

Next, start up your volume control program. Click the **Start** button, and you'll find the program in either **Programs**, **Accessories**, **Entertainment**, **Volume Control** or **Programs**, **Accessories**, **Multimedia**, **Volume Control**. The program will display volume controls for several different sound sources. For example, take a look at the one marked Wave. That one set the sound level for the MP3 you just played (and, for that matter, any WAV, MP3, or other digitized sound file you play). It's got a slider up top to adjust the balance between the left and right speakers, and a vertical slider for setting the total volume for audio from that source. It also has a Mute check box, which you would check if you didn't want to hear any audio coming from that source.

Your volume control window may look different, depending on the options you have selected.

Wave volume controls   Auxiliary volume controls

The volume control that you really want to use may not be visible, however. There are so many possible audio sources these days that you can't display them all. If you don't see a volume control marked *Auxiliary* (which is the one we want), here's what you do:

1. Choose **Options**, **Properties**.
2. In the dialog box that appears, click the **Playback** option button.
3. On the scrollable list below that, put a check in the **Auxiliary** check box.
4. Click **OK**.

Setting the Volume Levels

The volume controls for the sound you'll be playing into the computer will be marked Auxiliary. Set the volume level for this control to the same level that the Wave control is set for. Put a check in the **Mute** check box for each of the other input volume controls, to turn them off for now. *Don't* put a check in the **Mute All** check box, or you won't be able to hear anything.

If you connected your cables to the Line Out connectors on your audio player, you can start the audio player playing and the sound will come out through your computer. If you connected it to a headphone output jack, however, you'll need to turn the player's volume all the way down first. Then, after the player has started playing, slowly turn the player's volume control up. You should start hearing the sound come out of your computer's speakers. When the sound is about as loud as the MP3 file you played earlier, you've got the player's volume at the right setting. (This step is important; playing too loud an audio signal into your computer may possibly damage some components.)

When you're done with this test, and done doing all your digitizing, clear all those **Mute** check boxes on the volume control. Otherwise, you won't be able to hear all your system sounds or listen to that hot new MP3 of Cher and Madonna's duet, "We Want Our Last Names Back!"

Other Volume Controls

Your PC may have an additional volume control program already installed. Many sound cards come with their own *mixer* programs, which do pretty much the same things as the Volume Control program, but may have added features. You can search your Programs directory for these, or just try double-clicking the Volume Control or Mixer icon on the right end of your taskbar to see what appears!

WAV Hello!

Now that you know you can successfully play sound from your record or cassette player through your computer, it's time to try using the computer to catch some of that sound. In order to do this, you're going to need a sound recorder program.

The good news is that Windows comes with a sound recorder program built in, cryptically named *Sound Recorder*. The bad news is that Sound Recorder isn't very good. It doesn't have a lot of features (although it has the basic ones that you need). The real problem, though, is that it tries to record all the sound into your RAM, and high-quality sound will fill up your RAM right quickly. On my system, Sound Recorder usually quits recording after about one minute. The only song you can fit in that space is Michael Jackson's "Everything I Know About Repairing Late-Model Dodge Trucks."

You may already have a good sound recording and editing program. Many sound cards come with a bundle of programs, including those. Also, some advanced CD creation programs include recording programs for people who are trying to convert their LPs to CDs. Easy CD-Creator Deluxe Edition, for example, includes a recording software which will help you get rid of the noise from old records.

Jam on This

Depopping Pop Music

If you're turning old records into WAV files, you may be picking up a lot of popping noises. If you don't want to shell out the money for Easy CD Creator Deluxe Edition, you can try using the shareware program Popfix. This is free to try, $25 to register. Download it from `www.newave.net.au/~voskulen/popfix/popfix.html`.

Recording WAVs with MusicMatch Jukebox

If you have a proper WAV file recording/editing program, you are probably best off using that to record your WAV files. Those programs generally offer a lot of handy recording features, as well as the ability to trim excess material from the beginning or end of a recording. However, if you don't have such a program, MusicMatch Jukebox can both handle basic recording needs, although it doesn't handle editing.

To record using MusicMatch, click on the **Record** button. The Recorder window opens up. Right-click on an unused part of the Recorder window and choose

Recorder, **Settings** from the pop-up menu. On the Options dialog box that appears (why can't software manufacturers ever decide if these are *settings*, *options*, or *preferences*?), click the **WAV Format** option button, to choose to record to a WAV file rather than directly recording an MP3.

Why *Not* Record Directly to MP3?

Because programs like MusicMatch can record directly to MP3 format, you may be tempted to use that ability. When you try recording directly to MP3, the program has to compress very quickly in order to keep from falling behind, and it may not make the best choices in compressing. If you record to a WAV file and then compress the WAV file, the program can compress at its leisure, and you are likely to end up with better sound quality. Also, having the WAV file first lets you do things like trimming the file in a standard sound editor. If you're encoding your own performances, you'll want to keep the WAV file for your own permanent records. The WAV file doesn't have the data loss that your MP3 file has, and you can back it up to avoid the decay concerns that will hit your audio tape original.

This isn't to say that you should never record directly to MP3. However, if you want to do that, make sure that you have a fairly powerful computer, and test it out on a couple of tracks before making it your usual way of recording. And again, if you're recording your own original performances, you should always make and keep a WAV file of it.

While you have this tab open, there's a couple other things you should take a look at. You should make sure there isn't a check in the **Mute While Recording** check box. Otherwise, you won't be able to hear the song your recording to know when it ends. Click **Song Directory** to get a dialog box that lets you select which directory the WAV file ends up in. This dialog box has a lot of options, which are described in Chapter 8, "Sound Squishing." Click **OK** to get rid of the New Songs Directory Options dialog box, and then click **OK** to get rid of the Options dialog box.

Right-click on the Recorder window again and select **Recorder**, **Source**, **Line In**. This lets the recorder know that you will be recording from the auxiliary audio input. When you select this, the Recorder display changes somewhat from the way it looks when you're recording material from CD.

113

You probably won't use MusicMatch to record the album Nat Gertler's Greatest Hits, but I will!

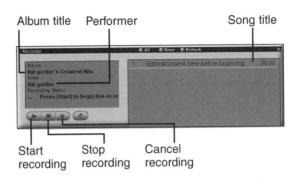

Album title　Performer　　　　　　　　Song title

Start recording　Stop recording　Cancel recording

Before you start recording your first track, MusicMatch wants you to name three things. Click the album name area on the left side, and type a title for the album the track comes from. Click the artist name area below it, and type a name for the musician. Finally, on the right side of the window, click **Edit Track Name Here Before Beginning** and type a name for the individual track. MusicMatch will use these three pieces of information in naming and placing the file. (Recorded WAV files do not get added to the music library.)

Jam on This

Microphone Master

Most of the instructions in this chapter will also serve if you are recording live from a microphone that's plugged into your sound card's Mic In port. Just substitute the terms *Microphone* or *Mic In* for the terms *Auxiliary* or *Line In*. Also, put a check in the **Mute While Recording** check box on the **Recorder** tab of the options dialog box.

Cording and Re-Cording

Click the **Record** button, and start your audio player. When the song is done playing, click **Stop**, and then stop your audio player. MusicMatch will finish writing the track to the hard disk. Then it's time for the next track.

For each additional track, click **Edit Track Name Here Before Beginning** and type a name for the individual track. Click **Record**, restart the music, and click **Stop** when the song is done.

The Complete Idiot's Quick MP3 Reference
MP3 Web Resources

cut here

Sources for MP3 Recordings

URL	Contents
www.mp3.com	A huge library of free, legal music MP3s
www.audible.com/mp3	Spoken-word MP3s
www.amp3.com	Quality, free, and legal MP3s with brief ads
www.emusic.com	MP3s by known artists for sale
www.rioport.com	A small but quality list of MP3s
www.betalounge.com	A weekly new music forum with old shows in MP3
www.blindfrog.com	Cutting-edge new bands
www.getsigned.com	Unsigned band MP3s, plus information for musicians
www.ihearyou.com	A friendly, free MP3 site
www.layer3recordings.com	A small-but-growing MP3 site
www.mammoth.com	An indie label with free MP3 samples
www.mjuice.com	MP3s for sale
www.wiredplanet.com	A Shockwave-powered music site
www.heartsongs.org	Christian music
www.jazzpromo.com	Jazz—cool and hot
www.bluesrevue.com	A magazine site with blues MP3s
www.pghblueswomen.com	Women from Pittsburgh sing the blues
mp3.songs.com	New bands screened for recording quality
www.epitonic.com	Reviewed and selected MP3 music
www.worldwidebands.com	Unsigned bands
www.resortrecords.com	Label-supported free MP3s

MP3 Reference Sites

URL	Content
www.narcopop.com	A guide to legal MP3 sites
www.mp3now.com	MP3 links and info
drogo.cselt.stet.it/mpeg/	The MPEG organization
www.mpeg.org	FAQs and links
www.soundbyting.com	A site on the stances of MP3-foe RIAA
www.iis.fhg.de/amm/	Fraunhofer, the developer of the MP3 format

MP3 Player and Encoder Software

URL	Player
www.sonique.com	Sonique player for Windows
www.winamp.com	Winamp player for Windows
www.xingtech.com/mp3/player/	XingMP3 player for Windows
www.macamp.org	MacAmp player for Mac
www.audioactive.com/player/	AudioActive player for Windows
www.freeamp.org	FreeAmp player for Windows and Linux
www.xmms.org	Xmms player for UNIX
www.musicmatch.com	MusicMatch player/encoder for Windows
www.audiosoft.com/virtuosa/	Virtuosa Gold player/encoder for Windows
www.RealJukebox.com	RealJukebox player/encoder for Windows
www.audiocatalyst.com	AudioCatalyst encoder for Mac and Windows
www.audioactive.com/mp3/	MP3 Production Studio encoder for Windows

MP3 Hardware Player Manufacturers

URL	Hardware
www.RioPort.com	Diamond Rio portable player
www.eigerlabs.com	MPMan portable players
www.nomadworld.com	Creative Labs Nomad portable player
www.mp3ijam.com	Cherokee Electronics I-Jam portable player
yepp.co.kr/eng/	Samsung Yepp portable players
www.empeg.com	Empeg car player
www.impy3.com/impy3	Impy3 car player
www.audiorequest.com	AudioRequest home MP3 player

Now I know what you're thinking: You can just play the album all the way through, quickly clicking Stop and Record between tracks. After all, you've got a quick mouse button finger. Unfortunately, that's not going to work; every time you click Stop, the system takes up a few seconds taking care of the file. When you click Record before it's finished stopping the previous track, it'll put up a dialog box telling you that it already is recording. By this time, the next song has started, and you're out of luck.

How Much Space Is Enough?

A WAV file in CD-quality resolution takes up about 10 megabytes per minute of recording.

But what you can do, if you have enough disk space, is record the entire album side as one track. Then you can use a good WAV editor to select portions of that long recording and save them as separate WAV files.

Tips to Tops Taping

To make sure that your taping goes smoothly, you should avoid running any other programs while recording. Make sure you have plenty of space on your hard disk, and defragment your hard disk at least once a month.

If you've been running your computer for a while without rebooting it, you may want to reboot it. The more you do with your system without rebooting it, the more it slows down.

Digitoshing for the Macintize

There are a number of good audio recorders and editors for the Macintosh. The AudioCatalyst all-in-one MP3 program from Xing (www.xingtech.com) can also handle recording.

The Least You Need to Know

➤ *Digitizing* means converting analog audio into a digital format.

➤ You can digitize music from cassettes, LPs, and other media by hooking the player up to the Line In or Auxiliary socket on the sound card.

➤ A special sound recorder/editor program is the best thing to use to digitize songs. One may have come with your sound card.

➤ To tell MusicMatch that you want to record the input from sound card's Line In connector, right-click a blank area on the Recorder window and choose **Recorder**, **Source**, **Line In**.

➤ You can tell MusicMatch that you want to store files in WAV format using the Recorder tab on the Option dialog box.

➤ To record in MusicMatch, enter the album name, artist name, and song title and then click **Record**. When the song is done playing, click **Stop**.

Chapter 8

Sound Squishing

In This Chapter

➤ Turn a CD track into an MP3

➤ Turn a WAV file into an MP3

➤ Turn an MP3 into a WAV file

Finally, it's time to actually make MP3s. To do this, you will need one pound of sugar, a can of evaporated milk, a quarter pound of butter....

Oh, wait, I almost gave you the secret family fudge recipe. To make MP3, all you need is digitized music (a CD or a WAV file), an MP3 encoding program (such as MusicMatch Jukebox, Virtuosa Gold, or RealJukebox), and a computer to run it on. But if you went and made the fudge anyway, I'll be glad to help you get rid of it.

How Much to Squish?

Before you compress your music, you're going to have to decide how much to compress it. Compression is measured in how many *kilobits per second* (Kbps) the compressed sound takes up. A *bit* is the smallest unit of computer data, able to hold either a 0 or a 1. A *kilobit* is 1,024 bits, about enough space to store the following sentence: The word "problematic" always seemed to me to be a very good name for a machine that the world really doesn't need at this time.

Most of the MP3s you'll find on the Internet are compressed to 128Kbps, which means it takes roughly a megabyte to store a minute of music. This rate provides fairly high quality, which some people refer to as *near CD-quality* and other people will claim to be *CD-quality*. It's certainly good enough to be giving people a sample of your music over the Net. Some hardcore audiophiles insist that to really get CD quality, you have to compress your files less, giving larger files (up to 256Kbps, which takes about two megabytes of disk space per minute). And there are always some purists who will tell you that any compressed sound can't be as good as the original, and that even CDs aren't as good as the high-quality nondigitized audio you get from a good record played on an expensive record player. Sometimes, people get so smug about it that you want to tell them to take an analog walk off an uncompressed pier.

You'll have to judge for yourself how much compression is acceptable for you and your favorite music. Part of the decision will probably rest on how much disk space you have available, and on the quality of the sound system you'll be playing the music through. A high-quality sound system will let you hear the difference between 112Kbps and 128Kbps, but you may not hear the difference in the same files when heard through cheap computer speakers.

Tune Talk

Variable Bit Rate

Some encoders now support *variable bit rate* (VBR) encoding. This term means that the whole song is not compressed at the same rate. Most of the song is compressed at a standard rate, but detailed sections of the music that would lose quality from such compression are compressed less. This process leads to larger files, but better sound. However, not all players will play VBR MP3s.

To help you work it out for yourself, we've thrown something special on the CD-ROM. The fine folks with Wacky Lemon Hello have let us take their song "Trust" and compress it at several different rates. In the directory RATES, you will find these files:

- ➤ TRUST.WAV (the source file)
- ➤ TRUST256.MP3 (compressed to 256Kbps)
- ➤ TRUST160.MP3 (compressed to 160Kbps)
- ➤ TRUST128.MP3 (compressed to 128Kbps)
- ➤ TRUST112.MP3 (compressed to 112Kbps)

➤ TRUST096.MP3 (compressed to 96Kbps)

➤ TRUST080.MP3 (compressed to 80Kbps)

➤ TRUST064.MP3 (compressed to 64Kbps)

➤ TRUST032.MP3 (compressed to 32Kbps)

➤ TRUST016.MP3 (compressed to 16Kbps)

➤ TRUSTV75.MP3 (variable bit rate compression set at 75%)

➤ TRUSTV25.MP3 (variable bit rate compression set at 25%)

This song was selected not because it tests the limits of compression, but to be a pretty typical example. It's really going to sound lousy at the smaller bit rates; anything below 48Kbps you will probably use only for spoken word recording, since it takes away all the magic that gives music its power. You can still hear the song at 16Kbps, but it sounds like it's playing in the car next to you, with the volume turned up but all the windows closed. Notice also that the sound difference is more apparent in the booming sections of the song with more instruments and complexity than it is during the song's quieter moments.

Compressing with MusicMatch

The unregistered version of MusicMatch included on the CD-ROM can encode any CD track or WAV file. It does, however, have one strong limitation: it will not encode at any bit rate greater than 96Kbps, nor will it encode using variable bit rate. You can use it to learn to encode, or to encode music for cases where you want to fit a lot onto a disk. If you want the higher sound quality that comes with larger bit rates, you will need to register your copy. If you surf over to www.musicmatch.com and register (it costs $29.99), they'll transmit to your PC a secret key that will unlock MusicMatch's ability to encode at bit rates as high as 320Kbps.

For instructions on installing and starting MusicMatch, see Chapter 3, "Installing and Using MP3 Player Software."

Optimal Options

To set the MP3 recording options, click **Option** and choose **Recorder, Settings**. The Option dialog box opens up showing the Recorder tab. It's full of MP3 recording settings and options. In fact, the settings look just like the options, so it doesn't matter what you call them.

The most important option to set is your recording rate. You can use an option button to choose 64, 96, 128, or 160Kbps MP3s. Select the **CBR** option, and you can use the adjacent slider to select from 15 different bit rates ranging from the hard-to-hear 16Kbps to the huge 320Kbps. If you have registered your copy of MusicMatch, choose **VBR** if you want to use variable bit rate encoding, choosing a variation rate from 1% (worst quality) to 100% (best).

MusicMatch recording options give you a lot of control over your recording.

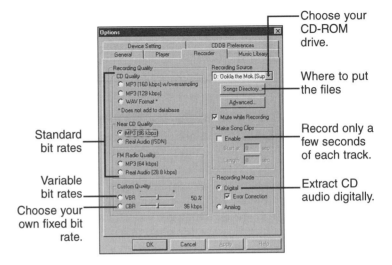

Choose your CD-ROM drive.

Where to put the files

Standard bit rates

Variable bit rates

Choose your own fixed bit rate.

Record only a few seconds of each track.

Extract CD audio digitally.

If you're going to encode from CDs, use the **Recording Source** drop list to select the CD-ROM drive you'll be using for your CDs. Next, head down to the Recording Mode area and click **Digital**, to choose to read the digital audio data directly from the CD. Putting a check in the **Error Correction** check box will slow down the process somewhat, but will avoid some noises that might be added to your music if the CD isn't read properly.

Where the Music Lurks

Click the **Songs Directory** button to get a separate dialog box that controls where on your computer the MP3s you encode will be stored and what the files will be named.

You can spend more time deciding where to put your files than you spend encoding them!

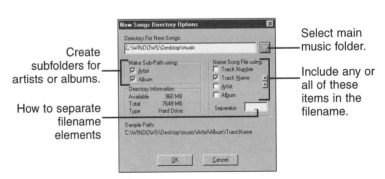

Create subfolders for artists or albums.

How to separate filename elements

Select main music folder.

Include any or all of these items in the filename.

To pick the main directory, click the enigmatically marked **...** button. (It might help if you realize that . . . is Morse code for the letter *S*, which perhaps is short for *Select-a-directory.*) A dialog box opens up listing devices and folders on your system. Double-click any device or folder to see the subdirectories it contains. When you find the folder you want to use as your main music folder, click it and then click **OK**.

The **Make Sub-Path Using** options are used to create individual subfolders for each artist or each album, making it easier to find songs so they aren't all in one huge folder. If, for example, you are MP3ing the song "A Hole in the Head" from the album *This Is Not a Drill* by the group Savage Dentists, and you didn't have either of these options selected, the song would end up in your main music folder. If you had just the **Artist** option selected, MusicMatch would create a subfolder called Savage Dentists, and the song would reside in there. If you had just the **Album** options selected, the main folder would have a subfolder called This Is Not a Drill, which would hold the song. If both options were selected, in the main folder would be a Savage Dentists folder, and in that folder would be a This Is Not a Drill folder, and that's the folder where MusicMatch would place the song.

All Songs Should Be Named "Eric"

MusicMatch can automatically name MP3 tracks using any combination you want of the album name, the artist name, the track number, and the track name. To design your own name order, first clear all the check boxes in the **Name Song File Using** area. Next, click on the check box for the element you want to be first in the file-name, and then click the up-arrow button. The element you want will move up in the list of elements. Keep clicking the up-arrow button until it has moved up to the top spot.

If you want a second element in the filename, click the check box for that element and then use the up arrow to move it into second place on the list. If you want a third element, click the check box and then move it up to the third place on the list. If you want all four elements included, put a check in the last remaining check box.

If you're using more than one element, you can also use the **Separator** field to choose how to mark the end of one element and the start of the next. Usually, you'll just put one character in here, such as a dash, an underline, or an exclamation point. However, you can put more characters in there. For example, if you were using album name, artist name, and track name (in that order) as the elements of your filename, and you typed QUACK into your separator, you would end up with files like this:

```
GordonQUACKBarenaked LadiesQUACKBe My Yoko Ono.MP3
```

As you work on setting up the folder and filename, the dialog box shows an example filename and path.

When you're done with this dialog box, click **OK**. When you're finished with the Options dialog box, click **OK**.

Optionmania!

Click the **Advanced** button on the Recorder tab, and you'll have access to a handful of other options. If you're getting clicks and noises in your recording, go here and turn the **Multipass** option on; this will slow the recording but eliminate the errors.

Recording from CD

Before you open up MusicMatch's recorder window for the first time, put an audio CD in each of your PC's CD-ROM drives. The program will test out your CD-ROM drives to see if it can read the digital audio data directly, or if it will have to play the CD into your sound card and have the sound card redigitize the music. The former method is both faster and gives better quality sound.

Be aware that MusicMatch is about to try to use the Internet, so if your modem is using your main phone line, it's time to hang up from talking to Grandma. When you start the recorder, MusicMatch reads an identification number off of your CD, and sends it to an online source called CDDB. The CDDB site responds with the name of the album, the artist, and song names...if it knows them. Their database will have most of the CDs in your collection, as they have an awful lot of the commercially released CDs. They won't have that homemade CD of your Uncle Chester yodeling the theme from *Mission: Impossible*, however.

To open the recorder window, click the **Record** button on the player window. (That's the button with the red circle on it.) The first time you open the recorder window, MusicMatch will run the CD-ROM test I mentioned earlier.

The left side of the window displays the name of the album and the artist. The right side of the window lists the name of each track, with a check box for each. If you don't see actual track names, click **Refresh** to force MusicMatch to check the CDDB for the information. If CDDB doesn't have the CD on record, you can click on the artist name, album

CD Not Found?

Do everyone a favor and enter the information about that CD into the CDDB database! Surf on over to www.cddb.com/userfaq.html to find out how.

name, and each track area, and type in the appropriate name. (If you don't see the check boxes, MusicMatch was probably last used to record from some other source than the CD-ROM drive. Choose **Options**, **Recorder**, **Source** and select your CD-ROM drive from the list.)

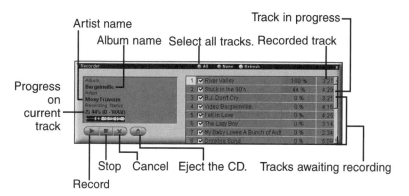

Artist name
Album name   Select all tracks.   Recorded track
Track in progress
Progress on current track
Stop   Cancel   Eject the CD.   Tracks awaiting recording
Record

MusicMatch's Recorder: better than those plastic recorders they taught you to play in fourth-grade music class!

Put a check in the check boxes of each track you want to record. If you want to record all the tracks, just click **All**. If you don't want to record any of the tracks, you can click **None**, but then if you don't want to record any of the tracks, what are you doing here in the first place?

Start the recording by pushing the **Start** button. The speed at which MusicMatch will record depends on what record options you chose and the speed of your CD-ROM drive. In most cases, it will record in a fraction of the time it takes to play the CD. If you need to interrupt the recording process, click **Cancel**.

Making a Little Splash with Compressed WAVs

As you saw in Chapter 6, "Rippin' Good Music," and Chapter 7, "Digitizing" (unless you skipped them, after I spent all those long days slaving over them—sigh), there are a number of ways that you can end up with uncompressed audio in the form of WAV files. To convert these, choose **Options**, **File**, **Convert**. A File Format Conversion dialog box opens up.

First, select **WAV** on the **Source Data Type** drop list. Then, find the folder with the WAV files in the Source Directory list. You can see the subfolders in any folder or device by clicking on the **+** next to it. Once you've found the right folder and click on it, a list of the WAV files in that directory will appear on the list below.

Converting MP3s to WAV files is a very efficient way to fill up your hard disk.

What folder has the WAVs?

Put the MP3s in what folder?

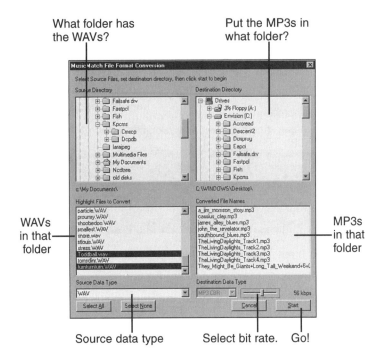

WAVs in that folder

MP3s in that folder

Source data type

Select bit rate.   Go!

Click the name of each file on the list that you want to convert. When you click it, it becomes highlighted. If you change your mind about converting a file, click it again, and it becomes unhighlighted. If you change your mind again, you are too indecisive, and should resort to flipping a coin. If you can't decide between a nickel and a quarter, then you're beyond my help.

Next, choose a folder to put the files into, using the Destination Directory section. (Don't be freaked out when a list of files appears below that; they're just whatever MP3 files were already in the folder.) Use the slider near the bottom of the window to choose the bit rate of the MP3s you're making. Finally, click **Start**, and let your PC do its work!

Jam on This

Some Things Need Editttting

Remember, you want to sample a song as a WAV (despite its size) if you plan to edit the resulting file.

Mono: The Space-Saving Kissing Disease

If you're doing a recording that isn't going to rely on sound quality (such as recording an audio letter that you're going to email to someone, or perhaps a book read aloud), you can choose to forego the stereo signal. Choose **Options**,

Recording, **Settings**. On the Options dialog box that appears, click **Advanced**. On the Advanced Recording Options dialog that appears, choose **Mono** from the Channels drop menu. With this option selected, MP3 file space will not be used up storing the information that normally separates what the left ear hears from what the right ear hears, leaving it more room to properly track a single signal.

For an example of high-compression mono recording of spoken words, check the directory book on the CD-ROM. The files `natstar.mp3`, `monkey.mp3`, and `angel.mp3` are recordings of me, telling the tales of my work as an acting extra on the films *Primary Colors* and *Mighty Joe Young*, and the TV show *Teen Angel*. Because these recordings were made with a typical cheap PC microphone, they aren't going to sound great even in high resolution, but they are certainly clear enough to hear compressed to 32Kbps.

WAVing Back

To convert MP3s into WAV files, start a new playlist with only those MP3s on it. Next, choose **Options**, **Playlist**, **Convert Playlist to WAV**. A dialog box appears where you can select a directory to put the WAVs and enter names for the WAVs. Take care of that and then click **Start**, and you'll be making WAVs!

Tag, You're "Beat It"!

MusicMatch lets you edit *tags*, little pieces of information about the song that get embedded into your MP3 file. These can be useful when you're creating your playlists. They can be extremely useful when you're going to be distributing your own original music, since you can put lyrics, your biography, your Web address, and even a picture of your album cover where the listeners will be able to find them. Many MP3 players automatically display tag information while the song is playing.

To add tags, first open up the Music Library window by choosing **Options**, **View**, **Music Library**. The window appears, and among the songs it lists are all the songs you compressed from CD. MusicMatch automatically added them to the database when you compressed them. (If you compressed a file from a WAV, drag the icon for the compressed version onto the Music Library window to add it to the library.) Find the song you want to add tags to, right-click it, and choose **Edit Track Tag** from the pop-up menu. A Tag Songs dialog box appears, filled with spaces for you to add tag information.

You may end up with more words in your tags than there are words in the song!

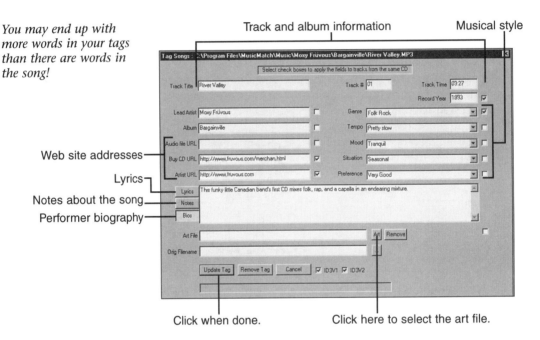

Track and album information   Musical style

Web site addresses

Lyrics

Notes about the song

Performer biography

Click when done.   Click here to select the art file.

The form has many different tag entries that you can edit to give more information about the song. These fall into five basic categories:

➤ Basic track information—This includes the song name, which track it was on the CD, the year it was recorded, the artist name, and the album title. If you encoded this track from a CD, MusicMatch will probably have already added most of this information (except the year) using the information it downloaded from the CDDB.

➤ Style information—The drop-down lists running down the left side let you describe the song in terms of genre, tempo, mood, quality, and the situation where you'd want to listen to the music. For all the categories except genre, you can type in your own description instead of selecting one from the list. These selections can be very useful for building playlists, as described in Chapter 3.

➤ Web addresses—You can enter three Web addresses (*URLs*), one where the song file is available on the Web, another for a Web site that sells the CD, and one for the performer's home page.

➤ Detailed information—Click **Lyrics**, and you can enter the words to the song into the big text field. Click **Notes**, and the field becomes a place for the story behind the song, or the names of the musicians, or any other information you want. Click **Bio**, and you can use the field for the performer's history.

➤ Song art—You can scan the CD cover into your computer, or design your own art to accompany the individual song. The only limitation is that the art must be stored in the Windows Bitmap format (files ending with .bmp) or the JPEG format (files ending with .jpg), and should be 100 pixels wide by 100 pixels high. Click **Art**, and a file browser appears. Select the file with the art in it and then click **Open** to add this tag.

Most of the fields have a check box next to them. Put a check in one of those fields, and MusicMatch will add that tag info to all the songs compressed from the same CD. That way, you can quickly mark all the songs from TLC's latest album as being polkas or apply a photo of your pet puppy Peanut to all the tunes from the musical version of *Death of a Salesman*.

When you're done, click **Update Tag**, and all the information you entered will be added to the MP3 file.

Squishing with Virtuosa Gold

The edition of Virtuosa Gold that comes on the CD-ROM has two substantial limitations when it comes to creating MP3s. First is that this ability will only work for 15 days. Second is that even within those 15 days, you can only encode the first track on any CD. They figure that this is enough for you to learn how well Virtuosa Gold works.

If you want to use the program as your main encoder, choose **Online**, **Register** to bring up the Virtuosa Gold Web site. There, you can enter your credit card information and then download a *patch* (a program that exists to change another program). You can then run the patch to turn this evaluation version into the unlimited version, which can encode any track (and will keep doing that beyond 15 days, or even 15 years). The price? $29.99.

For instructions on installing and starting Virtuosa, see Chapter 3.

Virtuosa has the ability to encode to MP3, or to a separate format (developed by Virtuosa's creator, AudioSoft) called *Secure ASFS File*. In order to encourage you to use their file format, Virtuosa defaults to using this other format when initially installed. Choose **Preference**, **Options**, and on the **CD-Player** tab select **Mpeg Layer-3 File** from the Output File drop menu. To pick the bit rate, click **Advanced** and select the bit rate from the drop list on the dialog box that appears. Be forewarned, however, that Virtuosa only supports three bit rates: 128Kbps, 112Kbps, and 96Kbps. Click the check mark button to accept the bit rate you select. Next, click the **Folder** tab. Click the **...** button in the Songs area, and use the file browser that appears to choose the folder to store your MP3s in. Finally, click the **OK** button to close the options dialog box.

For Fee Beats for Free

You may have heard that there are free unrestricted MP3 encoders out there, and wonder why Rod and I didn't include those on the CD-ROM. The folks who came up with the MP3 audio format have patents on it, and they make their money licensing the right to make encoders out to software companies. These free encoders are generally made without getting a license, meaning that they are violating patents. Just as musicians deserve to be paid for their labor, so do inventors, and giving out these encoders would work against that. (It also would open us up for womping-big lawsuits. I can barely afford to take a suit to the cleaners, much less to court.) Give your support to the software makers who support the inventors...and who, by the way, are more likely to offer you support and timely upgrades.

Compacting Compressed Discs...er, Compressing Compact Discs

To compress the songs on a CD (or, if you still haven't registered your copy of Virtuosa, the first song), open the CD Player window by selecting **View**, **CD Player** (shortcut: **F7**). Put your CD player in the drive. If Virtuosa already knows this CD, a list of song titles will appear in the CD player window.

If it doesn't know this CD, the songs will be listed as Track 01, Track 02, and so on. Click the **Query CDDB** button (the next-to-last button in the window), and Virtuosa will connect to the Internet, and get the album title, performer, and song information from the CDDB database.

While pressing **Ctrl**, click on each song that you want to record. (To select the whole album quickly, press **Ctrl+A**.) Click the **Record** button (the first button in the row). A copyright notice pops up, warning you about the possible copyright concerns and complications in compressing music. Read this through, learn from it, and put a check in the **Do Not Show This Message Again** check box; then click the check mark button. You'll only have to do this the first time you compress anything.

Virtuosa sets about compressing. The program takes two passes on each song. In the first pass, it just copies the track to the hard disk, without compressing. In the second pass, it compresses the track into an MP3 file and then deletes the original file.

Because it works in this manner, you may want to check to make sure that you have plenty of disk space—at least 10 megabytes left on your hard disk for each minute of the longest song you're compressing.

Virtuosa automatically adds any file you compress to the music data base. If you want to edit the tags on an MP3 file, find it in the data base, right-click it, and select **Properties** from the pop-up menu. Virtuosa doesn't track as many properties as MusicMatch does; you can only set the artist, album, song title, and a picture file.

Can't Compress WAVs

Virtuosa doesn't include the ability to convert WAVs into MP3s. Despite the fact that all the individual techniques needed for it are built into the program (reading WAVs, converting uncompressed audio into MP3), they didn't provide a command to tell Virtuosa you want to convert a file. There's no way to do it.

Do the Impossible

If you happen to have a CD-R or CD-RW drive, there is an awkward trick to turn WAVs into MP3s. Virtuosa has commands to take a playlist and burn those songs onto an audio CD. You could take a WAV, tell Virtuosa to burn it onto an audio CD, and then use the techniques described earlier to compress the track from the audio CD into an MP3. This is a heck of a pain in the neck to get that done. You'd be better off getting a compressor designed to convert WAVs.

Similarly, Virtuosa has no straightforward way to uncompress an MP3 file into a WAV. If you're feeling tricky, you can use the CD burning features to make an audio CD which will have an uncompressed version of the MP3. Once you do that, you can use the ripping techniques discussed in Chapter 6 to copy that audio track into a WAV file.

Mac Compression

AudioCatalyst from Xing (www.xingtech.com) can compress from CD and from WAV files. As I write this, MusicMatch is working on a Macintosh version of their Windows product; it may be available for download by the time you read this. Surf on over the www.musicmatch.com to see if it's available.

Decompression Without a Compressor

Winamp and Sonique can't be used to encode MP3s. That's how they can get away with being cheap shareware and free freeware, respectively; they don't have to pay the encoding license. They can, however, do quite a nice job of decoding MP3s and saving them as WAV files. Decoding, like butterflies, is free.

Windowsamplifier: Winamp Decompression

To turn an MP3 file into a WAV file, first click on the upper-left corner of Winamp's player window. On the menu that appears, choose **Options**, **Preferences**. A Preferences dialog box appears.

Click **Output** in the left pane of the window. A list of output plug-ins (different programs for handling Winamp's output) appears in the right pane. Normally, when you want Winamp's output to go to your speakers, Nullsoft WaveOut Plug-In will be highlighted. Click on **Nullsoft Disk Writer Plug-In** to choose to output to your disk instead of to the speakers.

To choose where on your disk the files end up, click **Configure**. A dialog box appears listing folders on your hard disk. Click the + next to any folder to see the subfolders in that folder. When you find the folder you want to store your WAV files in, click it and then click **OK**. Click **Close** on the Preferences dialog box.

Now you're set up to decompress! Just drag any MP3 file's icon onto the player portion (the upper left) of the Winamp window. Winamp will run the conversion, which it can do quite quickly. When you want to go back to using Winamp as a player rather than a decompressor, bring up the Preferences dialog box again, click **Output**, and reselect **Nullsoft WaveOut Plug-In**. (TheySure DoLike ToRun Words-Together!)

Decompressionique

The version of Sonique included in the CD-ROM has a feature to convert MP3s into WAVs—sort of. I say "sort of" because it has all the commands for the feature, but they don't work. However, the programmers know the problem, and by the time you read this, a newer, fixed version of Sonique will be available for download at the www.sonique.com Web site. The feature will work like this:

To turn Sonique into an impressive decompression contraption, click **Setup Options** on the main menu in large display mode. (If you don't see that, right-click the main display area, and it will appear.) On the Setup Options display, click **Audio**. Click the up arrow at the end of the Setup Options field, until **WAV Disk Writer** is displayed.

Next, click the **WAV Disk Writer Path** field. A dialog box appears listing storage drives on your system. Click the + next to any drive to see the folders on that drive, or the + next to any folder to see the subfolders in that folder. When you find the folder you want to store your WAV files in, click it and then click **OK**. Right-click the display window to return to the main menu. Then just use Sonique's standard commands to play any song, and instead of coming out of your speakers, it will end up in a file in the directory you selected.

The Least You Need to Know

➤ Compression quality is measured in *kilobits per second (Kbps)*. High Kbps rates mean big files but high-quality sound reproduction. Low rates mean small files but poor reproduction.

➤ A registered copy of MusicMatch Jukebox can convert CD files and WAV files into MP3s, ranging from 16 to 320Kbps. It can also convert MP3s into WAVs.

➤ An unregistered copy of MusicMatch is limited to creating MP3s at 96Kbps or less.

➤ Virtuosa Gold can compress CD files into MP3s ranging from 96 to 128Kbps.

➤ An unregistered copy of Virtuosa Gold will only encode the first song on any CD, and will only do that for 15 days after you install it.

➤ Winamp can convert MP3 files into uncompressed WAV files.

➤ The version of Sonique on the CD-ROM cannot properly convert MP3 files into WAV files, but the new version on the www.sonique.com Web site can.

Chapter 9

Spreading Your Sound Around: Distributing Your MP3s

In This Chapter

➤ Where is the best place on the Internet to put your MP3 files?

➤ How do you set up a free band page on the Internet?

➤ How do you upload MP3 files to your band page?

Hey World, Wanna Listen to My Song?

All artists want people to enjoy their artistic creations; musicians are no different from other artists. Well, some of them still wear tie-dyed clothing and say "Far out," but for the most part they are just like you and me. Isn't that far out? (Oops, I just spilled fruit juice on my tie-dyed shirt.)

Let's learn how to arrange for a whole lot of people to have a chance to listen to your music. Yes, friends, step right up and meet your potential audience: the world. All the world that is hooked up to the Internet, that is, which is certainly a large number of people. Just try fitting that many people into a concert hall. You could perform in a standing-room-only sports arena every night for a month and not begin to reach the number of potential fans waiting for you on the Internet. Distributing your MP3s on the World Wide Web allows your music to reach a staggering number of people from nearly every nation on planet Earth.

Before you will be able to entrance fans from France, or sing your heart away to some person from Mandalay, you'll need to find a home for your MP3s on the Internet.

Home Pages and "Home on the Range"

Certainly, if you have a home page of your own with enough space to house your MP3s, you could set them up there. You would simply place a link to your MP3 file and voilá! Your new fans in Sweden (and everywhere else) could download your song and groove to your musical genius.

Before you post your MP3s, however, be sure to check the arrangement with your Internet service provider (ISP). Some ISPs offer free Web space, but limit either the amount of storage space or the amount of information you can transmit to the Web per month. A popular MP3 site could rapidly exceed both of those restrictions, which in turn could cause your ISP to charge extra.

Newsgroup No-No's

You could also find an MP3-related Internet newsgroup where you could post your MP3s. Before you do, however, take one important fact into consideration: Never place an MP3 or other digital file into a newsgroup unless you are absolutely certain that binary files are accepted. The newsgroup will usually include the word *binaries* someplace in the title. If you are not certain that MP3 files are welcome in the newsgroup that you are interested in, don't upload them. If you do, you'll make a very large number of people very upset. That much concentrated ill will could—broadcast your way from across the globe, even—cause you to have a nasty headache.

That doesn't mean you can't take advantage of the non-binary newsgroups. Post your latest rap, "Hard 2B a Gangsta When You're Stuck in Alaska," on `alt.binaries.sounds.mp3.1990s`, which has the word *binaries*; then go to `alt.music.gangsta.rap` and post a message telling everyone to head over to the binary group to check out your new track. You can also post a message containing a link to your MP3 file on a Web page.

Newsgroups

Want to learn more about news-groups? Go check out `www.dejanews.com` for more info. Learn how to find discussions on just about any topic imaginable.

Songs in the Key of Email

Emailing your MP3s as an attachment to your friends is also a lot of fun. If you mail them, make sure you alert your friends that you are sending an MP3. Better yet, send them a short email first asking if it's okay to send them an MP3.

Why? Because as emails go, MP3s are pretty big. Your friend may be sitting there, tapping her fingers, waiting for this all-important contract via email, or perhaps a steamy love letter from her boyfriend. When the mail program finds your letter first, the modem line could be tied up for 15 minutes while downloading your latest masterpiece, "My Girlfriend Done Left Me Crying (and She Took My Kleenex Too")."

134

Binaries, Binaries, Who Has the Binaries?

The binary newsgroups that exist to carry MP3s include

➤ alt.binaries.sounds.mp3.1950s

➤ alt.binaries.sounds.mp3.1960s

➤ alt.binaries.sounds.mp3.1970s

➤ alt.binaries.sounds.mp3.1980s

➤ alt.binaries.sounds.mp3.1990s

➤ alt.binaries.sounds.country.mp3

Go to dejanews.com to learn about newsgroups.

American Online and CompuServe have music forums with file libraries, which may very well be places for you to place your MP3s. (Check the forum rules to make sure that what you want to upload is acceptable.) While this might be a wonderful place for you to put your MP3s, you'll find that the World Wide Web is the most popular location for MP3s. Why? Because of the "world" part of World Wide Web. Only members of AOL or CompuServe can access those libraries, but the Web is open to everyone.

135

The Internet allows you to reach a very large number of people. A whole world's worth of people.

MP3.com: The King of All MP3 Sites

The largest and most famous of Internet locations for MP3s is clearly MP3.com. (Rod should know, he works there as the fabulous music director.) More than six million people come to MP3.com each month looking for music to listen to. Here your songs will mingle with both new artists and some of the most famous musical artists in history. Billy Idol, The Band, The Beach Boys, Dionne Warwick, Willy Nelson, Ice-T, and Tom Petty have each placed MP3s on MP3.com for the world to enjoy.

MP3.com boasts hundreds of musical areas, *genres*, which helps you find the best possible spot for your music. For example, instead of offering simply an electronic area, MP3.com offers acid, ambient, break beat/breaks, dance, drum and bass, house, techno, industrial, detroit, goa, rave, trance, and many more. They'll have a home for whatever type of music you make.

Best of all, their service is completely free to all artists. You'll be able to obtain a Web page, have your music available for download, hear your music play on one of their genre-specific Internet radio stations, and enjoy tons of other cool features—all for free. Isn't that great? MP3.com is located at www.MP3.com. Regardless of how many Internet sites you select to house your MP3s, your first stop should be MP3.com.

MP3.com and You

MP3.com is located at—where else?—www.MP3.com. Once your friendly computer takes you to its home page, scroll down and you'll find a portion of the front page that says Artists/Labels. The sign-up process begins when you click **New Artist Signup**. You'll see the first of a series of helpful pages that will walk you through the artist sign-up procedure. Before you go any further, look for a link to Artist FAQs. This link refers to Frequently Asked Questions (also known as *FAQs*) that relate to artists.

Guess what? You might not be able to draw, but you are an artist in the eyes of MP3.com. When they mention "artists," they are talking about you. Make sure you follow that link and read all the FAQs so that you can learn about any recently added features.

The MP3.com homepage lets you post your own recordings.

MP3.com's services to artists are completely without charge. All they ask is that you place one complete song on their site. Many cool things can happen once your music is on MP3.com. Some MP3.com artists have ended up being on MTV, as well as other national television and radio programs.

Successful artists on MP3.com can find many doors opening that might have otherwise been closed. If you are a talented performer, your new fans will surely find you. MP3.com is always coming up with new ways to promote their resident musicians.

No doubt your eyes are open wide at this point as you think about all the exciting possibilities for your own music. Are you wondering what happens if MP3.com doesn't like your music?

Fear not! You will never face rejection from MP3.com as long as you own the music that you want to upload. MP3.com is happy to let the world judge your music. They accept every artist who wants to place an MP3 on their site. Aren't they wonderful?

No Strings, No Obligations, No Lie

Here are two magic words that apply to MP3.com: no obligation. MP3.com doesn't require an exclusive relationship with its artists. You are free to put your files on MP3.com and any other MP3 Internet site that you want. You can also terminate your relationship with MP3.com at any time and remove your music. The only strings around here are the ones on your sneakers.

The Free MP3.com Band Page

MP3.com offers you a free band page on their site, and they've already gone to the trouble of doing the basic design work for you. They know how busy a talented musician can be. All you have to do is sign up for their service and give them some information—away you go to set up your page.

How long does it take—from start to finish—to set up your page? Once you have a CD of your song in your hands, you could encode your song into an MP3, set up your band page, and have the world listening to your song within 48 hours after you've uploaded the MP3. That's fast.

Basic MP3.com Artist Requirements

The basic artist requirements are quite simple: You need a band name and an email address. Try to pick a unique band name—you already did, didn't you?—because MP3.com does not allow duplicate band names on their site. After all, the world doesn't need two bands named Pro-Life Cannibals. (In fact, it probably doesn't even need one.)

Do you need help selecting a clever band name? Here's my secret formula for dealing with this problem. Pick your favorite color. Now, pick your favorite style of peanut butter. (There are only two kinds, right?) Finally, ask your mother what her middle name is. Put a *The* in front and an *s* at the end; what do you get? I don't know about you, but I came up with The Purple Crunchy Estelles. No, no, don't thank me. I'm just doing my job.

Of course, if you're a solo performer, you probably already have a name. Thank your parents for that.

Your Own Secret Code (Sorry, No Secret Decoder Ring)

When you sign up as an artist with MP3.com, you are given a *password* and a *username*. This amounts to a secret code so that you and only you can log into your band page's *admin area*. You select the username; MP3.com selects the password. You must enter both the password and the username when you return to your MP3.com band page to make changes or additions.

Want to change the band photo? Add a new song? Exchange an updated version of one song for another? Your secret code (password and username) allows you to do so. Your password and your confirmed username are emailed to you automatically after you sign up with MP3.com.

I Just Know I Am Going to Lose My Secret Code

Don't feel bad. I've lost every single secret code that I have ever been given. If you lose your password or forget your username, don't panic. When you log into your MP3.com band page, you'll see a link that says Lost Your User Name Or Password? Click Here. If you click that link, you will find your password and username automatically sent to the email address that you gave MP3.com. No mucking about with questions about your mother's maiden name. The helpful little email will show up almost instantly, too.

Hey, Everyone! This Is a Photo of the Band I'm In!

While a one-of-a-kind band name and your email address are the minimum requirements for enrolling with MP3.com, there are several optional features that will help make your band page colorful and exciting. Do you have a cool photo of your band handy? You can scan that great work of art and load it to your band page if you want. Most CD covers aren't blank, right? Art helps sell CDs. You don't have to use this spot on your page for a band photo. You can also scan any original art that you happen to have on hand, or put up a photo of something that is meaningful to your band.

The image that you upload to MP3.com has to be in JPEG or GIF format and should be 270 pixels wide by 180 pixels high. You should make the images precisely these pixel dimensions.

I Joined a Band Because...

You are also encouraged by MP3.com to provide your fans with a description of your band, a statement about your musical influences, popular artists you sound similar to, a history of your band, and more. You can even list your band members, the instruments you play, albums you have recorded, upcoming concert dates, press releases, and other types of information designed to create excitement about your band.

It's best to organize all this information before you set up your page so that you don't find yourself making it up while you are filling out the online MP3.com forms. Take a look at some of the other band pages on MP3.com to get some ideas and then write your own material. This will make setting your band page up that much easier and will also help give your band page a more professional appearance.

Basic Requirements to Place an MP3 on MP3.com

As a new artist, you need to prepare before you sign up. You will, of course, need at least one MP3 file. You also need to know the title of your song and prepare a one-line description of your song. If your song is on a CD that you've already made, be prepared to list the name of that CD. If you have a record label, MP3.com will want you to tell the world about that, too. Some artists use this spot to say "I have no record label as of yet, but would like to be signed by one," or language to that effect. If you would like to be signed by a record label, you might as well go ahead and say as much.

MP3.com also provides a place to list the credits for the song. That area is most often used by artists to list who wrote the song and whether the songwriter is a member of ASCAP or BMI. You will also find that they provide a spot to place the entire song's lyrics.

Album Cover Art: Smaller but More Plentiful

You can also place a small JPEG or GIF version of your album cover. This image is different than the band photo. It's a lot smaller, for one thing—70 pixels by 70 pixels, or about a half-inch square. Plus, you are only given one spot for your band photo; the album cover art can be placed next to each and every song on your page. You can have a different image for each song, if you want.

Some people use this spot to put small animated GIFs if they don't have an album cover to show off. You can put any image there that you want. Again, you're sure to get some neat ideas for cool art when you look at several other band pages.

The only thing MP3.com actually requires is the MP3 file itself and the title of the song. The lyrics, cover art, credits, record label, and song description are all optional. MP3.com will give you a special password so that you can return to the site as often as you want and change things. You can put up cover art, change your song title, add lyrics, and so on, whenever you feel so inclined. If all you do at first is upload your MP3 file and name your song, that's perfectly okay; you can do the rest later.

Musical Genres: A Fancy Name for the Type of Music You Play

You'll also have the ability to select a genre for your individual songs. MP3.com has hundreds of musical categories that you can select from. Try to select the most appropriate genre for your song. Doing so helps people find your music. If you perform Gospel music, you'll want Gospel music fans to find you, right?

Don't purposely place your song in a genre that you know is inappropriate. For example, don't place your heavy metal song into the polka genre just because you think that would be funny or because you've decided that it is way past time for those silly polka lovers to learn about the pleasures of heavy metal. This advice isn't limited to MP3s that you might put on MP3.com, but is for all the MP3-related sites that you find on the Internet.

Your Own Custom Band Name "URL"

MP3.com will also provide a *custom MP3.com* Internet address: http://www.mp3.com/
yourbandname. This unique address will make it easy for you to tell your friends how
to find your band page on MP3.com. When you sign up as an artist, you'll find an
easy form to complete regarding this feature.

Why Isn't My MP3 on My Page Yet? I Uploaded It Hours Ago

After you've uploaded your MP3 file, the song will become available to the public to
listen to in a day or so. The encoding of your song must first be verified, and your
song is actually listened to by a real living person (or at least an MP3.com staff
member, which is almost the same thing) before it is released to the public.

Trouble Tickets: Reporting Problems

If at any point you have trouble creating your band page or uploading your art or
songs, you can fill out a *trouble ticket*. If you click the corresponding link, you can
report to MP3.com any problems you are having during sign up. A helpful MP3.com
person will respond to you within a day or so. You can also use the Trouble Ticket
link to report problems with your page at any time during your relationship with
MP3.com.

Overview of the Sign-up Process

Here's a quick sketch of what you do to sign up as an artist on MP3.com. Remember
that the New Artist Signup link is on the front page of MP3.com, underneath the
Artists/Labels heading. Click that. Now you are in the Artist Area-New Artist Sign Up
section. Remember to follow the link to Artist FAQs if you haven't already.

Now click **Go Straight to Step One**.

MP3.com Music Submission Agreement

Step 1: This is an online contract that you must read and sign before you can go any
further in the sign-up process. Read this contract carefully (don't worry, there isn't
too much fine print); if you agree to the terms of the agreement, complete the blanks
and move on to the next step. You must be at least 18 to sign this contract. If you are
under 18, you need your parent or guardian to do it for you. If your parents won't
sign the contract, you can hold band practice in the hall bathroom until they see
reason.

You don't exactly sign the contract. Instead, you type in your name and click a few
boxes that MP3.com ends up accepting as a signature.

141

You click a few boxes to accept the MP3.com Artist Agreement.

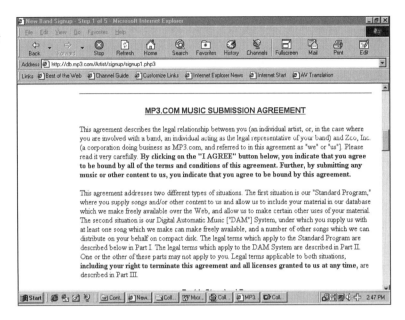

Step 2: Here you supply MP3.com with a mailing address. Not an email address, but a street address. This step is very important because MP3.com sometimes mails out freebies such as t-shirts and the like to their artists. If you make up an address, somebody that you don't know might get some great stuff meant for you.

Supplying your mailing address is vitally important if you plan to use MP3.com to make and distribute CDs. This is something covered in detail in the next chapter. No fair reading ahead! I don't want you to spoil any surprises. You can supply MP3.com with a post office box address if you would like. In any event, your address is not for viewing by the general public and does not show up on your page.

Step 3: This page asks you to review and confirm the artist information that you've entered. After you've double-checked your entries and made any corrections that are warranted, go on to the next step.

Step 4: Upload your band picture. Remember, it should be exactly 270 pixels wide and 180 pixels high. If your image doesn't appear on your page for some reason, try increasing the size of your image by one or two pixels more than 270×180. Research has shown that more people download songs from bands who have their photo on their band page, so don't be shy.

MP3.com has also recently added the ability to have full-color cover art for the CDs that they can make for you. We'll cover that in more detail in an upcoming chapter.

As you build your band page, you will see a preview of what the page will look like, including the art. Remember, this is simply a preview. The art won't show up on your page until your band has been approved by MP3.com.

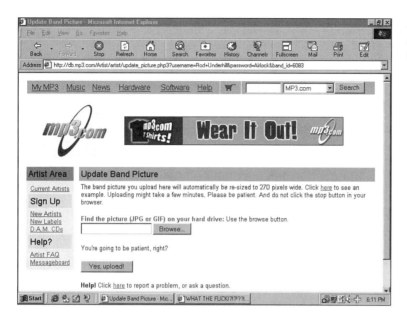

Uploading your band art on MP3.com doesn't take much time.

Step 5: You are now finished with the Artist Management menu. You have to upload a song. Click the **Add New Song** link and move on to the next step.

Adding Your Music: The Most Fun Step of All

Step 1: Enter your song information, which consists of the song title, a brief description, and your credits. Here is an example:

> **Song Title:** "My Parakeet Bill"
>
> **Song Description:** "I love my Parakeet Bill so much that I made up a song about him. Sadly, he flew away yesterday before I finished this tune and he never had a chance to hear it."
>
> **Credits:** "I wrote this myself."

Step 2: Find the MP3 file on your hard drive and upload the file. You'll notice a line on this particular page of the MP3.com sign-up process screen that reads like this: Find the MP3 file on your hard drive: use the Browse button. You will also notice an empty rectangle next to this statement. Empty rectangles are boring, so fill it with something appropriate. A window will open when you select the Browse button, showing you various files on your hard drive.

Simply follow the path to the file where your encoding software has stored your MP3 file and click the actual file when you locate it. You will see the file (and its path) automatically appear in the once-empty window. Windows users will see something like C:\Program Files\Encoderdelux\Music\Songs\music.mp3.

143

Now click the **Upload MP3** button. Your song will automatically be sent to MP3.com. Depending on your Internet connection speed, this process might take up to 45 minutes for every song you upload. If you have a slow modem connection, this might be a good time for you to write another song. After the song is uploaded, proceed to the next page in the sign-up process.

Step 3: Upload the album cover image. Remember that this picture must be 70×70 pixels. The art will appear next to your song on your page. You can provide a different one for every song that you upload. If you have several songs on your page, having matching cover art for each song really looks great. The uploading of your art will be quite brief compared to the time it takes to upload your MP3. You'll only have enough time to write a title for a song at this point.

Step 4: MP3.com provides a special button for pushing if your song should have a *parental advisory* warning. If your lyrics are a little on the adult side, please put a parental advisory on the page next to your song. The warning is set up by you, but someone at MP3.com might request that you do this if you forget.

Here's a good rule of thumb: Songs that contain profanity or explicit lyrics should bear a parental warning. Also, please keep your band names and song titles relatively clean as well, or you might find your band sequestered in an adults-only area on MP3.com. This would limit the exposure that your music would get because these areas aren't as well traveled by music fans.

Now decide where you want the song to be available. Remember, at least one complete song has to be available to the public as a free MP3. You can also allow MP3 to play the song on its Internet radio network and to place your song on one of its great promotional CDs—all at no charge to you. Three check boxes are selected automatically for you; the selections allow your songs to be on MP3, on radio stations, and on possible compilation CDs. Simply deselect those you are not interested in for a particular song.

You're done! Repeat the uploading process for each song that you want to place on MP3.com. You can return to MP3.com and to your band page as often as you want to add new songs, update current songs by giving them a new version (which retires the older version automatically), delete songs, and change where the songs are available.

The Artist Currently Known As "You"

After you've joined MP3.com as an artist member and successfully set up your band page (complete with at least one MP3 version of a song), you no longer have to go through the artist sign-up procedure. Instead, you'll return to MP3.com's front page and once again go to the area marked Artists/Labels; this time, however, you click **Artist Login**.

You then see a page where you type in your username and password. Remember that the usernames and passwords are case sensitive. In other words, if your username is John Smith, type `John Smith`, not `john smith`.

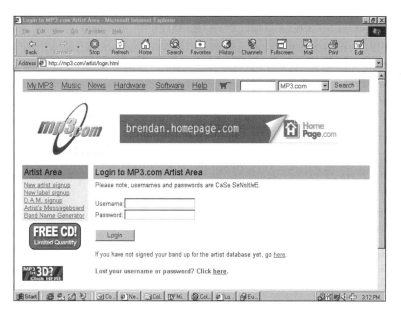

Here's where you log in to add songs and make other changes on your artist page.

Afteryou log in, you see a friendly greeting from MP3.com welcoming you back to the site. You also see a list of fun activities. Want to change your band info? Upload a new MP3? Change the art? Each function is clearly marked for you to follow with ease.

MP3.com Internet Radio

MP3.com will convert your MP3 file into a RealAudio file and play it on one of its Internet radio stations. All you have to do is give permission to do it. They have a Top 40 program, plus a station for every one of their many genres. Since MP3.com also breaks the larger genres down into smaller ones, you could also find your electric blues music playing on their electric blues station, and your acoustic blues songs playing on their acoustic blues station. They will also provide you with an Internet radio station of your very own—that plays only your music. Your very own private radio station! Besides being yet another free service for artists, MP3.com does all the work for you. All you have to do is upload your MP3s and let them know that you want your music to be played on their various Internet radio programs. You could find your song being played on several different Internet radio stations at the same time. What a great way to get new fans!

145

MP3.com's "We'll Do It For You" Program

If you don't want to bother encoding your song into a MP3 file and uploading it to MP3.com, you're in luck. MP3.com has a special program you should love. It's called the "We'll Do It For You" plan. Perhaps they should have called it the "I Got Better Things to Do with My Time Than Wait 45 Minutes to Upload an MP3" program, but they didn't.

MP3.com will encode your songs for you. However, while they will encode your MP3s, you still have to complete all the steps required to sign up as an artist, as well as those for setting up your band page and list of songs. That means doing those steps online at the MP3.com site.

However, you will simply skip over the one step that requires you to upload your MP3s to MP3.com. Instead, you'll mail your CD to MP3.com with a check for $20, and they will do the encoding for you. The fee covers all the songs on your CD that you want encoded, from one song to a full CD's worth. Remember, they won't set up your band page or scan your art. This program only includes the encoding of your CD, and they can't work from any medium other than an audio CD.

Because it can take up to 40 minutes to send a song to MP3.com over a standard 56K modem, this service is quite a bargain if you are planning to upload several MP3s. Look how much time you save if you are going to upload an entire CD's worth of MP3s. You'll find a set of FAQs regarding this program in the Artist area of MP3.com. Check it out to see if there are any recent updates to the "We'll Do It For You" program.

Remember the basic facts of this program: You must set up your band page with the band photo, cover images, band information, and song information just like you normally would, but here you skip over the upload MP3 part of the process. You then complete the online "We'll Do It For You" program forms. The forms tell MP3.com what songs to encode. Finally, you mail your CD to MP3.com, who does the encoding for you.

MP3.com will not return your CD, but will keep it in their library in case they have to re-encode the songs.

Don't have an audio CD of your music? Are your tunes on DAT, ADAT, or some other format? In the Artist FAQs you will find a link to one or more companies that can inexpensively burn an audio CD for you from these and other formats.

Setting Your Sites Further

Of course, MP3.com is not the only MP3 site out there. It's the biggest and the best one to start with, but you should take advantage of the other sites out there as well. Take a quick look at Chapter 4, "Where to Get `Em and How to Download `Em," for a list of some of the other major MP3 sites. Those that distribute tracks for free are generally glad to have you upload yours. Each site has a different procedure, so read through their guidelines carefully.

The Least You Need to Know

➤ The most popular place to put your MP3 on the Internet is MP3.com.

➤ Your band page can contain photos, art, lyrics, and other promotional information along with your MP3s.

➤ Scan your photos, title your songs, and prepare your band-related text before you begin setting up your page on MP3.com or any other MP3-related site.

Band of Gold

MP3s on CD: A Lot of Music on One Disc

Take a look at any one of your commercial audio CDs and count the number of songs on it. You'll discover maybe 10 to 12 songs, right? The average blank CD can actually hold up to about 74 minutes of music, but few people take advantage of this capacity. But some CDs contain a full 70 plus minutes of music, and I get really excited about them. More is better, usually.

Now consider this: If you put music in the form of MP3s on a CD, it can hold nearly 10 times as much music as a standard audio CD—that's a whole lot of music. Of course, having an MP3-filled CD means that you have to upload the MP3s to your computer and play the songs on the computer's speakers, or perhaps download the MP3s to a Diamond Rio or some similar device. But wouldn't it be great if you could play a 100-plus song MP3 CD in your car, or on a home CD player?

Soon you will be able to. MP3s are a very new technology and hardware manufacturers are just starting to catch up. Soon CD players will be able to handle both formats: standard CD audio tracks and MP3s. That means you can pop in an MP3-based CD and rock for hours without having to put in a new CD. How come? Because the new players will instantly know if the CD is a standard audio CD or an MP3 CD and will play both types of recordings.

This is where you come in. Let's say you have an album's worth of material ready to go. Why stop there? You could place loads of material on the CD that fans would be interested in. Start of course by putting your basic collection of 12 (or so) songs on the CD. Then, why not add a few bonus tracks, such as some demos that you might have done? After that, why not add a half an hour of interviews with the band, broken into five-minute segments?

You could also add a few live tracks, and a couple versions of your songs with the vocals mixed out so that your fans could have some fun and sing along with your band. In short, jam that CD with as much cool audio material as you can possibly think of.

Then, sell the CD at your live shows. You could be the first band on your block to be ready with a lengthy, and interesting, MP3 CD, when the new players start showing up in neighborhood stores. You could also sell your CD on the Internet from various locations like www.cdbaby.com or from your own Web page. The point is that you should be ready to exploit the new MP3 technology by preparing in advance your MP3 CD and have it ready to sell when the MP3 home and auto players first come out. It will be a while before the major record companies come out with 10-hour long CDs at any affordable price. You will be able to be ahead of the game if you plan now.

Naturally, it might be difficult for you to come up with 10 hours of material for your CD, or even two hours of material. So, why not team up with other bands and get a great, massive CD together? You can easily meet bands that you like on MP3.com or other MP3-related communities.

MP3.com and the "DAM CDs"

MP3.com has a pretty neat way of setting you up to sell your MP3s. The "DAM CD" system, which stands for "Digital Automatic Music."

Once you have enrolled as an artist on MP3.com, you can elect to sell your music on CD. You set the price for the CD, which is offered for sale on MP3.com. Your fans can download samples of your album, since you have to give at least one free MP3 away to qualify for a band page on MP3.com. The rest of your music, including the free MP3, can be available on the CD that MP3.com will manufacture for you.

MP3.com prints the CD and full-color cover art, places the CD in a jewel box, and ships the CD for you. The fans pay for the CD with their credit cards. You are given a full 50% from the sale of the CD, which you collect after a $100 worth of CDs are sold.

And, here's something really neat: The DAM CD contains both MP3 versions of your songs and standard CD tracks that MP3.com automatically creates for you. That means your CD can be played both on a standard CD player, like in your car, and on your computer!

The Future of "Getting" Paid for Your MP3s on the Internet

It is important to remember that the concept of MP3s is very new to the Internet. Because of this, ideas for helping bands to make money with their MP3s are undoubtedly under development. As *MP3* becomes more of a household term, the popularity of the format will surely grow. Now is the time to get your music into MP3 format and on the Internet. Better and more effective ways of making money with your MP3s will surely follow. Remember: the current main goal for you should be getting tons of fans. After you achieve that goal, hopefully some money may follow.

Enrolling in the DAM CD Program

Once you've signed up as an artist on MP3.com and your MP3s have been approved for release, simply log in to your artist page on MP3.com. Remember how you do that? Go to the MP3.com home page and find the link that says **Artist Login**. Click on that and you'll be taken to a new page that has two boxes: one for your username and one for your password. Just fill that information in, and you'll be taken to the Artist Admin Area, where you can make changes to your band page.

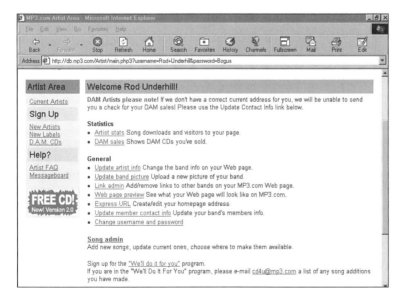

The Artist Admin Area.

Creating Your DAM CD on MP3.com

In the Artist Admin Area, scroll down the page until you find the link that says **DAM CD Admin**. Click on that and then scroll down the next page until you see a link that says **CREATE NEW CD**. Click on that.

Click on the link ***DAM CD Admin****.*

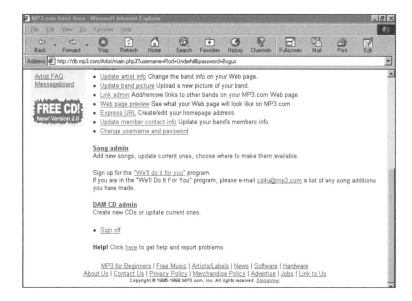

Now you will see a list of your approved songs. All you have to do here is click in the box next to every song that you want to appear on your album.

You will also give your CD a title by filling in that information in the CD Name box. You can use only a maximum of 30 characters. You will also set your CD price on this page by going to the pull-down CD Price window and scrolling down the available prices ranging from $5.99 to $10.00. Pick the price that you want, and then you are ready to move on to the next step.

After you are ready to go on to the next page, just click on the **Continue to Step 2** box.

Step 2 of the CD creation process is a breeze. (But all these steps have been easy, haven't they?) Here you just list the order of the songs for your CD. See the boxes next to each song. Just pull down the little windows and scroll to the order number that you want to set for each song. See! Easy as pie. (Why do people say that? I don't know how to bake a pie and I've been to college.)

When you have finished, click on the box on the bottom of the page and move on to step 3.

New! Cover Art for Your DAM CD!

This is a relatively new feature on MP3.com: color cover art for your CD. Step 3 is where you set up your album cover art. This is not to be confused with the "cover" art that is mentioned elsewhere on MP3.com that refers to the small, 70 pixel by 70 pixel images that go on your band page next to your songs. Those images are essentially small thumbnail pictures of any art that you want to use to jazz up your page. The "cover art" that we are talking about here is specifically the cover art that will be printed for your CD.

This would probably be a good time for me to tell you the specifics that you should know so that you can do a good job on creating your cover art, huh? Well, okay, since you bought this book and everything....

You will be sending the image to MP3.com through the Internet, and that means that the picture will have to be turned into a certain type of graphics file. You've learned already that an MP3 is actually a compressed file format for music. Now, I am going to tell you about a certain type of compressed file for pictures called a *JPEG*.

The JPEG, or ".jpg file" as it is also called, is created by any one of several computer art/photo programs. Perhaps you already have own one such program such as Painter or Photoshop. If you do own such a graphics program, please refer to the instructions that came with it for more information about JPEGs.

If you don't own any art or photo software, don't get upset and stick your tongue out at this book. What good would that do? I can't even see you! Well, actually I can, but that's because of the secret camera we have built in to page 99 that I'm not supposed to tell you about. Isn't miniaturized electronic technology coming along nicely? Hey! That picture on the wall behind you is crooked!

You can obtain the shareware program Paint Shop Pro if you are using a Windows-based computer, or, the shareware program GraphicConverter if you are using a Mac. These programs will happily create JPEGs for you. GraphicConverter can be located at `www.lemkesoft.de` and Paint Shop Pro can be found at `www.jasc.com` on the Web.

Where should you get the art for your CD cover? You can paint your own picture, take a photo, or create your own original art in any way that you want. Digital cameras are great for this sort of thing. But one thing that you can't do is use art that you do not own. That means you can't simply scan in somebody's art that you find in a book, a magazine, or a postcard.

Tune Talk

Two PEGs from the Same Hole

JPEG stands for *Joint Photographic Experts Group*, a committee of the ISO, the same folks who brought you *MPEG*.

Use your graphics program to create a file that is sized 1,435 pixels wide and 1,425 pixels high. Your resolution must be set at 300 dpi to make sure that the resulting CD cover appears nice and crisp.

If you don't want to create your own CD cover art, MP3.com will provide you with some nice default art.

Additional Hot Tips for Making Money!

While you may experience various levels of success regarding selling your MP3s, you can make additional money by selling t-shirts and other promotional materials and by getting people to come to your shows! Make sure that you collect the email addresses for all the people you meet on and off the Internet and set up mailing lists so that you can tell your fans about your new songs, your shows, and your products. Ask your fans to tell other people about your band! The future of music may not be in selling your music, but giving it away freely, and making money on shows and other product sales.

Additional Revenue Ideas

A few Internet MP3 sites are experimenting with paying bands for the downloads of their MP3s. One such company, AMP3.com, offers two cents per download. The downside to this is that the company adds a three to five second jingle advertisement to the beginning of your song. That means that if people download their songs from AMP3.com and add them to their playlist, they'll have to put up with an advertisement as an intro to each song that they listen to, which can be rather disconcerting.

AMP3.com may also be able to help you find a higher-paying sponsor for your music. Again, a brief ad would be added to your song, but you would qualify for some sort of compensation. Check out `www.amp3.com` for the latest details on this and other revenue-sharing programs for their artists.

MP3.com regularly runs news stories regarding MP3s and the Internet. If you read these news stories on a steady basis, you will pick up information regarding MP3 sites from all over the Internet and learn of any new ways you can earn a buck with your MP3s.

The Least You Need to Know

➤ Get ready for the upcoming CD players that will handle both MP3 CDs and regular CDs by preparing your lengthy MP3 CDs now.

➤ Sell your MP3s on CD at MP3.com through their DAM CD program.

➤ Keep your eye on upcoming ways that you can make money with your MP3s by visiting MP3.com often.

Part 4

Music Police 3: MP3 and the Law

No, the Music Police won't come over to your house and get your noisy neighbors to turn down their loud stereo in the wee hours of the morning. And Music Police isn't the name of a Cheap Trick album. There are, however, serious laws that you need to be aware of that affect MP3s.

In this part, you will learn about the legal history surrounding MP3s, pirated music (avast, mateys!), and legitimate sources from which you can encode MP3 files. You will also learn how you can get permission to record your favorite song and release it as an MP3 on the Internet. We'll also tell you a true story about a famous rock star and his MP3s.

Chapter 11

Making Money from MP3s When You Aren't a Musician

In This Chapter

➤ What is bootlegging?

➤ What is a music review site?

➤ What are the different types of review sites?

➤ How do I make money with a review site?

Be a Music Tycoon!

Perhaps you love music a great deal, but have absolutely no ability to play an instrument or sing. Maybe you can't even carry a tune in a bucket. Don't worry! There's still a place for you in the world of MP3-related commerce. Doesn't that make you want to sing a happy tune? No, don't thank us, we're here to help.

There are at least two great ways to earn some money by using your newfound knowledge of MP3s. But before we walk down either of those golden paths, let's take a look at one way you *can't* make money with MP3s—at least legally.

Bootlegging: A Quick Trip to Troubleland

Some people might think that the rich bounty of CD-quality MP3 music on the Internet is a license to steal. These unprincipled persons might consider downloading oodles of fantastic MP3s and then use them to burn their own custom CDs, which they would in turn sell to their friends. They might even come up with the idea of selling them at stores or even swap meets. Is this a good idea? No! It's a serious crime.

This activity is known as *bootlegging*, and is illegal, whether it's smuggling liquor or copying recorded music or movies. Don't even consider doing it. After all, it got Al Capone in trouble, and he probably had a better lawyer than you do. Besides, there are other, *legal* methods to earn a living within the exciting musical world of MP3s.

Music Review Sites: The Land of Gold

The Internet is rich with tens of thousands of free MP3s. Many of them are recorded by artists with little talent. Although there are huge numbers of gems, searching through the chaff can be daunting and time consuming. This is where you come in.

You can easily establish an Internet site where you review MP3s of high quality. Are you an expert in a particular type of music? Wonderful! If not, you can always partner up with someone who is an expert in a certain type of music. Or, you can list MP3s by artists who are playing live in your own city and let your users make their own decisions about the abilities of the acts in question.

Here's the coolest part of this whole idea: You don't have to keep the MP3s on your own server space, but can merely link to the remote location where the MP3s are kept. This keeps your space requirement for your page down to a minimum. In fact, such a site can easily fit on the free Web space many ISPs offer with your email account. Low overhead means higher profits!

Make sure that you set up links to MP3s that are legitimate and authorized by the performers. Never link to pirated music because doing so can still get you in loads of trouble.

Lycos Falls into Copyright Trouble

Lycos operates a very powerful and popular Internet search engine. The International Federation of the Phonographic Industry (IFPI) became upset when Lycos licensed an MP3 search engine and database that was owned and operated by a Norwegian business called FAST Search & Transfer ASA. Essentially, the FAST company provided links to hundreds of thousands of MP3s on the Internet. Evidently, the IFPI must have felt that a certain number of these MP3s were actually pirated from various record companies that the IFPI represents. The issue of whether FAST has in some way violated Norwegian copyright law remains unresolved at this point, as the case remains in litigation. It is important to remember that record companies are very serious about protecting their copyrights.

Thinking of Linking

Before you set up your review page on the World Wide Web, make sure that the locations that you are linking to are okay with what you are doing. Most MP3 sites *encourage* other Internet sites to link to them, but you should always ask if you aren't certain. MP3.com *encourages* review sites to link to their site, and even provides art that you can use on your page for just that purpose.

But some MP3 sites will become angry if you link to them. For sites other than MP3.com, you should ask first before you set up your links. You can usually find a link on the page to email the Webmaster, which is a fancy title for the person who runs the site. (Hey, after you're done, you'll be a Webmaster too!) Also, read the materials on any site carefully to see if it has posted its policy on this subject.

You should also check with each artist whose MP3 you intend to review (and link to) to make sure that it's okay with them. You should find that nearly every artist will absolutely love the idea! Why? Because you are helping to drive new fans to their Internet pages and they want all the new fans that they can possibly get. You'll be a hero! On MP3.com, each artist has a special email link on their page that makes contacting them easy to do. Tell them that you only review music that you like, and they'll jump at giving you permission!

You can see the MP3.com listing of review sites at `http://mp3.com/artistspotlight/`. If you want to submit your own review site to MP3.com for listing on this page, you'll find a handy link right there just for that purpose. Click it; an email window opens up, and you can send MP3.com details and the URL address of your review site. Good luck!

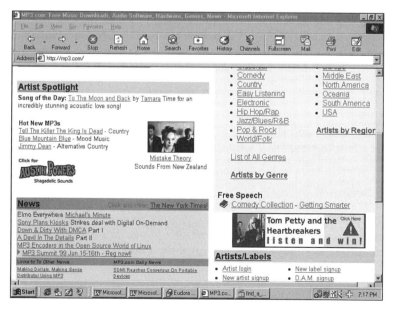

The Artist Spotlight page offers a listing of review sites.

MP3 Review Model One: The "Specialist"

The first example of a possible review page is one that concentrates on one type of music. For purposes of having a good example, let's arbitrarily select "The Blues" for our genre of music. Not that either you or I have the Blues right now. How could we? We're having so much fun learning how to make a buck with MP3s!

Your first step is to search out the best blues music on the Web that's offered in free MP3 format. The starting point for your search should always be MP3.com, the recognized mother lode of free, authorized MP3s.

You'll need to listen to all the blues music that you can. If you have a slow modem, you'll find the going easier if you listen to the "Instant Play" version of the song, which streams out in low-fi, mono RealAudio format. If you need to study the music in greater sonic detail, you can download the actual MP3.

Make notes as you go and select only the tunes you consider to be the best blues music that you can find. As you find the best MP3s, make sure that you save their URL links as bookmarks or favorite places. You'll need them to set up the links from your page to the page where the MP3 resides.

Super Slick Trick: Try the "Right-Click"

When you have an MP3 that you want to download, you can simply click on the link with the right button on your mouse instead of the left button. A menu will appear from which you can choose to save the file the link points to. A dialog box then appears from which you can easily select just the right location to place your MP3 file. Give it a try!

Make some notes about the artists and the songs as you go, so you won't have to listen to the music all over again to remember why the heck you liked them in the first place.

After you've collected the URLs to whatever number of hot MP3s you want to review, write a brief description of each of the bands and their songs. Because you're writing about music that you love, try and state clearly what's so great about the music. Don't be fancy or overly inventive in your descriptions. Remember, your fans want to be guided to the best music more than they want to be impressed by your prose.

Yet *Another* Way to Make Money in the MP3 Business

As easy as setting up MP3-related Web pages is, many people don't want to take the time to learn how. A lot of musicians have heard about MP3s but they don't want to be bothered with learning how to encode MP3s, scan art, or any of the other tasks necessary to set up their band page on the Internet. Some musicians don't even have a computer!

You can help them for a fee! I suggest a minimum fee of $25 an hour, but that's up to you. Make sure you ask for an hourly fee rather than a flat, one-time charge, so that you can make any changes and additions to their page without feeling like you've been underpaid.

Take out a small ad in the musician's section of your local newspaper, and you'll be surprised about how many clients you'll get. You can also send flyers to all the recording studios in your town. You'll be an Internet Music Guru in no time!

Adding Photos and Artwork to Your Review Page

Add artwork to your review page to make it sparkle! You'll find cool art on most MP3 pages that has been provided by the artists themselves. Because some MP3 sites, such as MP3.com, have a space limitation regarding artwork and photos, you might also see if their page links to another site where you can find additional art. You can save the art to your own computer by right-clicking on the particular image that you want and then choosing the save option from the resulting pop-up menu.

Don't forget to ask the band or performer if it is okay to use the art as part of your review page. Most performers will be glad to give you permission because it will help you promote their music. Remember, if you tell a musician that you are going to give their MP3 a glowing review, they will bend over backwards to

Free Art! No Strings Attached!

There are many Web sites that provide free clip art to enhance your pages. You'll find a nice collection of images that you can use for your Web page at `http://members. aye.net/~gharris/Groovy/ grafix.htm`.

help you set up your review page. If you don't watch out, they might even try to come over and cook your dinner, bathe your dog, and cut your grass while you are working on your review page! That's how happy they will be.

The Specialist Page: Some Hot Tips

Because you want people to return to your review page on a regular basis, try and feature a different song every day. You could call it "The Daily Blues" or something clever like that. But regardless of *which* type of review page you create, try to change your featured content on a daily or at least a weekly basis.

Make sure that you check the links to the MP3s on a frequent basis as well. When a band retires their MP3s, the links no longer work. Make sure that you remove all links to retired songs every day. Otherwise, your users will quickly get frustrated and unhappy with your review page.

Add some new links to MP3s every day. Fresh content is the key to success for any review page. Your specialist page should also have something of interest other than MP3s. In this blues example, you could write an article about the history of the blues. Later you could write articles about blues masters such as Eric Clapton, B.B. King, Robert Cray, or John Mayall. With all specialty review pages you should easily be able to find interesting topics to write about, regardless of the genre you select.

MP3 Review Model Two: The "Generalist"

This approach could be described as a "MP3 Greatest Hits" sort of page. The secret here is to find cool music from several types of genres. The easiest way to do this is to peruse the music on MP3.com, or some other MP3 Internet site that you like. Try to stick to the most popular genres: Classical, Rock, Pop, Blues, Soul, Hip-Hop, Rap, Electronic, Techno, Alternative Rock, Country, and so on, at least at first. As your page grows, you can add more genres.

With a little work, you should be able to create an interesting series of links for songs that people might be overlooking. See, you provide a valued service! Don't forget to write up a brief review about each of the songs. Remember, you're the expert, so don't be afraid to act like one. If you select wisely, you will be able to create your own fan following and become an MP3 guru. Bands will crave your attention! Fans will look to you to point out great MP3s!

MP3 Review Model Three: "The Local Expert"

If you live in a large city, this approach might be your best bet. This page should concentrate on local artists that play live in your city. Do some research and find all the clubs in your town that support live music from local acts. If you call the clubs, they will probably be glad to provide you with a list of their upcoming shows.

You can also usually find a list of bands that play locally by looking in your newspaper. Most of these bands will be glad to put you on their mailing list (either email or normal "snail mail") and you'll be constantly updated regarding their shows.

The best way to get revenue for this type of page is to charge something to the local clubs for a prominent listing on your Web page. You'll have to promote your page by spreading the word among bands, fans, and clubs. You can do so by telephoning bands, handing out flyers at clubs, and so on.

Have some business cards printed that list your name and your review site Web address. Business cards are an inexpensive form of advertising, and you can design them yourself.

If you register with the various search engines, the following key phrases would no doubt serve you well: (Your City) Local Music Scene, (Your City) Live Music, (Your City) Concert Guide. Signing up at a search engine should help bring many readers to your Web page.

Make sure you write reviews regarding some concerts. Change your major content at least every week. You'll probably want to post new information on Monday so that people can get a head start on planning their weekend.

Link to MP3s recorded by the musicians in your town. That way, people can check out the band's music in advance.

How to Obtain Advertising Money for Your Site

Many companies offer money to Web page owners if you put banner ads on your site. It's best to do some investigation regarding these companies before you sign up. A good Internet spot for information regarding such advertising possibilities, and other helpful Web page information and links, can be found at: `http://www.howtoweb.com/corner/advert.htm`.

Each company has different rules about how and when you'll get paid for these ads. Read their rules carefully before you agree to partner up with them.

Amazon.com has a referral program where you get a percentage of book and CD sales if you send them customers. Because Amazon sells CDs, you can include a link to the CD containing the songs on your MP3 page. That way, your MP3s can spur a purchase of the CD!

Amazon calls this referral arrangement the "Amazon.com Associates program." Through this program, you can offer links to books and CDs of your selection. Try to pick items that make sense for your Web site. If you are doing a specialty page, like one about the blues, you could list both popular blues CDs and books about the blues. You can also add a search link, which enables people to search Amazon's catalog from your Web site, and pay you if they order anything they find.

When you can, don't just list the books and CDs. Include honest reviews. Although the negative reviews may drive people away from certain items, it will get people to trust your positive reviews, making them much more likely to order those items.

If you have a general review page, list the top-selling CDs and general books on music so that you can make some additional money.

As for a local page, see if Amazon.com offers books about your town. If you live in a major city, you should be able to find plenty of books available. Don't forget to list CDs from famous bands that got their start in your city, too.

Go to Amazon.com for full details about the Associate program. While you are there, order several extra copies of this book to give to your friends and family. They make wonderful gifts.

The Least You Need to Know

➤ Selling MP3s that you don't own is illegal.

➤ MP3 review sites are a valuable service because people need extra help locating the best free music.

➤ There are several types of review sites to choose from.

➤ You earn money with a review site through various forms of advertising.

Chapter 12

Pirates, Legal Troubles, and Big Business

In This Chapter

➤ What is the Audio Home Recording Act?

➤ What is the Digital Millennium Copyright Act and how does it affect MP3s?

➤ What was the Diamond Rio dispute about?

➤ What if my own music gets pirated?

I Got Dem Pirate Blues, Mama!

A couple of centuries ago, pirates were a real problem for people. There you were, sailing cheerfully along on your galleon, drinking grog and minding your own business, and you would suddenly find your ship boarded by a group of smelly, unshaven louts who would promptly proceed to ruin your day. Their idea of a good time was pretty unpleasant, too. They would take all your stuff, snarl at you, and generally act in a rude manner. Nobody in their right mind would ever invite a pirate to a sailing party.

I don't know if there are any more pirates plying their violent trade on the High Seas, but I know this: We've got a few still hanging out on land. Oh, not the eye-patch wearin', "Avast, ye maties" talkin', parrot befriendin' type of pirates (and not the baseball players!), but something just as alarming. Yes, friends, I am talking about music pirates.

Who are the music pirates? For the most part, they are people that copy recorded music that they don't own and then sell the copies for a tidy profit. That really annoys the actual owners of the music because pirates usually forget to send the real owners a check when they burn off a few hundred bootleg copies of somebody's album. Pirates are absent-minded that way.

In the past, music pirates also included an awful lot of people who just wanted a copy of an album they couldn't find or they didn't feel like paying retail price for, so they taped a friend's album for themselves. Although there were a lot of these small-scale music pirates, the cops and lawyers never cracked down on them because copying any one album seemed like such a minor infringement. Cumulatively, however, they were getting an awful lot of music for free that the musicians and record companies deserved to get paid for.

Audio Home Recording Act

Not liking commercial music pirates much, and also wanting to take large groups of ordinary people out of the "scofflaw" category, our lawmakers in Washington decided to fire a broadside at music piracy. To help out music copyright holders in their fight against these musical outlaws, they passed the *Audio Home Recording Act* in 1992. This law imposes a 3 percent surcharge on the sales of blank digital tape, discs, and cartridges. Digital audio recording devices (such as DAT and Minidisc) have an added 2 percent to their price of sale.

This law also required that certain digital music devices meant for personal use have a Serial Copy Management System built in so that copies of copies of digital music cannot be easily made. The record companies want to make sure that if you're digitally copying an album, at least you're copying directly from the original, rather than copying from a copy of a copy of a copy. Some recording devices just won't let you copy a copy, while others copy it as an analog rather than a digital track, reducing the quality of the recording.

As for the money collected from the sale of the tapes and such: Where does it go? It is gathered up and distributed to songwriters, record companies, publishers, and so on. All of us pay this surcharge even if we aren't pirates. That seems fair, doesn't it?

"Who Gets the Audio Home Recording Act Money, Anyway?"

The money collected goes to the Register of Copyrights and the Librarian of Congress. These are both U.S. government agencies, of course. Two-thirds of the money goes to a "Sound Recording Fund." Most of this money goes to record companies, but 40% of this two-thirds goes to famous artists. A small bit of it goes to nonfamous artists and backup musicians. The other third goes into a "Musical Works Fund" and is split evenly between songwriters and music publishers. Aren't they lucky guys?

Sometimes I think that this law might have come about because in the late 1980s, Sony (a major manufacturer of private recording equipment) purchased CBS Records (a major producer of commercially recorded music). Plus, Matsushita (another large manufacturer of private recording equipment) purchased MCA, another large record company. In the sunny days prior to the passing of the Audio Home Recording Act, Matsushita and Sony were, uh, *against* this type of law. After investing in the Recording Industry, they decided to *support* passing this interesting tax.

But perhaps that was a coincidence of some sort. (I'll pause for a moment while you snort and slap your knee. Really, I am quite shocked at what you are suggesting, Dear Reader. You don't think that Big Business has the ability to have us taxed for their own direct benefit, do you?)

So, we are all picking up the tab for the pirates. How do I know this? Because in 1989, a study by the U.S. Congress determined that there was no real evidence that home audio taping was reducing sales of prerecorded, commercially released material. In fact, they concluded that home taping actually increased sales for the record companies. The law was passed anyway.

The Act Stinks

My beloved co-author Rod, who wrote most of this chapter, isn't nasty enough towards the Audio Home Recording Act. This new tax (signed into law by Mr. "No New Taxes" himself, George Bush) has ugly causes and ugly effects:

➤ It is based on the assumption that some folks were breaking the law (which is true), and that the proper thing to do is not to enforce the law, but rather to treat everyone as if they had been breaking the law, and had to pay for it.

➤ It weakens the control that copyright is supposed to provide, which was already weakened for musicians. Now, they don't have the right to say "people at home can't make copies of my song and pass it around." Instead, the musician has to accept it and hope he gets some cut of the money pile.

➤ It puts limits and added complications on information technology.

➤ The little guy is being taxed not to feed the poor or provide for our national defense, but to pad the bank accounts of multinational media conglomerates.

➤ Buying a DAT recorder to make high-quality tapes of your cutting edge band that is nothing like that commercial music you so hate? Congratulations, you're supporting Capital Records. Recording an audio letter to your Mom on your Minidisc recorder? Way to go, you're funding the Backstreet Boys.

New taxes, weaker copyright, crippled and expensive technology, all in the name of funding international multimedia conglomerates. This act is a loser all around.

Copying Without Fear

There were two major benefits for consumers, however. After the AHRA was passed, manufacturers felt more comfortable making digital home music equipment. Now we could buy digital recording equipment that would perfectly duplicate music. More important than even that: We could now digitally copy prerecorded music for our own personal, noncommercial use without fear of breaking any laws.

That's pretty cool, too. It is perfectly okay to make your own CD of your favorite songs drawing from music in your own, purchased collection. Strictly speaking, making copies of something that was copyrighted wasn't necessarily something that you could do. Now you can. You pay for the privilege to do this via the surcharge added to your CD recorder and the blank CDs. But this law does not give you the right to start mass-distributing MP3s of your favorite songs.

The Digital Millennium Copyright Act

In 1990 Congress passed the Digital Millennium Copyright Act (DMCA). The purpose of the act was to help the Copyright law catch up to the reality of modern music technology.

If an Internet service provider allowed, either intentionally or not, users to keep illegal MP3s on its site, that storage of unauthorized, pirated MP3s could potentially cause them some legal problems. Or, even if an Internet service provider provides some helpful hyperlinks to surfers looking for pirated material, that could also cause the referring service some legal trouble, as well.

The DMCA provides a "safe Harbor" for these types of Internet-related businesses. See how we keep getting nautical references coming up in this chapter? Just a coincidence, I assure you. (Hand me my bottle of grog, ye scurvy land lubber.)

This issue concerns an Internet service provider giving someone space to store something that may be copyrighted when the copyright owner hasn't given permission for the duplication. Like if somebody puts up an MP3 version of the latest major hit record. That could be embarrassing. It could result in an unpleasant phone call from an unpleasant person:

> Hello. This is John Dewey, Esq., from the law firm of Dewey, Cheatem, and Howe. We represent Billy and the Boingers. We found a copy of their latest major hit record (available at all major stores now) on your online service. That fact has made Billy's teeth fall out, his hair stand on end, and generally hurt his feelings. It also violates his copyright in at least a contributory fashion. Therefore, we would like you to contribute a very large sum of money to his bank account in the form of compensatory damages. We also have a lengthy list of demands. Let's discuss it over lunch, shall we? Please bring your checkbook.

That communication could ruin any ISP's day. Who wants to be responsible for someone's poor dental health?

In their wisdom, Congress passed a law that protects an ISP from being sued for copyright infringement when infringing material is on their Web site if certain conditions are met. The rules are fairly simple.

The ISP shouldn't be aware that the material is infringing. That simply means that if they know a song or composition is pirated or unauthorized, then they should promptly remove it from their site. So far, pretty easy, huh?

Making money from illegal MP3s will bar an ISP from the "safe harbor." Simply put: The ISP shouldn't get paid by anyone who is accessing the infringing material. Making money from illegal MP3s, even if you don't know they are unauthorized, can potentially bar the ISP from the safe harbor.

After someone alerts the ISP of a copyright violation, the ISP should comply with certain reasonable "notice and take down" procedures. The law provides a process that the ISP can safely follow in the event somebody complains about the copyright violation and the ISP is reasonably unsure of who actually owns the particular copyright. If you've been looking on the Web for MP3s, you may have seen notices that ISPs have removed MP3s from their site.

Lycos Moves into Tricky Waters

Interested in the fad in MP3s, Lycos (the popular Internet search engine) established a special MP3 search engine. People could pop over to Lycos on the Internet and easily find MP3s from all over the world. The International Federation of the Phonographic Industry (IFPI), located in London, decided to sue the Lycos partner company, which was involved with the actual search engine. That company, called FAST, is located in Norway. FAST was sued because the IFPI felt that the Lycos search engine amounted to a violation of copyright law because it contributed to copyright infringement by leading fans to unauthorized, pirated MP3s. Lycos will no doubt counter that they deserve the benefits of the "safe harbor" provided by the DMCA. At press time, the matter remains in litigation.

Diamonds on the Souls of My Ears

I have this great little toy called a Diamond Rio. It easily fits into the palm of my hand, has no moving parts, and plays MP3s. You can download MP3s to your computer, and then transfer some of them to your Rio and then enjoy the music through a pair of headphones. It sounds pretty good, too. Trouble is, it also sounded sort of scary to the king of the anti-MP3 forces, the Recording Industry Association of America (RIAA) , a group representing the record companies of the United States.

Prior to the Rio being released, the RIAA filed for an injunction in federal court to stop the sale of the Rio. They claimed that the device did not meet the specifications of the Audio Home Recording Act. That law, remember, requires money to be paid in the form of royalties and a serial copy management system to be placed in the device itself so that zillions of unauthorized copies can't be easily created with the device.

The Federal Court did issue a preliminary injunction that kept the Diamond Corporation from selling the Rio for a period of 10 days. However, after that 10-day period elapsed, the court ruled that there was no relationship between the Diamond Rio and unauthorized copying of MP3s. The Audio Home Recording Act was also not violated, according to the judge in the case, because there was no way of taking a copy of a song out of the Rio, and thus it doesn't qualify as a copying device.

The Rio was set free, sort of. After some continued litigation, the Diamond Corporation agreed to produce the next generation of Rios with an added feature. They will play both MP3s, which can be easily duplicated, and another format other than normal MP3s, which won't be able to be copied, due to encryption being added to the compressed sound file.

Although there are several types of handheld MP3 players available now, the Diamond Rio is quite popular and makes for a good example of how they work. They come in two editions, the first of which is the Rio RMP300. This cute little unit holds up to 60 minutes of digital-quality music and up to 12 hours of voice-quality audio. Plus, it has no moving parts and is about the same size as an audio cassette. You can also add on flash memory cards that give you room for several new songs per card and take the memory from the standard 32MB up to 64MB. Figure that 1MB is not quite a minute of music at the highest-quality setting.

The Rio PMP300 "Special Edition" comes in a transparent teal case and has 64MB of onboard memory right out of the box. The memory can be increased with an add-on module to 96MB.

Other companies that are putting out similar players include Creative Labs (the Nomad), ATLM Taiwan, Inc. (the Etman), and I-JAM MultiMedia Corp (the IJ-100). There are others, too. Have fun shopping!

Billy Idol: Cyberpunk

In December of 1998, Billy Idol decided to give his fans an early holiday present. He released two new singles on MP3.com. The songs were free to all takers. These MP3s were the first new Billy Idol music since his 1993 album *Cyberpunk*. The two songs, "Sleeping with an Angel" and "Find a Way," turned out to be very popular. While it lasted, that is.

Idol's label, Capitol Records, evidently requested that the songs be removed from his MP3.com Web page only a few days after they were released, according to a press release posted on MP3.com at the time.

Other recording stars were quick to jump on the MP3 bandwagon, to the dismay of their record labels. Tom Petty released "Free Girl Now," from his *Echo* CD, on the Internet as a free MP3. It didn't stay up for more than a day or so, either. The Beastie

Boys also experimented with MP3s for a while. One doesn't get the impression that the major record companies loved this sort of experimentation.

The Grateful Dead were pretty famous for letting fans tape their concerts, going so far as to designate a section of the venue just for tapers. But the Dead recently cracked down on MP3s of their music being distributed online. On the other side of things, Julian Lennon and Cheap Trick both cheerfully distributed free MP3s on the Internet without any real problems.

MP3s are wildly popular and appear to be the grassroots' favorite format. Meanwhile, record companies and others are trying to surplant MP3s with various formats that cannot be easily copied. MP3s appear, given their support by fans, to be on solid ground. However, whether sites that contain MP3s can survive legal challenges remains to be seen.

The Mighty Six

There are really only six major record companies: Bertelsmann, EMI-Capital, Universal, PolyGram, Sony Music, and Warner Music. That's it. They own the whole ball of wax.

They hate pirated music, too. But they only hand over to their bands about a dollar for every $16 CD sold. They aren't giving much of a deal to the consumers, either. CDs are cheap to manufacture, yet prices keep going up and up (contrary to promises made when the format was introduced). Yet U.S. record companies made about three billion dollars in profits in 1998. That's a lot of money.

Pirates seem to think this is an excuse for stealing music. Of course, it isn't. But the music industry isn't helping anything with their high prices.

What If You Have Been Pirated?

If you're a musician, you might find out someday that your music has been placed on a Web site without your permission. There are two things that you can do.

You can just allow it to stay where it is. After all, it is free publicity for your act, right? Of course, you are going to want to make sure that the song is properly credited to you. You don't want other people taking your music and putting it up as an MP3 in their name.

Or, you might simply want to have the music removed from the unauthorized Internet site. If you do, let the managers of the Web page know by sending them an email. Most MP3-related music sites do not want to have unauthorized music on their pages and will swiftly move to remove music when they get a complaint.

Remember, the law establishes a responsibility for Internet service providers to respond to your reasonable request to have unauthorized MP3s removed. If there is a dispute as to whether you are the actual copyright holder of the song, they still have to respond to you so that you, and your lawyer, can attempt to resolve your complaint.

If you want to shut down an out-and-out pirate site using your music, and you can't figure out how to locate its actual ISP, there are ways to track them down. You will find a wonderful article on how to accomplish this on MP3.com at `http://mp3. com/news/119.html`, written by MP3 guru Michael Robertson. Essentially, what you will learn is that you can find and verify unlicensed MP3s by using Internet search engines. You'll learn how to locate the server containing the suspect music and then how to identify the server owner or the ISP that the server uses. Finally, you will learn how to best make contact with the owner of the server so that you can have the offending music removed.

The Least You Need to Know

➤ The Audio Home Recording Act allows you to make copies of commercial music for you own personal use.

➤ You pay for the right to make personal copies through higher costs for certain digital home stereo recording equipment and blank tapes and CDs.

➤ Internet service providers have certain responsibilities regarding housing unauthorized MP3s on their services.

➤ If your own music has been pirated, you have certain recourses to get the music removed from the offending site.

Chapter 13

Permission for Distribution

In This Chapter

➤ How do you get a copyright for your music?

➤ How do you get permission to release a cover version of a song you like?

➤ How and why should you join ASCAP or BMI?

➤ What are the rules about sampling music?

Step Right Up Folks and Grab Your Free Instant Copyright!

Feel like writing a song? I bet you're feeling quite creative about now, so go ahead, don't mind me. I'll wait right here.

Finished? Now go record it. Sing it into a cheap cassette recorder. It doesn't have to sound great. I'll wait again while you do that. (I'm getting paid by the hour, not by the word.)

Done? Wonderful! Now you don't only have a song, you own a copyright. Copyright is a legal term. Having the song's *copyright* means that right now, nobody can record that song without your permission. Once a recording of that song is released, if anyone wants to sell recordings of his own version of that song, he has to pay you money. A copyright gives you music, control, and money; what more could you want out of life? (Well, maybe some chocolate cake.)

Once you have written and recorded the song, even in a rough demo form, the copyright is established for you automatically, according to federal law. It doesn't matter if you record a live version of it while you're playing a show, record a highly produced version at the best recording studio in the world, or sing by yourself into a Fisher-Price tape recorder—the copyright exists as soon as you've gotten the song on tape. Presto! It's legal magic.

There is another way you can establish your copyright. You can write the sheet music and lyrics on a piece of paper just as Wolfgang Amadeus Mozart did when he wrote his greatest hits. Doing so also establishes, or "fixes" the copyright. You don't have to be able to write musical notation to get the job done—recording it in any fashion does the job just as well. If tape recorders had been around when Mozart was doing his musical thing, maybe he wouldn't have bothered to learn to read and write musical notation.

Registering Your Copyright

You can make your copyright even stronger by registering your song with your friends at the U.S. Government Copyright Office. Doing that makes it a lot easier to take legal action against anyone who steals your song. Registering your copyright gives you the evidence you need if you ever have to prove that you own your song. You can get the copyright registration forms for free by calling the Copyright Office at 202-707-3000 or by writing to the Library of Congress, Washington D.C., 20559. My favorite way to get the copyright forms is online at `http://www.bmi.com/cright/cright/html`. Registering each song will set you back only 20 bucks.

The forms are offered at BMI in PDF format. You can obtain free software needed to open and read the PDF versions of the copyright documents: Pick up this very helpful Adobe Acrobat Reader at `http://www.adobe.com/acrobat`.

Simply print the forms and complete them, and then mail them to the Copyright Office. The address is right there for you on the forms, along with helpful instructions. Proof of your copyright will be mailed back to you for each song that you register.

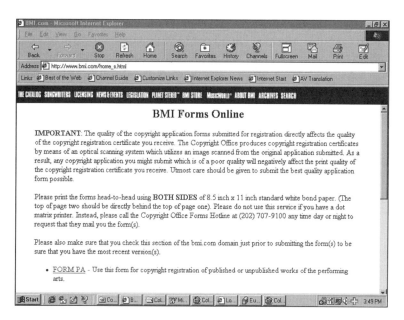

Getting your copyright forms is easy from www.bmi.com.

The Poor Man's Copyright

Some people take a tape of the song that they have written and then mail it to themselves. When they get the letter from the post office, they keep the envelope sealed and put it away in some safe place. Unopened and postmarked, the letter (with the tape containing the song inside) offers proof of their ownership of the song. However, the legal value of this action is dubious. At best, this practice offers a form of evidence regarding the creation and copyright ownership of the song or musical work in question. It's a clever thing to do, but it is far better to register your copyright with the U.S. Copyright Office. Sure, it's fun getting mail, even from yourself, but there is really no need to do this if you register your copyright with Uncle Sam.

Recording Other People's Songs

If you own the song, you can do anything you want with it (except, of course, whistle it in outer space, because there's no air there). If you want to make an MP3 version of the song and put it up on a Web site, there's no one to stop you. (In fact, as you read in Chapter 9, "Spreading Your Sound Around: Distributing Your MP3s," it's a good way to reach a wider audience.) So far so good. What if you didn't write the song? What if you want to record and release an MP3 of a song or musical composition that someone else wrote?

Remember, this is a different issue than when you rip (that is, copy a song from) an MP3 from a commercial CD that you own. We covered that in a previous chapter, as you will recall.

Tune Talk

What Is a Cover Song?

A *cover* is nothing more than when you record your own version of a song that you didn't write yourself. If you decided to record your own version of your favorite Beatles song, you would be doing a cover of that song. Many famous recording artists have done their own covers of songs that they like, sometimes doing entire albums of cover songs. The upside of doing a cover song is that you don't have to write it and can select a song that might be familiar to the general public. The downside is that you have to pay for the right to use the song because you didn't write it and therefore don't own it.

Public Domain: Free Music for All My Friends

Copyright doesn't last forever. If you write "Kiss Me Now, Cook for Me Later," you own it for the rest of your life. At that point your inheritors own it for another 50 years. That's it; nobody owns it anymore. Any fan of kissing and cooking can record that song for free. Legalese for "nobody owns a song" is *in the public domain.*

There's a lot of music in the public domain. Much of it got there simply by being old. Other songs are in the public domain because their owners forgot to take some legal steps that were important under old copyright laws that don't apply to new music. Generally speaking, if a song is fewer than 50 years old, it probably isn't in the public domain, so you can't issue a CD of you whistling the *Gilligan's Island* theme without paying someone. If a song's more than 100 years old, it almost certainly is in the public domain, so feel free to do that rap version of "Greensleeves." (Don't, however, sample parts of someone else's version of "Greensleeves" because that is probably copyright protected, at least as far as the arrangement and sound recording goes.)

If you are not certain whether a song is in the public domain, there are two *performances rights organizations*—groups that specialize in licensing the performance rights to music—that you can contact to find out.

The American Society of Composers, Authors, and Publishers (ASCAP) can be reached at its World Wide Web site (www.ascap.com). Broadcast Music, Inc. (BMI) can be reached at—you guessed it—www.bmi.com. The ever-cheerful Harry Fox Agency, discussed shortly, can also help you in this regard.

Let's Cover Covering a Cover Song

You've decided you want to cover Calling All Vampires' new hit single, "If I Can't Suck Your Blood, Can I Nibble Your Ear?" That's a brand-new song, though, so it's highly unlikely that it's in the public domain. You're hosed, right?

Wrong. You're welcome to record that song. In fact, the song owners even want you to do so. They hope that your own version hits the big time because they get to share in your success. How? You'll pay them 7.1 cents for every copy of their song sold on a CD or cassette (a bit more if the song is more than five minutes long). That is a pretty good deal for you.

Is there a catch? Of course there's a catch. (After all, if it weren't a catchy tune, you wouldn't be covering it, would you?) The catch is that you have to obtain a license for using the song, and you must pay some money up front for the right to release it. The excellent Harry Fox Agency (HFA) will be most pleased to give you all the forms that you need to obtain permission to do your favorite song.

The Harry Fox Agency has been around since 1927 and represents more than 20,000 American music publishers. Music publishers manage the various songs that they own. Some people, such as Sir Paul McCartney, have invested a great deal of money in buying the rights to famous songs. Sir Paul owns not only many of his own songs, but also songs written by Buddy Holly and other famed artists, making him one of the most important music publishers in the world. HFA acts as a go-between publishers such as McCartney's publishing company (MPL) and you, the aspiring musician. HFA makes it very easy to obtain the license that you desire.

Let's Go on a (Harry) Fox Hunt

The best way to contact the HFA is via its Web site, at http://www.nmpa.org/hfa.html.

181

The Harry Fox Agency is where you get mechanical licenses so that you can record somebody else's song.

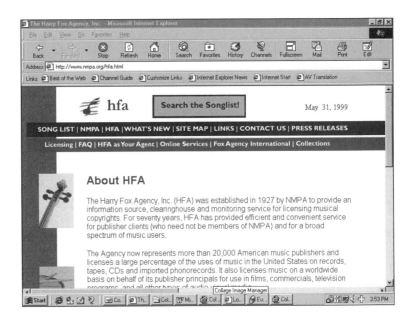

You can also contact the HFA at the following street address:

HFA
711 Third Ave
New York City, NY, 10017

HFA also offers a special telephone number for licensing requests (212-834-0100). Any way you look at it, this one particular fox is as close as your computer, your mailbox, or your telephone.

Remember, this license is for the use of the composition—that is, the right to record your own version of a song you like—or for the use of a sample from a commercial CD to incorporate in your own musical work. Don't call them for permission to rip an MP3 from your favorite CD for your own home use.

The Mechanical License

The *mechanical license* is the permission you need to issue your cover song on CD, cassette, LP, or one of those old Edison phonograph cylinders that you can also use as a rolling pin. Obtaining a mechanical license is even easier than getting a driver's license because there is no test. They don't even examine your vision. The HFA Web site is easy to use and clearly explains the types of licenses that are offered. After you've completed the forms, you simply mail them to HFA along with the required fee. If you are selling a CD of your music with a cover song on it via an Internet retail site, you pay a little more than $35 for a license that covers a maximum of 500 CDs.

The Internet License

What if you don't want to sell CDs? That is, what if you don't want to put your cover song on a CD that you intend to sell, but instead merely want your song to be available as a free MP3 from your Internet Web site? Do you need a license for that? Or is it okay to give away a free MP3 of a cover song?

The HFA knows what it wants you to do. It has an Internet license form that it wants you to complete and file with its office. The HFA also will set some sort of fee for the Internet license, but what that might be is uncertain at this time. Evidently, the entire concept of an Internet license for cover songs is still under development.

The Internet license is not a new creation, but one that is the subject of some debate. Is an MP3 a performance? Or a reproduction? Or neither? If it is a reproduction of a song, the Harry Fox Agency would have jurisdiction. If an MP3 played on the Internet is actually a performance, the various performance rights organizations (BMI, ASCAP, SESAC) would have jurisdiction.

Presently, it would seem that you should contact both the Harry Fox Agency and ASCAP, BMI, SESAC, or whatever performance rights organization applies regarding the song in question and see what their opinions are regarding Internet use of an MP3 version of a cover song that you have recorded.

At this point, MP3.com and the other major MP3 Internet sites each have house rules about cover songs. Some of them might not require you to have an Internet license, but you must have at least a mechanical license for each. Check the FAQ (*Frequently Asked Questions*) list on each site that you are interested in uploading your cover to. Remember, though, that just because the site lets you put the song up for download, that doesn't mean that you are legally protected if the music publisher feels you are infringing on his copyright.

Please, don't release CDs or cassettes of a cover song without first obtaining the necessary licenses. You might otherwise find yourself in serious trouble! Commercial use of somebody else's song without his or her written permission can bring you a lot of legal trouble. As much as you might love doing a smashing cover of Smashing Pumpkins, it's not worth spending years smashing rocks for.

Covering a Song Your Sister Wrote

Your sister writes a catchy little ditty called "My Family Sucks." You want to record it. Of course you can—if she gives you permission.

As the songwriter, she should copyright the song before you release it via the Internet (or anywhere else, for that matter).

The creator of the song should also consider joining ASCAP or BMI, one of the performance royalties organizations. That way, if your version of the song should ever become a smash hit on the radio, she'll get her well-earned performance royalties. If you are a songwriter or composer, you should join up, too. What if, after releasing your song on MP3.com or another Internet site, scads of traditional radio stations discover your musical genius and start playing it in major rotation? What if a thousand bands want to record cover songs of the song that you wrote? Don't you want to get rich?

Getting paid will be difficult if they don't know where to mail the check, which is where ASCAP and BMI come into the picture. ASCAP and BMI are more than willing to collect the money that you are owed, deduct a small fee, and forward the balance to you. It's a pretty good deal.

Joining ASCAP, BMI, or SESAC

Becoming a member of either of the two major performance rights organizations is easy. ASCAP lets you join as a writing member if someone has commercially recorded a musical composition of yours. If you haven't seen any of your music commercially released, don't panic. You can also join as an associate member if you have registered one musical work with the U.S. Copyright Office. You can read all about this and other great stuff about ASCAP at www.ascap.com.

The ASCAP home page is packed with useful information for aspiring recording stars.

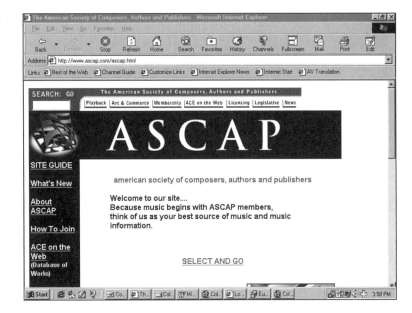

BMI is very similar. You can join if your musical composition has been commercially recorded or published, or if it is otherwise likely to be performed. If you are interested in joining BMI, its Web page (www.bmi.com) helps put you in contact with an official BMI Writer's Relations office near where you live.

There is a third performance rights group, SESAC. It is not as easy to join as BMI or ASCAP because SESAC uses a "selective process" through which it allows new members to join its organization. If you are interested in learning more about SESAC, you can check out its home page at www.sesac.com.

If you are a songwriter, you'll want ASCAP, SESAC, or BMI to collect your royalties for hit songs. I'm pulling for you because I know that you are loaded with both talent and good sense; otherwise, you wouldn't be reading this fine book.

ASCAP, BMI, or SESAC?

Which is better for you to join? Each one offers different options beyond helping you collect song performance royalties. It's best for you to carefully read the promotional materials that they mail you or that you find on their Internet pages. You will only be able to join one of these groups at a time, so carefully select which one seems to be the best for you.

What About Sampling?

Sampling is the process of taking a piece of someone else's recording and making it part of your own. You might want to take a bit of the vocals from the Beatles' song "Get Back," mix it with some of the guitar from Offspring's "Pretty Fly for a White Guy," and round off your new creation with some of the drum beats of any one of a dozen songs by your favorite rap star. Each bit that you copy and use from somebody else's sound recording is called a *sample*.

Sampling is somewhat easy to do and a lot of fun. Simply turn on the trusty MIDI-equipped computer or sampling keyboard, grab a commercially released CD, and away you go. A lot of very creative music is done via sampling, and as a form of musical expression, it is insanely popular.

However, sampling the music of another artist without permission is not only unfair, but also illegal. A payment of a license fee is usually required to get permission. Why? Because the songwriter owns the copyright to his or her music and you don't. Taking a bit of music from another song that you don't own and incorporating it into a new song that you've made up is usually forbidden. You won't go to jail for it, but you'll find yourself with a huge whompin' lawsuit.

If you like to use sampling in your own music, don't despair. You can get permission to use samples of songs that you don't own or otherwise have the right to use by contacting the Harry Fox Agency. Isn't that place helpful? Look into this permission before you do your recording! Licensing the recorded music or sounds from a famous song can cost thousands of dollars. The safest route for a sampling musician is to use the sounds that you create on your own. You may come across samples on the Internet, on CD-ROMs, or other sources that you believe you might have the right to use in your own music. Owning a recording of a song does not automatically give you the right to sample it. Carefully check to see if you are allowed to use the samples in any way that you want. If you are not sure, don't use them in songs that you intend to release, as you may be engaging in a copyright infringement.

What About Fair Use?

That's a fair question. Of course, if it were an unfair question, I'd still answer it because you've paid for this book. *Fair use* refers to a section of the copyright laws that permits you to use "reasonable" amounts from a copyrighted work without you having to first obtain a license. What's "reasonable?" Legally, reasonable requires that your sampling not substantially impair the value of the original work.

This may sound simple, but it isn't. Some people assume that a sampling artist can use 20 seconds or less of a copyrighted musical work without getting into trouble. This assumption is more wrong than a banana and tuna fish sandwich.

There is no clear formula available to lead us along this slippery legal path. The rules in this area of the law are quite difficult for anyone to understand. Not even an experienced copyright attorney can safely tell you how to be sure that fair use will protect you from a nasty copyright infringement suit. I'd like to be able to tell you that you can safely use small bits of somebody else's recorded music, but I can't. It is simply much safer for you to obtain a license for the use of somebody else's recorded sounds and music.

The Least You Need to Know

➤ Copyright your original music before you release it on the Internet.

➤ If you haven't written the song you want to release, you must obtain a license from the song publisher.

➤ You can freely use songs or music from the public domain.

➤ The Harry Fox Agency is the place to get licenses for cover songs.

➤ If you are a songwriter or composer, you should probably join ASCAP or BMI.

➤ The safest thing is to avoid sampling the recorded music of another performer into your musical work unless you get written permission to do so.

Chapter 14

Compressed Successes

In This Chapter

➤ How can having an MP3 on the Internet promote my act?

➤ How are some MP3 bands getting to become opening acts for major performers?

➤ What types of extra promotion is available for my MP3s? Is it free?

➤ What about television, magazines, and other non-Internet media? Are they interested in MP3 bands?

From Russia with Love

Andrey Vinogradov is a gifted composer who lightly sprinkles his romantic Russian music with exquisite pop and folk influences. Andrey obtains the finest Moscow musicians and singers to perform his marvelous works, accompanying them on piano or some other keyboard instrument.

The final musical result is really quite stunning. Such songs as "Again, White Campanulas" and "Pearl-Divers" are so beautiful that they nearly move me to tears when I listen to them. If I spoke Russian I probably would actually cry, which could be quite embarrassing for a big, tough, book writer like me. Don't let anyone know how sensitive I am, okay?

Anyone anywhere who might have an Internet connection can freely download one of several wonderful Vinogradov songs or instrumentals. Rather than waiting for the recording industry to discover him, he has found a great way to offer his music to the world: via MP3s. As for selling his wares, rather than giving them away, he also offers to sell his audio CDs to his fans via his MP3.com Web site.

Such is the most typical success story for many MP3 bands. They are finding a world-wide audience by simply offering their music to the people of the world. Language is not a barrier. They don't need an agent or a music attorney. They don't require a contract with a recording company. MP3s have opened a very large door to a new world of musical freedom, and thousands are stepping through.

But, to what final success? To be fair, the MP3 movement is really still in its infancy. Will major stars spring from the world of free MP3s? Only time will tell, but every indication is "heck, yes."

Meanwhile, some MP3 bands have obtained some notable successes.

Mickey Dean and His "Song of the Day"

Country artist Mickey Dean was lucky enough to have one of his MP3s selected to be "Song of the Day" on MP3.com. Within a few days of that event, he got a record deal, a distribution arrangement, and an experienced manager. Not bad, huh? To further add to Mickey's excitement, Newsweek called him up and interviewed him about the whole deal.

The artist currently known as "Chaz" is no stranger to MP3s. Sometime after posting his first MP3 on the Internet, he was selected by the President to perform during the White House's 1999 Easter Egg Roll. That event brings forth a lot of children, which was handy, since Chaz is a most excellent composer and performer of children's music.

Meanwhile, in sunny San Diego, about the same time as the Easter Egg Roll, local retro-rocker Cobain Morrisson was performing live for a CBS Evening News camera crew. Why? They had discovered his MP3s on MP3.com. Sure, they teased him a bit about his funny name, but they featured his great band on national news anyway.

A few weeks later, another MP3 savvy Rock band was also featured on CBS News. This band, called Red Delicious, is extremely popular on the Internet and could very well end up being the first MP3 band to make the big time. If they do, I promise to call you up and let you know.

More MP3s, More Television Crews

MP3 artists *Ashcan School*, who live in Seattle, got a visit from a Japanese news crew who filmed them over the course of two days. The resulting news article was broadcast to an audience of 30 million people.

One Japanese computer magazine selected an MP3 by John Powers to be featured on a CD given away with every copy of one month's issue. Since the magazine's circulation is over 100 thousand copies each month, this distribution was a major bit of promotion.

Check These Great Artists Out!

You can find Red Delicious at `http://www.mp3.com/artists/12/red_delicious_.html`, Chaz at `http://www.mp3.com/artists/13/chaz_the_unity_guy.html`, Mickey Dean at `http://www.mp3.com/artists/9/mickey_dean_and_his_talking_gu.html`, and Ashcan School at `http://www.mp3.com/artists/8/ashcan_school.html`. Meanwhile, Andrey Vinogradov's music is found on the CD-ROM that comes with this book!

Many such opportunities are striking MP3 bands all over the world. It is only a matter of time before a band "breaks" via MP3s and hits the big time. We are living in the great golden age of MP3. Now is the time to get your music on the Internet and get discovered!

Hey, Mom! We're on 250 Thousand Albums!

Twenty very lucky MP3.com bands were selected for a musical CD-ROM entitled "It's Not a Revolt It's a Revolution." MP3.com printed 100 thousand copies and distributed them for free during university spring breaks around the nation. Not a bad way for a band to get some wonderful promotion. Plus, unlike similar promotional CDs designed to bring attention to unsigned bands that you might have come across in the traditional or non-MP3 field of music promotion, not one band paid a cent to be on this promotional album.

MP3.com followed up with a second CD collection of MP3s, "103 of The Best Songs That You've Never Heard," which featured, naturally, 103 different performers. This time 250 thousand copies were printed and distributed for free. This CD was also packed with a computer game, a contest, and other fun stuff. Again, the bands were admitted to this special CD at no cost. Each of these collections contained the songs in MP3 version only.

However, several other promotional CDs are coming soon, some of them with both MP3s and standard audio tracks!

And the Lucky Winner Is...

MP3.com also ran a very exciting contest designed to promote MP3 savvy bands. Entitled the "Tom Petty Cover Contest," it encouraged bands to record and place on MP3.com their own version of any song from Tom's Echo album. The usual legal restrictions regarding covering a Tom Petty song were relaxed for the contest. The winning band was awarded a free round trip to a Tom Petty concert, where they were invited to perform their version of the song.

Alanis Morrisette and Tori Amos joined together in 1999 for their "Five and 1/2 Weeks Tour." They selected their opening acts exclusively from bands on MP3.com.

How to Get Special Attention for Your MP3s

Most bands want to get Song of the Day or other feature spots. There isn't any sure-fire way to obtain such extra promotion from an MP3 site, but it can't hurt to send review copies of your CDs, press clippings, and newsletters to the MP3 Internet provider of your choice. Remember, they are hunting for great bands and are usually happy to hear about a great band, even if the tip is coming directly from the band. Trust me, I know; I pick the MP3.com Song of the Day!

I Heard It on the Radio

Many MP3 acts have been discovered by local radio stations. One band, Sutrobath, was profiled in depth on British Columbia's "Home Grown" radio program. Other MP3 bands have been contacted by various radio stations in Europe and ended up having their songs placed on the airwaves.

Folk artist Toby Leflang was lucky enough to have one of his MP3s played during a National Public Radio news segment covering MP3.com. Other MP3 artists have had their music selected as background music for various radio commercials promoting MP3s in general.

The July 1999 issue of Macworld Magazine issued a CD-ROM featuring the hilarious MP3 "I Wanna Be a Stormtrooper," as performed by the comedy troupe Anarchy Steering Committee. The rock band Belly Puddle also had one of their own MP3s featured in the same issue.

"Ice-Picks" by Ice-T

Famed rapper and all around media star Ice-T hand picked several rap and hip-hop bands as "Ice-Picks." He selected these acts from MP3.com as what he considered to be the best rap and hip-hop music on the Internet. This was certainly a very exciting thing for the acts selected. It isn't just any performer who can brag, "Ice-T thought my song was dope."

More and more MP3 bands are getting press, radio play, and even record contracts. Expect to see many bands to "break" via MP3s in the near future.

Reality Check!

Everything Rod says in this chapter is true. However, these are all *possibilities* of what could happen to your band. Remember this:

➤ If you upload a song, people *might* download it.

➤ If they download it, they *might* listen to it.

➤ If they listen to it, they *might* like it.

➤ If they like it, you *might* build a reputation.

➤ If you build a reputation, you *might* get media and record label attention.

➤ If you get attention, you *might* end up with hit music and financial success.

But that's a heck of a lot of *mights*. The real truth is that only a small percentage of the thousands of musicians making MP3s (like most of those not making MP3s) will ever make a substantial portion of their living off their music. Only a very small portion of those will ever have a hit song, and most of those will be flashes in the pan. If you're making music because you want to be a superstar, you'll likely be crushed. If you're making music because you love making music, however, you're already a success.

The Least You Need to Know

➤ Having a popular MP3 band can lead to many types of media attention including radio, magazine, and television exposure.

➤ You may want to mail promotional materials to MP3.com or other MP3 sites in an attempt to call attention to your band.

➤ Not every band will get selected for some major, extra promotion, but more opportunities are coming up all the time.

➤ The business of making music is a difficult, longshot fight. The art of making music, however, can be a lifelong source of joy.

MP3 Musicians: Their Music and Opinions

In This Appendix

➤ Listen to MP3s from the best artists on the Internet.

➤ Read their opinions about what MP3s have done for them.

➤ Learn from fellow musicians how you can best promote your music with MP3s.

To close our look at music on the Internet with MP3, we'll turn the spotlight on some outstanding artists who have achieved some measure of fame by distributing their music electronically. We're helping them out by providing their MP3 files on the CD-ROM that accompanies this book.

We've broken this appendix down by genre; hopefully, everyone will find something they like by an artist they might not have known about before.

Blues/Jazz

Here are a number of artists who've made a stir in blues and jazz circles.

Beyond Blue

➤ Virginia Norwood—Vocals
➤ Joe Norwood—Lead guitar

An Unsung Blues Giant

Beyond Blue guitarist Joe Norwood is one of the best guitarists in the United States, although not quite famous (yet). If you are a fan of electric guitar, you'll be quite impressed by his playing on this track.

➤ Bruce Crossley—Bass guitar
➤ David Penny—Drums

Stylistic influences: Duane Allman, Eric Clapton, Jimi Hendrix, Ann and Nancy Wilson, Lydia Pense, Rod Underhill, Carlos Santana, Pat Benatar, and Billy Gibbons

Album available: *Live at Etta's*

Live performances: San Diego, Los Angeles

Song on the CD: "Make Me Sweat"

About the song: "'Make Me Sweat' deals with frustration that couples may go through when the fire has gone out of their relationship and needs to be re-ignited."

Song file location on CD-ROM: Jazz_blues/make_me_sweat/mp3

About the MP3 experience: "MP3 has been a great help in exposing our music to a worldwide audience which we would not have reached otherwise. Our DAM CDs have sold to fans as far away as Sweden and Brazil."

Other MP3 bands they recommend:

➤ Mickey Dean
➤ Blue By Nature
➤ Kristin Banks

Beyond Blue info on the Web: beyondblue@ixpres.com

Blue By Nature

➤ Karen Lawrence—Vocals
➤ Fred Hostetler—Rhythm guitar
➤ Rick Dufay—Lead guitar
➤ Charlie Diaz—Bass guitar
➤ Billy Ward—Drums

Albums available:

➤ *Blue to the Bone*
➤ *Hard Daze*
➤ *Live at the Lake*

Live performances: Based in Southern California

Song on the CD: "Cadillac Blues"

About the song: "Recorded in a converted bus in Malibu, CA, by ex-Aerosmith guitarist Rick Dufay and rhythm guitarist Fred Hostetler producing. The song was remixed by Jack Douglas."

Song file location on CD-ROM: Jazz_blues/cadillac_blues/mp3

About the MP3 experience: "Let there by music! Let it be heard!"

Blue By Nature info on the Web: www.bluebynature.com

Chauncey Canfield

Stylistic influences: "Too numerous to mention, but Bill Evans, Horace Silver, and Jimmy Smith are definitely in the mix."

Albums available:

➤ *The Adjustable Waistband Collection*

➤ *Big Box Retail Experience*

Live performances: Washington, DC

Song on the CD: "Sane to You"

A One-Man Band

Mr. Canfield plays all the instruments on this track: keyboards, bass, and percussion!

About the song: "I put the song up on the site as an afterthought, actually, and it was picked as an MP3.com 'Song of the Day.' It evolved from some chords I was noodling around on one day. I liked the lush, melancholy sound, and I decided to shift to a trip-hop rhythm with a trumpet solo toward the end to give it some momentum."

Song file location on CD-ROM: Jazz_blues/sane_to_you/mp3

About the MP3 experience: "I've had enormous exposure to audiences around the world, and close to 50 thousand copies of my songs are out there now. I think it is fantastic that artists have this option to do an end-run around the traditional label distribution, and listeners seem to be very responsive."

Other MP3 bands he recommends:

➤ Dan Cox

➤ Dave Salvator

Chauncey Canfield info on the Web: www.mp3.com/chaunceycanfield

A Jazz Master

Ray is another very talented performer who performs all the instruments on his track.

Ray Palfreyman

Stylistic influences: "Just about everything I've ever heard. Started off with Blues in the `60s then 'progressed' to Jazz, especially E.C.M. label stuff."

Album available: *Solo*

Live performances: Liverpool

Song on the CD: "MJ3"

Song file location on CD-ROM: Jazz_blues/mj3/mp3

Artist history: "Picked up the guitar at age 14 and played in various bands as guitarist/bass player. Took up sax seven years ago and also learned musical theory and how to read music."

About the MP3 experience: "Great. My stuff is selling to the world, including the world wide sales of three different CDs."

Other MP3 bands he recommends: Adam Pfeffer

Ray Palfreyman info on the Web: www.mp3.com

Oriental Jazz

This Japanese jazz rock fusion band is one of the most exciting new groups that I have heard in years. Dramatic and colorful, every track is a winner.

Powered Express

➤ Nobauka Takahashi—Guitar and composition
➤ Hideyuki Sato—Soprano saxophone
➤ Norimasa Kawagoe—Keyboards
➤ Takumi Kajiura—Electric bass
➤ Katusuji Miyama—Drums

Album available: See http/www.asahi-net-or.jp/~hu8h-stu/ for details.

Live performances: Tokyo, Japan

Song on the CD: "Blue Snow"

About the song: "'Blue Snow' is one of our most popular live tunes. It was originally composed with the image of crowd and silence in a big city like Tokyo. You should feel as if you were in a large city when you listen to the tune. The first part of the melody is meant to give you a taste of the mystery that surrounds a large city."

Song file location on CD-ROM: Jazz_blues/blue_snow/mp3

198

Powered Express.

Artist history: "In 1991, Powered Express was established. In 1998, our present members came together and independently released the first album fully included original sound. We hold live concerts at jazz clubs, sometimes on open-air stages, around Tokyo five or six times a year. All our original tunes are composed by Nobuaki Takahashi, who is our guitarist."

About the MP3 experience: "MP3.com should be the most useful Web site for amateur musicians, like us, because it gives the artist a great deal of opportunity. We have received many messages from fans from all over the world and several offers to feature information about us in various books. MP3 is creating a brand new culture, but one that must be utilized legally."

Other MP3 artists they recommend: New York Horns

Rogues on the Run

Rogues on the Run.

➤ Jack Hoban—Vocals, songwriter, guitars

➤ Wayne Gronberg—Bass guitar

➤ Mario Cicerello—Piano, organ, keyboards

➤ Robert Sozanski—Percussion

➤ Vel Johnson—Saxophones

➤ Greg O'Keefe—Drums

Stylistic influences: Steely Dan, Allman Brothers, B. B. King, Chris Rea

Album available: *Something's Cookin'*

Live performances: Jersey Shore

Song on the CD: "Bogeyman"

About the song: "Rockin' Blues. Two thumbs up from our seven year old fans who can relate. But the Bogey Man is even nastier when you got mortgages and kids. And that's what the song is really about."

Song file location on CD-ROM: Jazz_blues/bogey_man1/mp3

About the MP3 experience: "We love it and have gotten great exposure worldwide."

Other MP3 bands they recommend: Line Drive

Rogues on the Run info on the Web: http://www.livingvalues.com/rogues

Lee Totten

Live performances: Northeast USA

Song on the CD: "The Jagermeister Song (electric version)"

Song file location on CD-ROM: Jazz_blues/the_jagermeister_song/mp3

About the MP3 experience: "Amazing exposure."

Other MP3 bands he recommends: Bellypuddle

Lee Totten info on the Web: www.leetotten.com

Care for Some "Fusion"?

Solo performer Lee Totten mixes rock with classical, jazz, and hiphop influences and produces some pretty amazing music.

Randell Young

Randell Young.

- ➤ Randell Young—Guitar and vocals
- ➤ Diedra Lang—Backup vocals
- ➤ Rick Shlosser—Drums
- ➤ Stu Elster—Keyboards
- ➤ Pasquale Carlucci—Bass

Albums available:

- ➤ *Nefarious Rhythms*
- ➤ *Guitar Noire*

Live performances: Southern California

Song on the CD: "Don't Know How to Love You"

Song file location on CD-ROM:
Jazz_blues/quotdontknowhowtoloveyouquot/mp3

Artist history: "Everhart Records' blues guitarist/vocalist Randell Young has recorded two solo albums and worked with such artists as Nicollette Larson, Rob Mullins, Billy Mitchell, Poncho Sanchez, Tony Guerrero, Harmonica Fats, Jeff 'Skunk' Baxter, Four20, Tyrone 'The Smurf' Brunson, and the Jazz Crusaders' Stix Hooper. He holds an honorary Doctor of Music degree from City University, Los Angeles.'

"Young's performances have generated numerous and favorable reviews from a variety of sources. *LA Times* music critic Bill Kohlhaase appraises Randell's technique as 'a tight, cosmopolitan sound.' Register columnist Alan Bock describes the guitarist as 'genuinely accomplished and inventive…one of my favorite artists.' KSBR's Aaron Blackwell assesses Young as 'World Class' while Register music critic Robert Kinsler touts Young as 'a master blues player.'

"This well-traveled blues man has been featured at numerous jazz and blues festivals and has performed in clubs and concerts world-wide for nearly 25 years. Young emphasizes a groove-oriented presentation with due respect for the idiom yet still manages to bring something unique to the stage. As explained by Robert Kinsler: 'Just as every great guitarist from Robert Johnson and B.B. King to Alvin Le and Stevie Ray Vaughn has performed the blues with a distinctive style, so has Young taken creative strides to cut his own turf.'"

About the MP3 experience: "Our group is very pleased to participate in this compilation and hope that your listeners enjoy all of the music selected. We appreciate what you and other MP3 advocates are doing to provide artists with easier and less encumbered access to the marketplace."

Randell Young info on the Web: Netunes.com

Classical

If you're a classical-music fan, you might enjoy the MP3s provided by these artists.

James Bohn

Stylistic influences: Lejaren Hiller, George Antheil, Eric Lyons

Albums available:

➤ *Coloring Outside the Lines—The Media Café*

➤ *waveFORMation—The Experimental Music Studios*

➤ *The Frog Peak Collaborations Project—Frog Peak*

➤ *Electro-Acoustic Music*

➤ *Syncopated Lady—Capstone*

Rod Speaks

Something Unusual

This piece was composed by James Bohn and executed on vibraphone by Geoffrey Brady. The genre of music involved is best described as "Avant Gard."

Live performances: Normal, Illinois

Song on the CD: "Implosion for Vibraphone and Computer-Generated Tape"

About the song: "This was commissioned by Scott Wyatt for the University of Illinois School of Music Centennial Celebration (1995)."

Song file location on CD-ROM: \classical\implosion\mp3

Artist history: "James Bohn received his Bachelor of Music degree from the University of Wisconsin in 1992. At Madison he studied with Stephen Dembski, Joel Naumann, Robert Crane, and Tamar Diesendruck. He received his Master's degree in 1993 from the University of Illinois, where he completed his D.M.A. during 1997. At Illinois he studied with various faculty members. Since he earned his Doctorate, James has served as Coordinator of Labs and Web Services for the Office of Research in Arts Technology at Illinois State, in Normal, Illinois. He has received commissions from the School of Music at the University of Illinois and the Chicago Chapter of the American Composers Forum. His music has been performed throughout the Midwest, New York, Wyoming, Puerto Rico, and Germany."

About the MP3 experience: "The MP3.com Web site provides a great means of free international distribution. Consumers can download and listen to tracks before purchasing an album, relieving the 'leap of faith' attitude one normally has to take when purchasing a recording. The statistics that the Web site provides artists in terms of number of page hits and number of downloads reassures the artist that their music is reaching an audience. Artists can also view the number of downloads for any given composition, allowing them to get a degree of tangible feedback in terms of what the public seems to enjoy the most."

Other MP3 artists he recommends:

➤ David Dexler

➤ Tomm Roland

➤ Sean Vaugh

James Bohn info on the Web: `http://www.mp3.com/jbohn`

Rogerio Dec

Rogerio Dec.

Stylistic influences: Hector Villa-Lobos, Igor Stravinsky, Claude Debussy, Maurice Ravel, James Horner

Album available: *Phoenix*

Live performances: Brazil

Song on the CD: "Una Alegre Cancion"

About the song: "A happy song for Classical guitar, inspired in the aggressive style of Astor Piazolla."

Song file location on CD-ROM: \classsical\una_alegra_cancioacuten

Artist history: "Composing Classical music since 1983, Dec started to play guitar when 11 years old. In the next years he learned to play drums, bass, keyboards, electric guitar and followed with a auto-didactic learning of musical theory, transcriptions, arrangement, and orchestration."

About the MP3 experience: "I have discovered the potentiality of the MP3 file type a few months ago, and in also the MP3.com Web site, which seems to be undergoing an explosive growth."

Other MP3 bands he recommends: Jeff Harrington

Rogerio Dec info on the Web: http://mp3.com/dec

I Love This Track!

While not true classical music, but rather modern music influenced by Richard Wagner, this composition is quite beautiful and dramatic, and electronically realized.

Richard DeCosta

Stylistic influences: Danny Elfman, Richard Wagner, Isao Tomita

Album available: *Space Woozies*

Live performances: Maine, USA

Song on the CD: "Metropolis, Main Titles"

About the song: "This is the first piece in a series I am writing for Fritz Lang's 1927 film, Metropolis. Eventually, I will re-score the entire film, add Foley and Sound FX, and will seek to publish the new work on CD, VHS, and DVD."

Song file location on CD-ROM: \classical\metropolis\main_titles

Artist history: "Began writing music in 1981 at the age of 10. Has written several symphonies, cantatas, numerous piano pieces, an opera, and hundreds of experimental synthesizer pieces, as well as techno-industrial music."

About the MP3 experience: "MP3 is going to change the way people produce and listen to music. It already has for me. I now distribute my music almost entirely in MP3 format over the Internet. Where with CDs and tapes I could reach perhaps a hundred people a year, I can reach thousands a month with MP3s."

Other MP3 bands he recommends: Master Zap

Richard DeCosta on the Web: http://listen.to/thesystem

Antonio Genovino

Stylistic influences: Classical composers and symphonic music for films

Album available: *The Digital Style*

Track on the CD: "Overture Amadeus"

About the track: "This is a short orchestral composition written in the style of Mozart."

Song file location on CD-ROM: classical\overture_quotamadeus\mp3

Artist history: "Antonio Genovino (b.1964) is an Italian composer and pianist. He obtained a piano diploma from the Music Conservatory of Lainia (Italy) and a B.A. in Literature and Music from Rome University."

About the MP3 experience: "Very impressive. The MP3 format is an excellent and useful way to listen to music with high-quality audio on the Internet."

Antonio Genovino info on the Web: www.mp3.com/artists/8/antonio_genovino

Jeffrey Gold

Jeffrey Gold.

Stylistic influences: Ennio Morricone, Vangelis, John Barry, among others

Album available: *Prolegomenon: Music for Films and the Imagination*

Track on the CD: "Elegy: Adagio for Strings"

About the track: "An adagio dedicated to Irma Burgos, my most ardent fan."

Song file location on CD-ROM: classical\elegy_adagio_for_strings\mp3

Artist history: "Jeffrey Gold is a composer for films and music belonging to the self-styled genre of 'visual' music. He has scored for various film projects, including some of his own productions."

About the MP3 experience: "It is an excellent way to reach an international audience. The feedback I have received has been excellent. Listeners who enjoy my music are able to contact me directly."

Jeffrey Gold info on the Web: www.jeffreygold.com

Brent Hugh

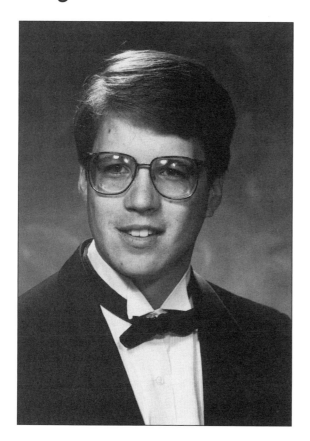

Brent Hugh.

Piano Magic

A solo piano work by a young master. All of his recordings are very well performed.

Stylistic influences: Glenn Gould, Dinu Lipatti, among others

Albums available:

➤ *Fantastic Rhapsodies*

➤ *Brent Hugh Live in Kansas City*

➤ *Christmas Dreams*

Live performances: Western and Midwestern USA

Song on the CD: "The Engulfed Cathedral"

About the song: "This was recorded before I had ready access to digital editing equipment, and so it is basically a one long unedited take, like a live performance."

Song file location on CD-ROM: classical\the_engulfed_cathedral\mp3

Artist history: "Hugh is a Classical composer, teacher, and performing artist and Assistant Professor of Piano at Missouri Western State College."

About the MP3 experience: "MP3 is really liberating for the artist. It gives you complete control over your work and freedom to use it the way you would like. There can be an immediacy there similar to a live performance—you can record something, post it, and start having dozens of downloads, all in the same day. Then in a week you can pull the track and replace it with an improved version of something completely different.'

"MP3.com allows composers and performers to find an audience that is interested in their sort of music. When I posted my first, rather obscure, track to MP3.com, I was thrilled to have maybe five listeners a week. When I posted some tracks I knew would be of wider interest, I was still floored to have, on many days, over 500 downloads.'

"I reach as many listeners on MP3.com in a week as I do in live performances during an entire year.'"

Brent Hugh info on the Web: www.mp3.com/brent_d_hugh

Stephan Malone

Stephan Malone.

Stylistic influences: "Many instrumental influences from ancient to contemporary."

Album available: *Relief*

Live performances: Florida

Song on the CD: "Night Dancer"

Song file location on CD-ROM: classical\night_dancer_47_mb/mp3

Innovative!

A New Age work from a talented new composer.

About the MP3 experience: "Very positive. I have made my music available in MP3 format for one year."

Other MP3 bands he recommends: Erika/Phillipe Pascal

Stephan Malone info on the Web: www.mp3.com/malone

Richard Morris

Richard Morris.

Album available: *Wapin Piano Bridge*

Live performances: Cincinnati, Ohio

Song on the CD: "Moonlight Sonata"

Song file location on CD-ROM:
classical\beethoven_moonlight_sonata_
op_14\mp3

About the track: "Daring is the word; to produce a fine recording such as this on such a small piano is a bold endeavor to say the least. Why? The producers are marketing a new invention for the piano called Wapin. Wapin is a patent pending method for attaching a string to a bridge on a piano that provides for clearer tone, with a richer harmonic spectrum and greater sustain. 'We tried to market our CD through normal channels. We always kept a few wave files on our Web site hoping that the interested parties would be patient enough to wait out a download, then came MP3...'

Extremely Talented!

This gentleman is one of the most popular performers of classical music on the Internet.

"Previous compression algorithms were too destructive to the quality of the sound, rendering them useless for our purposes. Cassettes could not display this clarity, CDs could. 'We feel that the MP3 format displays the distinctive Wapin sound quite well. We dare you to compare the sound of this little piano with that of any commercial produced CD piano sound. It's truly amazing!'"

Artist history: "Richard Morris is a professor of piano for the College Conservatory of Music of the University of Cincinnati. Morris is a featured clinician, adjudicator, and a conductor of master classes throughout the United States. He is past president of Music Teachers National Association. His specialty as a recitalist is performing complete sets of the Chopin Preludes, Chopin Scherzi, and the 24 Debussy Preludes."

Richard Morris/Wapin info on the Web: www.wapin.com

Moscow Virtuals

➤ Lev Guelbard—Violin

➤ Sergej Rossokha—Cello

➤ Mikhail Mouler—Viola

➤ Elena Kuschnerova—Piano

Stylistic influences: Yehudy Menuhin, Artur Rubinstein

Album available: *Classic Open Air*

Live performances: Germany and beyond

Song on the CD: "Brahms, piano quartet n.3, 2/4"

Song file location on CD-ROM: classical\brahms_piano_quartet_n3_24\mp3

Artist history: "On his way from Germany to Venezuela, Lev Guelbard met in a plane a Moscow pianist named Irina Ossipova who told him that Elena Kuschnerova had left Russia and moved to Germany. This occasion was a new start for both artists who once upon a time played in Moscow together."

Moscow Virtuals info on the Web: `http://home.t-online.de/home/elena.kuscherova`

Country and Folk

Make your computer two-step with the country and folk MP3s by these artists.

Ricky Lynne

Ricky Lynne.

Stylistic influences: Elvis, Trisha Yearwood, among others

Album available: *Live to Love*

Live performances: All over the USA

Artist history: Studied musical theatre at Ohio University.

About the MP3 experience: "Everyone is putting songs in MP3 format."

Ricky Lynne info on the Web: `http://rickylynne.freeservers.com`

The Singing Hayes Family

➤ Earl Hayes—Lead vocals
➤ Delores Hayes—Harmony vocals
➤ Bill Hammond—Drums/percussion
➤ Deana Hammond—Harmony vocals
➤ Kemra Vanhoose—Harmony vocals
➤ James Vanhoose—Rhythm guitar
➤ Paul Hayes—Bass guitar, harmony vocals
➤ Angela Hayes—Keyboards
➤ Norman Hayes—Lead guitar
➤ Tonya Hayes—Piano

Stylistic influences: The Goodmans, the Hinsons, the Downings, the Spencers

Albums available:

➤ *After a Little While*
➤ *Jesus is Coming*
➤ *Bread of Life*
➤ *Love and Prayer*
➤ *Singing Hayes Sampler*

Live performances: The Southern USA

Song on the CD: "Wait on Jesus"

About the song: "This was written as a very slow, sad song written almost 20 years before it was recorded. When recording the *Bread of Life* album we had space for one more song and the song we had slated for this space was not working. At the last minute "Wait on Jesus" was brought out. Once again the song was slow, very mellow. After about 10 minutes of toying with the song, Bill, our drummer, said that he didn't hear the song that way and kicked into an early '60s Pop beat and the song took off from there."

Song file location on CD-ROM: country\wait_on_jesus\mp3

Artist history: "The group is made up of a mother and father, their four living children, and their husbands and wives. The group has been singing in some form since 1979 and its present form since 1990. The family has had several songs on the national Southern Gospel charts."

About the MP3 experience: "This has been great for us. MP3 has allowed us to reach people all over the world that we would never have reached otherwise. We see this an extension of our ministry. We have sold quite a few MP3.com produced CDs and received orders for back catalog, soundtracks, and bookings through the MP3.com site."

The Singing Hayes Family info on the Web: www.mp3.com/singinghayesfamily

Bob "Bobby K" Kingston

Bob "Bobby K" Kingston.

➤ Bob Kingston—Lead vocal, rhythm guitar, train whistle, drums

➤ Mitch Potter—Bass, electric guitar

➤ Mike Rivera—Electric guitar

➤ Jay Buckey—Fiddle, dobro

Stylistic influences: "Traditional country performers like my father, Jack Kingston, Hank Williams, and Elton Britt."

Album available: *Since I Lost You*

Live performances: Las Vegas, Nevada

Song on the CD: "Freight Train Blues"

About the song: "Remake of an old Public Domain song from 1930."

Song file location on CD-ROM: country\freight_train_blues\mp3

About the MP3 experience: "MP3 has been a great outlet to expose my music to a new audience. I have had inquiries from other countries and music magazines."

Bob "Bobby K" Kingston info on the Web:
www.geocities.com/nashville/rodeo/3069

Robby RoBott Band

➤ Robert Goldring—Vocals and guitar

➤ Tony Trischka—Banjo

➤ Kenny Kosek—Fiddle

➤ Bob Gilbert—Bass

Stylistic influences: Lester Flatt and Earl Scruggs

Album available: *Kickin' Up the Mud*

Live performances: New York tristate area

Song on the CD: "Southland"

Song file location on CD-ROM: country\southland1\mp3

About the MP3 experience: "Great experience...it's helping out with sales very much!"

Robert Goldring and Robby RoBott Band info on the Web: MP3.com

Rod Speaks

Two Kinds of Music: Country AND Western!

Robert Goldring and the Robby RoBott Band is incredible! Mixing Bluegrass and Folk, Goldring and his band covers new ground in an exciting way.

Robert Goldring.

MP3.COM
USA
Cat#7835

DONK'S

Bobby RoBott
Tonight Only — 8 pm

Southland   New Camptown Races (with Bill Keith)
Journey Home   Ants on a log
Disturbed Phalanges   Uncle John
Groundspeed   Deep River Blues
Cowboy Blues   Nine Pound Hammer
Bull Frog Shuffle/Leap Frog So Long, Old Friend
Believe

R&B and C&W!

Southwest nicely straddles the gap between R&B and country music. That might seem like an unusual combination, but this band nicely pulls it off.

Southwest

➤ Charlie Orlofsky—Live show sound engineer, graphic art design

➤ Joe Pelick—Drums

➤ Sherri Orlofsky—Lead vocals, back up vocals, percussion

➤ Ken Yeaney—Lead vocals, back up vocals, bass guitar

➤ Mike Yeaney—Lead vocals, back up vocals, rhythm guitar

➤ Dan Yeaney—Studio engineer, pedal steel

Stylistic influences: "From the time I was a little kid I listened to all kinds of music so that's a hard one to answer. I suppose somewhere in between Hoagy Carmichael and Neil Young with a little Duke Ellington and some Gordon Lightfoot thrown in."

Album available: *Eye of the Storm*

Live performances: "Mostly in Pennsylvania but we have been out of state including playing at the Rock and Roll Hall of Fame in Cleveland, Ohio."

Southwest.

Song on the CD: "Baby Blue"

About the song: "Not a lot of deep philosophical meaning here. Just a boogie-woo-gie Be-bop fun song."

Song file location on CD-ROM: country\baby_blue\mp3

About the MP3 experience: "MP3.com as well as other Internet commerce sites provide an opportunity that never existed before for people like us. I should have out-grown this music stuff a long time a go but the MP3 trip has been interesting and fun."

Other MP3 bands they recommend:

➤ Spiral Mouth

➤ The Dead Engineers

➤ Joanie Chesiwick

Southwest info on the Web: www.southwestmusic.com

Electronic

Just as MP3s push the frontiers of musical distribution, these artists push the frontiers of electronic instrumentation.

Creative State of Mind

Creative State of Mind.

➤ Ed Patrick—Keyboards/synths

➤ Sam Young—Beats/samples

Stylistic influences: Prodigy, The Crystal Method, Goldie, Orbital, Photek

Album available: *COMPfear*

Song on the CD: "Mystikal Jungle"

About the song: "We were just sitting around throwing things around and this is what came out."

Song file location on CD-ROM: electronic\mystikal_jungle\mp3

Artist history: Formed six months ago, making serious music three months ago.

About the MP3 experience: "It made our name for us. Without it, we would've never been able to reach a fraction of the amount of the people we have. Using MP3, we created a world-wide fan base."

Creative State of Mind info on the Web: www.mp3.com/CSM

Redstorm

Album available: *Redstorm*

Song on the CD: "Artificial Love"

About the song: "Reflections of being single and physical attraction."

Song file location on CD-ROM: electronic\artificial_love\mp3

About the MP3 experience: "Great for Web promotion, and quick file transfer."

Redstorm info on the Web: www.redstorm-productions.com

Solo Star!

This track is the product of one artist, Rick R. Connor, who played all the instruments, wrote the song, and performed the vocals.

Rock/Pop

Put a dollar in your MP3 jukebox and jam to these tunes.

Allen B

➤ Allen B—Vocals, acoustic guitar, organ

➤ Marc Shawn—Lead guitar

➤ Neil Deverman—Drums and percussion

Stylistic influences: Matchbox 20, The Wallflowers

Album available: *Emotions*

Live performances: Detroit

Song on the CD: "Mr. Postman"

About the song: "This is the ninth single off his debut indie release. The song is a poppy love song with catchy guitar riffs and a beat that you can really dance to. This song is just one of the many songs from *Emotions* with a major label feel. The album is dedicated to his late father, who was his true inspiration for music."

Artist history: "Allen B (born 1977) grew up in the suburbs of Detroit, Michigan, where he studied music since the age of three. When he was 10, his parents bought his first guitar. When Allen was 11 he wrote his first song called '9N05-3A07,' and added it to his debut album."

Song file location on CD-ROM: rock_pop\mr_postman\mp3

About the MP3 experience: "MP3, despite its controversy with the major labels and artists is the main source for fans to listen to music and musicians they've never heard of. It gives us independent unsigned artists the chance to be heard, which is a very hard task in this tough business. It's very hard to give unsigned artists like myself notice to the public eyes and ears, but with MP3 it makes it a lot easier."

Other MP3 bands they recommend:

➤ Emily Richards

➤ Pokerface

Allen B info on the Web: http://www.allen-b.com

Amazon Mollies

Amazon Mollies.

> ➤ Antonette Goroch (Molly Coddle)—Vocals, bass

> ➤ Samantha Cabuluna (Molly By Golly)—Guitar, vocals

> ➤ Julie Snell (Molly Bolt)—Drums, vocals

Stylistic influences: Folk, Punk, Country, Rockabilly, Alternative, Nursery Rhymes

Album available: *Molly Rock*

Live performances: California/West Coast USA

Song on the CD: "Toast Sweat"

About the song: "Remember how David Lynch just wanted people to have better driving etiquette in 'lost Highway'? The mollies just want people to have better kitchen etiquette."

Song file location on CD-ROM: rock_pop\toast_sweat1\mp3

Artist history: "All children of government operatives in Panama, met there and performed a band, after playing on the base's field hockey team."

About the MP3 experience: "This has been an invaluable tool for reaching and extending our audience."

Other MP3 bands they recommend:

> ➤ Red Delicious

> ➤ Lucid

> ➤ L7

Amazon Mollies info on the Web: www.beinworld.com

Big Pooh Generator

> ➤ Ben—He plays stuff and dances around.

> ➤ John—Same thing as Ben.

> ➤ Rob—Same thing as Ben and John.

Album available: *Please Kill Us*

Live performances: Chicago, Los Angeles, The Bathroom

Song on the CD: "Mr. Poo (He's in You)"

About the song: "'Mr. Poo (He's in You)' is about a poo that is inside you."

Song file location on CD-ROM: rock_pop\mr_poo_hes_in_you1\mp3

About the MP3 experience: "Great. We've done really well. A great way for people to enjoy our music. It's fun."

Sounds (Scata)Logical to Me!

Big Pooh Generator is nasty and disgusting and I love them. They relish in being nasty and disgusting, which makes them all that much better. They don't want you to take them seriously but at the same time they expect you to. They are wallowing in dangerous visions and dark humor, bringing new respect to scatological humor. Girls think they are cute and boys think they are funny as can be. Somebody should pass a law requiring everybody to buy 15 of their albums even if simply used for drink coasters. One woefully uninformed critic has slammed this band and suggested that they be "flushed." The nerve.

Other MP3 bands they recommend: Usagipop

Big Pooh Generator info on the Web: www.mp3.com/bigpoogenerator

The Bottletones

➤ Scratch Bottletone—Vocals and percussion

➤ Crash Bottletone—Guitar

➤ Ace Bottletone—Guitar

➤ Speed Bottletone—Drums

➤ Thunk Bottletone—Bass

Stylistic influences: Old Surf, '30s and '40s Swing, Rockabilly, Punk Rock

Albums available:

➤ *Corn Rampin'*

➤ *The Sheriff of Bottletone County*

Live performances: Chicago and the Midwest

Song on the CD: "El Coolo"

About the song: "As five Anglos enamored with Latino culture, this was our first attempt at a basic Latin beat. This song has become one of our most popular live songs to date."

Song file location on CD-ROM: rock_pop\el_coolo\mp3

Artist history: "Formed in 1993, second album came out in 1999. We've played live continually since then."

About the MP3 experience: "We downloaded a CD ripper from a software link at MP3.com. We were pleasantly surprised at the ease of use and had our songs posted on MP3.com within three hours."

The Bottletones info on the Web: www.bottletones.com

Daisychain

> ➤ Jeff Farmer—Guitar, vocals
>
> ➤ Jimmy Ramage—Bass, vocals
>
> ➤ David Gulliver—Drums, vocals

Stylistic influences: Early Aerosmith, Led Zeppelin

Album available: *Daisychain*

Live performances: Southeast USA

Song on the CD: "Simon Says"

About the song: "This is one of the band's favorite songs. It has good energy and always 'kicks' live."

Song file location on CD-ROM: rock_pop\simon_says1\mp3

Artist history: Have been playing the circuit since 1993.

About the MP3 experience: "MP3 has opened doors for the unsigned musician or for a musician that doesn't like the 'deal' offered by labels. I see it as an asset for musicians for as long as they play."

Daisychain info on the Web: www.itusc.com/daisychain

The Dead Beats

> ➤ Steven Meloan—Guitar, vocals
>
> ➤ Michael Meloan—Vocals
>
> ➤ And guest starring on keyboards and drums—Ethan James

Stylistic influences: The Doors, The Velvet Underground, REM, Bob Dylan, David Bowie, Neil Young, Elvis Costello

Another Success Story

The Dead Beats' song included with this book is the sort of song that really gets under your skin. I love the organ sound as well as the lyrics. Two of their songs were featured on VH1 after their Internet debut, including "I'm Just a Cigarette."

The Dead Beats.

Album available: *Farewell to the Man*

Live performances: Los Angeles and San Francisco

Song on the CD: "I'm Just a Cigarette"

About the song: "She ordered mussels I recall, those fishnets hanging from the wall. The gypsy said 'best to beware,' I never could resist a dare."

Song file location on CD-ROM: rock_pop\im_just_a_cigarette\mp3

Artist history: "The band began in the subways of London, Paris, and Berlin—and has since been heard on KROQ's 'Rodney on the ROQ', KLOS's 'Best of the local licks,' as well as having garnered airplay on college radio in the U.S., and in Australia and Canada. Steven Meloan's written work has appeared in Wired, Rolling Stone, Playboy, SOMA, and American Cybercast's Web Episodic "The Pyramid." Michael Meloan has written for Wired, Buzz, the L.A. Weekly, and has contributed to Joe Frank's National Public Radio program."

About the MP3 experience: "It is the Punk of the New Millennium...we mean it, man."

Other MP3 bands they recommend: Damian Child

The Dead Beats info on the Web: www.mp3.com/thedeadbeats

Dizzy Park

Dizzy Park.

➤ Jimmy Walker—Vocals, guitar

➤ David Romweber—Bass

➤ Russell Bombik—Drums

Stylistic influences: The Beatles, Led Zeppelin, Lenny Kravitz, Sheryl Crow

Album available: *High Gloss Dope*

Live performances: East coast—Midwest

Song on the CD: "Sugar"

Song file location on CD-ROM: rock_pop\sugar11\mp3

About the MP3 experience: "Excellent forum for indie bands."

Artist history: "We have been writing and performing since 1997."

Other MP3 bands they recommend: Kid Wicked

Dizzy Park info on the Web: dizzypark@aol.com

dot Fash

dot Fash.

- ➤ Russ Rogers—Vocals, guitar
- ➤ James Coyle—Guitar
- ➤ Jarrett Shapiro—Bass
- ➤ Phil Tucciarone—Drums

Stylistic influences: Radiohead, The Cure, The Verve, Jeff Buckley

Album available: *dot Fash*

Live performances: Southeastern USA

Song on the CD: "When All Is Said and Done"

About the song: "About the battle between hope and despair. Ultimate outcome is usually decided by fate."

Song file location on CD-ROM: rock_pop\when_all_is_said_and_done\mp3

About the MP3 experience: "MP3 technology has only brought good things for us as a band. We're noticed on a more even level with major acts."

dot Fash info on the Web: www.dotfash.com

Tom Fidgen

➤ Tom Fidgen—Guitars, bass, vocals

➤ Steve Gaetz—Drums

Stylistic influences: "Folk inspired sound of the '70s to the progressive sound of the '90s."

Album available: *Human by Trade*

Live performances: Canada

Song on the CD: "Humans Being"

About the song: "Written one night in the kitchen after a good cup of tea and recorded in one take."

Song file location on CD-ROM: rock_pop\humans_being1\mp3

Artist history: "Singer-songwriter from Cape Breton, Canada, he released his debut solo CD to critical acclaim and his music is a combination of Folk, Pop, Rock, and even Celtic elements."

About the MP3 experience: "Great promotional tool and it sounds great, too!"

Other MP3 bands they recommend: "All the undiscovered artists!"

Tom Fidgen info on the Web: www.tomfidgen.com

Fisher

➤ Fisher—Vocals

➤ Raw—Piano

Stylistic influences: PJ Harvey

Album available: *One*—On Fish Records

Live performances: Throughout the United States

Song on the CD: "I Will Love You"

About the song: This song was originally written for the Kevin Costner/Paul Newman film *Message in a Bottle,* but never made it to the soundtrack.

A Huge Talent!

Fisher is easily one the most talented singers on the Internet today. Stunning vocals and wonderful song writing makes this artist a sure winner.

Fisher.

Song file location on CD-ROM: rock_pop\I_will_love_you1\mp3

Artist history: "In December of 1997 Fisher received a call from Atlantic Records. By a twist of fate they had heard one of our demo tracks called "Breakable" and wanted to know if they could use the song in their upcoming soundtrack for the 20th Century Fox film *Great Expectations*. Needless to say, we agreed immediately. The album was released in 1998 and did very well. So well in fact that it fell into the hands of the Lilith Fair folks who wanted to know if we were interested in doing three concert dates. In late June of 1998, we did our first Lilith date in Phoenix, then Oklahoma and Kansas where Sarah McLachlan, Sinead O'Connor, and Fisher performed Marvin Gaye's "What's Going On" to a packed stadium.'

"Over the following months Fisher received a RIAA certified Gold Record for *Great Expectations* and her itty bitty fan base grew from 500 to 7,000 due mainly to email. Everyone was requesting a full length Fisher CD.'

"We then decided it was time to complete and release our own product initially over the internet since the Atlantic Records deal was for one song only—leaving us no legal ties.'

"As of this writing, we are shipping product to all the online retailers. Things look very good especially when you consider our profit will be 800 to 1,000 percent higher per CD than 'signed' acts get.'"

Fisher info on the Web: `http://www.digitalsound.net`

The Graveyard Farmers

The Graveyard Farmers.

➤ Brandon Irons—Guitar

➤ Eric Gothold—Vocal

➤ Clayton Scott—Drums

➤ Scott Debauche—Bass

Something Fresh from the Graveyard

"Psychobilly" is a new type of music that combines Rockabilly and graveyard humor. I quite like it. Funny and fast moving, it's proving to be a very adventuresome new genre.

Stylistic influences: Ronnie Dawson, The Cramps, Rev'd Horton Heat, Elvis

Album available: *The Graveyard Farmers*

Live performances: USA

Song on the CD: "Formaldehyde"

About the song: "It is a song about a guy who wants to create his own kind of girl and love. Something I think he has control of. An inner feeling that we may have all had at one time."

Song file location on CD-ROM: rock_pop\formaldehyde1\mp3

Artist history: "The band has been together for about one year. We decided to form a group to play the kind of music that *we like* and to try to satisfy all the popular industry tastes."

About the MP3 experience: "MP3 is great. The opportunity to bypass the industry black hole and get your music out to the people. Let the people decide what they want to hear instead of being fed music on a radio. MP3 will revolutionize the music world."

The Graveyard Farmers info on the Web: www.thegraveyardfarmers.com

Hol'Fader

Hol'Fader.

➤ Mario Defazio—Bass, backup vocals

➤ Nigel Hunt—Drums

➤ Mike Valunate—Guitar, vocals

Stylistic influences: The Beatles, The Jam, Husker Du

Albums available:

➤ *In the Dreamshelter*

➤ *Kama*

➤ *In One Life*

Play It Loud!

Nice fuzz guitar on this one. Absolutely one of my favorites, very similar to the best tracks from REM's *Monster* CD.

Live performances: Montreal, Toronto, Ottawa, East Coast

Song on the CD: "Golddust"

Artist history: "Formed in 1993. Winners of CHOM FM Esprit competition in 1996 for their outstanding songwriting and performing."

Song file location on CD-ROM: rock_pop\gold_dust\mp3

About the MP3 experience: "When we uploaded our songs to MP3.com we never thought that "Golddust" would hit #1 on the Alternative Chart (3.1.99). Since then we've had an offer for that song to be used in a promo video for a video software company. Three of our songs will also be featured in a U.S. indie movie. We've made more contracts this way, than years of sending out CDs and tapes. Our new material will probably be available exclusively on MP3.com's DAM CD system."

Other MP3 acts they recommend:

➤ Lavalite

➤ Headboard

➤ Chelsea in Orbit

Hol'Fader info on the Web: http://members.xoom.com/holfader

Tracy Kash

➤ Tracy Kash—Singer/songwriter

➤ Henry Hey—Keyboards

➤ Pete McCann—Guitar

➤ Bob Roe—Bass

➤ Brian Delaney—Drums

Stylistic influences: Jonathan Brooke, Joni Mitchell, Dar Williams, Chaka Khan, Dianne Reeves

Album available: In progress

Live performances: Manhattan, New York

Song on the CD: "Home"

About the song: "This is a song about all the tremendously positive and powerful things of a healthy, happy childhood. I have a wonderful family and some ver vivid memories of what home was all about for me, which I managed to work into the song. Of course, childhood isn't always a cakewalk, but as a songwriter, you get to pick and choose exactly what to include in a song. I think it's called 'artistic license.' This song is a very meaningful one for me."

Song file location on CD-ROM: rock_pop\home\mp3

Artist history: "I am trained in Classical/Jazz music having a Bachelor's Degree from the University of Northern Texas and a Master's Degree from Boston Conservatory. I pursued a symphony career as a flutist before I turned to songwriting; definitely a good move.'

"I am originally from Detroit. The wonderful musicians on this track are friends from the Univ. of N. Texas who, luckily for me, all wound up in the same place: Manhattan!'"

About the MP3 experience: "My bass player is really the one who handles the sound files as far as Internet exposure goes. So far, however, it has been a very positive experience. Using MP3 files, we have been able to gain a great deal of exposure. These kinds of tools are invaluable for the independent and up and coming artist."

Tracy Kash info on the Web: http://roemusic/tracy

Bryan Kelley

Album available: *Charming the Gods*

Live performances: United States

Song on the CD: "Charming the Gods"

About the song: "From a 10 song tapestry of modern Folk-Rock-edgy, with traditional elements, such as acoustic guitar, fiddle, squeezebox and mandolin, woven throughout."

Song file location on CD-ROM: rock_pop\charming_the_gods\mp3

About the MP3 experience: "A wonderful tool that can help expand your listening audience and gain a fan base."

Bryan Kelley info on the Web: www.groovehouse.com

Bryan Kelley.

Bruce Lash

Stylistic influences: "On this track, anything thickly layered and psychedelic such as The Beatles or Brian Eno."

Albums available:

➤ *Innocent People*
➤ *Prozak for Lovers*
➤ *Sad Sack*

Song on the CD: "High Water"

Song file location on CD-ROM: rock_pop\high_water\mp3

Artist history: "I have played in bands since I was in high school. I started making my own records when I got a job as an audio editor for a commercial post production house in Chicago in 1990. I'm really drawn to artists that play and sing all of the parts on their records.'

"I record my records on non-linear digital audio workstations. From 1990 until last year, I used an AMS Audiofile, which is a 16 channel DAW. Now, I work on a Pro Tools 4.3 24 Mix Plus. Recently, my company acquired the tools to record CDs. Now, whenever I'm not booked, I'm either recording my own music or mastering it to CD.'

"I have no interest in playing in front of an audience. I really like the "painterly" aspect of making records. My style is dictated by the song at hand. The credo I follow is 'serve the song.'"

About the MP3 experience: "I first checked out MP3 about 18 months ago. The players were lousy and the files seemed too big, especially considering my 28.8 modem. I learned to encode MP3 from a guy with a Nirvana fan page. He had MP3s of all kinds of bootleg stuff. He did it because he loved the music. I stayed long enough to learn to encode MP3s. Geffen Records shut him down a few months later. I lost interest in MP3 after that.'

"I sated up again when the MP3 debate began in my neck of the woods in the Winter of 1999. The place that sells my CD, CD Baby, got a deal with Diamond, the Rio People, to bundle MP3s by CD Baby artists and offer them to Rio owners because the biggest customer complaint was that there wasn't enough legal MP3 on the market. I downloaded some freeware and a player. I was amazed at how far the player had come along. Play lists within a player. Wow! EQ within a player. Double wow! I have a 56k modem now so downloading isn't much of a problem. I rarely download anything, though. Usually it will be music by someone I know on the Web. I have yet to download anything illegal. I don't buy that many CDs either. I guess I like to record music more than listen to it.'"

Other MP3 bands he recommends:

➤ Creeping Myrtle

➤ Spiral Mouth

➤ The Dead Engineers

➤ Joanie Chesiwick

Bruce Lash info on the Web: `http://home.att.net/~bblash`

Mike Livingston

Stylistic influences: Jeff Lynne and Electric Light Orchestra, Paul McCartney, X.T.C.

Album available: *Tales of Love and Worry*

Live performances: New England

Song on the CD: "Crusin' Through the Afternoon"

About the song: "Just a typical day for my son and I with some nonsense lyrics thrown in for good measure."

Song file location on CD-ROM: rock_pop\cruisin_through_the_afternoon\mp3

Artist history: "Mike Livingston started out playing acoustic and electric lead in a variety of local bands, but went out 'on his own,' backed by the newly formed Mike Livingston band in 1985. It enjoyed a busy engagement schedule and a following that burgeoned in the course of five years until, in 1990, Nashville called his name, and Mike answered.'

"Two years in Music City saw Mike Livingston's fortunes turning as his name became known. But his time in Nashville ended up a what-might-have-been when Mike's equipment was stolen from his van as it stood parked outside a movie theatre. Disheartened and disillusioned, he gathered his belongings and headed home to New Hampshire. So profoundly disturbed was he by this cruel finale to his Nashville aspirations, a full year would elapse before Mike returned to public performing in 1993.'

"Before leaving Nashville, he bought an old Ovation Custom Legend guitar for $50.00 from a pawnshop. 'Ol Krusty' remains his preferred instrument in a live performance.'

"In the Spring of 1998, Mike and 'Ol Krusty' teamed up with TrebLLL Clef Promotions, a 2 woman organization with offices in Connecticut and Arizona. Their intent was to expand Mike's horizons as a cover artist, but when they heard his own music, there was an abrupt change in course. By the end of the year, a CD of original songs was in the bag and, as 1999 began, Mike was beginning to play the engagements that would showcase his own work.'"

About the MP3 experience: "I was astounded the first time I experienced MP3 sound! I played my own files over the studio monitors and could hear very little difference between the MP3 files and my own CD."

Mike Livingston info on the Web: www.mikelivingston.com

Nikki Loney and Justin Abedin

➤ Nikki Loney—Vocals

➤ Justin Abedin—Eight-string guitars and six-string electric and acoustic guitars

➤ Davide Di Renzo—Percussion

Stylistic influences: Suzanne Vega, Cassandra Wilson, Lyle Lovett, Charlie Hunter, Tuck Andress

Album available: *Tourists in My Life*

235

Nikki Loney and Justin Abedin.

Live performances: Toronto, Canada

Song on the CD: "Dandelion Girl"

About the song: "A funky tune about a bold, yet somewhat jaded young woman."

Song file location on CD-ROM: rock_pop\dandelion_girl\mp3

Artist history: "Veterans of the Toronto music scene, Nikki and Justin started working together in late 1994. Tired of the traditional routes, they decided to play as a duo. Without the aid of samplers, keyboards or drum machines, their unique approach began to take shape. Nikki's poignant lyrics combined with Justin's innovative eight-string guitar vision resulted in their stunning album."

About the MP3 experience: "A great opportunity to expose our music to an otherwise untapped market."

Other MP3 bands they recommend: Michael Keith

Nikki Loney and Justin Abedin info on the Web: www.interlog.com

Larry Loyet (Larry's World)

Stylistic influences: Dead, Allman Bros

Album available: *12 Times Around*

Live performances: Illinois

Song on the CD: "Breezy"

About the song: "I had the riff in my ear for a while, then the slide just set it off."

Song file location on CD-ROM: rock_pop\breezy\mp3

Artist history: "Musician, carpenter, worked out of my home most of my life, playing music on the weekends."

About the MP3 experience: "The greatest thing to happen to music since the dawn of time."

Other MP3 bands he recommends:

➤ Luther Ingram
➤ Stacey Collins

Lost Disciples

➤ Jason—Lead vocals, acoustic guitar
➤ Donovan—Electric guitar
➤ John—Lead guitars
➤ Larry—Bass
➤ Brad—Drums

Stylistic influences: Collective Soul, Creed, John Denver, Pearl Jam

Album available: *Lost Disciples*

Live performances: Southern California

Song on the CD: "Ant Hill"

About the song: "A song that questions the idiocy of our times."

Song file location on CD-ROM: rock_pop\ant_hill\mp3

Artist history: "San Diego based since 1994, we have created new paths and direction for San Diego Music, fresh and hard hitting, we will be sure to ignite you."

About the MP3 experience: "MP3 is the future. With MP3, independent artists finally have a chance to make an impact."

Lost Disciples info on the Web: www.redbutt.com/lost

Lotusland

Lotusland.

Very Talented!

Lotusland is a stunning new band with a big future in front of them. They are gaining new fans by the hundreds on a daily basis.

➤ Christy Schnabel—Vocals, guitar
➤ Jerry Dirienzo—Vocals
➤ Scott Mathers—Drums
➤ John Berry—Bass

Album available: *Lotusland*

Live performances: Los Angeles, California

Song on the CD: "Don't Bring Me Down"

About the song: "A demo track recorded in New York City in 1998."

Song file location on CD-ROM: rock_pop\don't_bring_me_down\mp3

Artist history: "Although its members boast formidable pedigrees as former players in indie and mainstream rock outfits, like Cell, Ugly Beauty, Sleepy and Idaho,

Lotusland's sound, somewhere between the raw, emotive power of PJ Harvey and the quiet intimacy of solo John Lennon, is entirely their own. Lotusland's songwriters, Christy Schnabel and Jerry Dirienzo, were the principal members of Ugly Beauty, whose major label debut *The Sweetness* caused a critical and commercial splash upon its 1997 release."

About the MP3 experience: "Amazing response: over 25 thousand downloads and 60 thousand unique visitors to our Web site in less than two months."

Lotusland info on the Web: `lotusland.simplenet.com`

Joe Mersch

Joe Mersch.

➤ Joe Mersch—Acoustic guitars, vocal, bass, synth, drum sequencing, shaker

➤ Janet Curci—Vocal

➤ Marc Burroughs—Mandolin

Stylistic influences: "Fingerstyle acoustic guitarists such as Pierre Bensusan, Ry Cooder, Bruce Cockburn, edgy Alternative-Pop icons like Crowded House, Stan Ridgeway, Peter Holsapple, T Bone Burnett, Brazilian music, Celtic music, and jazz"

Album available: *The Forbidden Anthems*

Live performances: San Diego, CA

Song on the CD: "Walk This Burden Down"

About the song: "The song was written with a close friend in mind, who was going through a rough time and was really down. I guess I was trying to cheer the guy up. The track was fun and easy to record-one that felt right all the way through the production process."

Song file location on CD-ROM: rock_pop\walk_this_burden_down\mp3

Artist history: "I started playing around in the San Diego area in the late 1980's as a solo artist and as a duo with vocalist Janet Curci. All prior releases have been on cassette and recorded in my home studio with the exception of *Foreshadow*, which was released on vinyl."

About the MP3 experience: "It's a great way to get my stuff heard, though fame and fortune haven't arrived yet."

Other MP3 bands they recommend: Dave Howard

Joe Mersch info on the Web: `http://www.mp3.com/artists/8/joe_mersch.html`

Steve Nolan

➤ Steve Nolan—Guitars, guitar synthesizer

➤ Robin Smith—Bass

➤ Ben Everlast—Drums

Stylistic influences: The Beatles, Jimi Hendrix, John McLaughlin

Song on the CD: "Ben James"

About the song: "This tune has an unusual history. The bass and drum tracks were recorded in 1983 and remained unknown to me until 1998 when the Internet reconnected me with Robin Smith, who I hadn't seen in 15 years. He dusted off the two-track master reel and digitized this and one other track, converted them to MP3 format and emailed them to me. I converted them back to WAV format and loaded them into a digital multitrack recorder and laid down all the guitar tracks, finishing the song some 15 years behind the production schedule."

Song file location on CD-ROM: rock_pop\ben_james\mp3

Artist history: "I started playing guitar in 1964 at age 10 and was playing in live bands by 13. After high school, I played in a long string of bands over a 22 year period during which I met bassist/vocalist Robin Smith. My current employment as a producer/director for a public television station still allows me to keep my involvement in music above a hobby stage."

About the MP3 experience: "MP3 is the first audio format to come along that allows decent audio fidelity within a reasonable bandwidth. In the past, doing music in the telecommunications world was limited to MIDI because of the bandwidth. Once WAV audio caught on and was incorporated into most MIDI recording programs, the medium was no longer limited to keyboard players alone, but the bandwidth involved with transferring WAV audio over a phone line still limited access to those musicians with high capacity connections. The advent of MP3 compression has finally bridged that gap and has opened the world of cross collaborative works to anyone who wants to be involved."

Reality Jones

- ➤ Tim McFadden—Lead vocals, acoustic guitar, backing vocals
- ➤ Tim Fowler—Bass, backing vocals
- ➤ Jon Peck—Drums
- ➤ Tom Russell—Lead guitar
- ➤ Paul Buono—Rhythm guitars, backing vocals
- ➤ Mookie Segal—Hammond organ

Stylistic influences: Van Morrison, Elton John, Sting

Album available: *All You Need To Know*

Live performances: Maryland, Washington, DC, Pennsylvania, and Virginia

Song on the CD: "Man Who Lost His Heart"

About the song: "It's a song about a man who lost touch with the simple things in life. He let the weight of his possessions blur his vision as to what was truly important."

Song file location on CD-ROM: rock_pop\man_who_lost_his_heart\mp3

Artist history: Reality Jones is a Baltimore-based, original pop/rock band, which was formed in 1997. Reality Jones is fronted by singer/songwriter Tim McFadden. Tim's writing provide insightful lyrics and memorable melodies for Reality Jones to arrange and mold into well crafted, unforgettable pop songs. The band is comprised of top-notch musicians, all of whom have many years of playing experience. The band prides itself on exceptional instrumentation, tight harmonies, and a unique

241

blend of personalities that all combine to keep and audience captivated. The band's debut CD, *All You Need To Know,* was released in 1999.

About the MP3 experience: "It has been a good experience enabling us to get our music heard by many listeners, who otherwise, may never have heard our music."

Reality Jones info on the Web: www.realityjones.com

Sedona

> ➤ Michael Fox—Lead vocals, guitar, bass, background vocals
> ➤ Darrell Hale—Drums, background vocals
> ➤ Mark Holley—Guitar

Stylistic influences: Soundgarden, Alice in Chains, Aerosmith, Journey, King's X, Fuel

Albums available:

> ➤ *Dragonfly*
> ➤ *Reel History*
> ➤ *Drift*

Live performances: Sacramento and the San Francisco Bay Area

Song on the CD: "Filling Up the Holes"

About the song: "The songs on Sedona's new release, *Dragonfly,* contain lyrics pulled straight from the scenes of songwriter Mike Fox's life just prior to the recording of the album. Nowhere is this more evident than on the album's opener, 'Filling Up the Holes,' which reflects on issues ranging from the death and burial of his mother to the consolation resulting from the birth of his mother to the consolation resulting from the birth of his first child. As personal and introspective as the lyrics are, however, 'Filling Up The Holes' is among the hardest rocking and heaviest hitting songs on the album."

Song file location on CD-ROM: rock_pop\filling_up_the_holes\mp3

Artist history: "For nearly a decade now, Sedona has been performing on some of the world's most renowned stages such as The Fillmore and the Great American Music Hall with legendary bands like Fleetwood Mac, King's X, Foreigner, Gin Blossoms, Heart, Cheap Trick, and many others. Nine and a half years later, the four original members of Sedona continue to create their own distinctive brand of rock."

About the MP3 experience: "MP3 has the potential to radically change the music industry, and is a godsend for the unsigned artist. Until now, only a tiny percentage of the world's musicians had the opportunity to be heard. This was due to the fact that the only way to be heard was to be signed to a record label that had significant worldwide distribution and promotional resources. Now, an unsigned artist can upload his or her music to an MP3 site, where the entire world has unlimited access to it, eliminating the need for distribution by a record company. It also eliminates most of the cost involved in dispensing the music to the public. No materials cost, no production costs, no transportation costs. None of the enormous overhead that distribution via a record company involves. The distribution is exactly as it should be, between artist and consumer. The role of the record company will be reduced to a promotional capacity. And you don't need some record mogul taking 85% of the artist's earnings just to do promotion.'

"I foresee the promotional market becoming highly competitive, with the highly qualified marketing pros on Madison Avenue giving record execs a serious run for the money.'

"There are still serious matters that need to be resolved. Once the artist achieves world wide recognition, distribution by MP3 stops becoming a promotional venture, and becomes a chief source of commerce. The technology needs to evolve to a point where copyright protection can be implemented when desired, preventing multiple copies of an MP3 file to be made. I believe that once well organized, ultra-fast MP3 distribution centers are established, users would be willing to pay for downloading their favorite music without the hassle of searching the Web for a pirate server, attempting the frustrating feat of actually obtaining access to one, only to find a meager selection of music from which to choose.'

"A fee of, perhaps $1.00 per download would be worthwhile to the consumer for extreme ease of use, large selection, and fast download. The proceeds would go largely to the artist, with a small percentage being kept by the distribution house to cover expenses such as Internet connection and hardware. A vast improvement over today's distribution methods, where the record companies pocket the vast majority of revenue collected on behalf of the artist.'

"And the MP3 experience will only bolster the entire musical community. No longer will record stores be limited to carrying today's top 40. Searching MP3 sites today, you can find music spanning four decades, from 50s Doo Wop to modern day Classical. Once the copy protection and pay-per-download kinks are worked out, musical genres will see unprecedented returns on their creative work. Artists like Tommy James and the Shondells, who probably haven't sold a record in twenty years, will suddenly benefit from worldwide instant availability to fans willing to shell out a dollar for a pristine copy of 'Crimson and Clover' instead of climbing into the attic to retrieve their scratchy vinyl version from the fiberglass infested rafters.'"

Yes, But...

The writer brings up some interesting points. However, it is unlikely that Tommy James and the Shondells would be able to sell their famous song on the Internet because the master recording is no doubt owned by their record company. They could, however, newly record a version that they could sell, as long as they paid the proper license fees to whoever owns the publishing rights to the song.

Other MP3 bands they recommend: Hollowman

Sedona info on the Web: www.sedonaworld.com

Eve Selis

Eve Selis.

➤ Eve Selis—Vocals

➤ Bob Sale—Knee slapping

➤ Marc Intraraia—Guitars

➤ Jim Reeves—Bass

➤ Mike Peters—Keyboard

Stylistic influences: Steve Earle, Emmy Lou Harris, Lucinda Williams, Sheryl Crow, Maria McKee

Albums available:

➤ *Into the Sun*

➤ *Out on a Wire*

Live performances: San Diego, CA

Song on the CD: "Show Me What Love Is"

About the song: "The track is completely live: one take! Except Marc overdubbed a second guitar part."

Song file location on CD-ROM: rock_pop\show_me_what_love_is\mp3

Artist history: "Marc Intraia and Eve Selis have been songwriting partners since 1991. They formed a band called King's Road in 1992 and released two CDs."

About the MP3 experience: "Very cool! As an artist it has been great exposure for our music. We couldn't afford to pay someone for the kind of exposure MP3 provides. We've had emails from all over the world, even from Russia. I actually found a third cousin in Belgium because of our MP3 site."

Other MP3 bands Eve recommends:

➤ Loam

➤ Jason Sinay

Eve Selis info on the Web: www.kingsroadmusic.com

The Selzers

The Selzers.

> ➤ Ryan Gentles—Vocals, guitar
> ➤ Ian Cartwright—Guitar, vocals
> ➤ Gary Zampin—Bass, vocals
> ➤ Jeff Weber—Drums

Stylistic influences: The Beatles, The Beach Boys, Sloan

Album available: *The Bus Ride Home EP*

Live performances: New York-New Jersey and beyond

Song on the CD: "Supermodel"

Song file location on CD-ROM: rock_pop\super_model\mp3

Artist history: "Formed in 1996, old '60s style Pop with modern angst and falsetto harmonies add to the classic Pop sound. The Selzers have opened for numerous famed bands such as Fountains of Wayne and The Connells."

About the MP3 experience: "MP3 has given the band more exposure than the touring and shows we've done put together."

Other MP3 bands they recommend: 52nd Stream Media Compilations

The Selzers info on the Web: www.selzers.com

Jeff Shuck

Jeff Shuck.

Stylistic influences: The Sea and Cake, The Cocteau Twins, Fountains of Wayne, Ivy, The Smiths, The Carpenters, The Fifth Dimension

Album available: *brightest coldest blue*

Song on the CD: "Sidewinder"

About the song: "This song is about trying to figure out if the person holding out an apple to you is genuine or just another snake in the grass."

Song file location on CD-ROM: rock_pop\sidewinder\mp3

Artist history: "Jeff Shuck is a Chicago and Salt Lake City-based singer and song-writer who performs nationally. All the instruments and sounds on 'Sidewinder' were played or created by Mr. Shuck. His first album was released to exceptional reviews in 1998. 'Sidewinder' is his first single of 1999."

About the MP3 experience: "MP3s—and MP3.com in particular—are a wonderful way to bring your music to the world. The sound quality is excellent, and the ability to reach anyone in the world with a computer is truly invigorating. We all get into this business because we want to reach people with our ideas, and MP3s provide an incredibly rewarding way of doing just that."

Jeff Shuck info on the Web: `http://members.aol.com/oneschool`

James Simmons

Stylistic influences: Allman Brothers, Eric Clapton, Jeff Beck

Live performances: Northeast Georgia

Song on the CD: "Tribute to Duane"

About the song: "A tribute to my guitar hero, Duane Allman."

Song file location on CD-ROM: rock_pop\tribute_to_duane\mp3

Artist history: "I started playing guitar and drums when I was 12. I played in bands ranging from County to Blues and Rock. Played mostly in South Carolina and Texas before settling in Georgia."

About the MP3 experience: "It has been really great. The people at MP3.com really take a personal interest in making music careers happen."

Other MP3 bands he recommends:

➤ Beyond Blue
➤ Big Bill and the Cool Tones
➤ Marc Pattison

James Simmons info on the Web: `http:www.localnoise.com/jamessimmons`

Skavenjah

➤ Hugh (Pappy) Dixon—Vocals, driver of the tour bus
➤ Rick (Rico) Gelsinger—Guitars
➤ Scot (SkaT) Beaumont—Bari and tenor sax
➤ Dave (Claude) Kapp—Low frequency death ray dispenser
➤ Kendra (Spicegirl) Smyznyk—Keyboards

➤ Colin (Polka King) Neufeld—T-bone

➤ Nathan (Gus) Lowey—Trumpet

➤ Andre (Big Jim) Boehn—Drums

➤ Terry (Bulldog) Quinney—Alto sax

Live performances: Canada

Song on the CD: "Stop Thief"

About the song: "Written by Rick, and available on *Little Monsters.*"

Song file location on CD-ROM: rock_pop\stop_theif\mp3

Artist history: "Skavenjah is a nine-piece Ska band hailing from Regina, Saskatchewan. While their music is based on traditional Jamaican Ska, it defies categorization and is further supercharged with healthy doses of Punk, Funk, Latin, Swing and other stuff. Its fast, its slow, it rocks, it rolls, its all over the place! Their albums include *Put Some Skank in Your Tank*, *Little Monsters* and *All Dressed Up.*"

Skavenjah info on the Web: www.skavenjah.regina.sk.ca

The Joey Skidmore Band

The Joey Skidmore Band.

- ➤ Joey Skidmore—Vocals and guitars
- ➤ Eric "Roscoe" Ambel—Lead guitar
- ➤ D. Clinton Thompson—Guitars
- ➤ Mike Costelow—Guitars
- ➤ Joe Terry—Piano
- ➤ Walter Paisley—Bass
- ➤ John Marshall—Drums
- ➤ Lou Whitney—Producer

Stylistic influences: The Rolling Stones, Iggy and the Stooges, Creedence Clearwater Revival

Albums available:

- ➤ *The Word is Out*
- ➤ *Welcome to Humansville*
- ➤ *Joey Skidmore*
- ➤ *Bent*

Live performances: Kansas City and the Midwest. We have done two small tours of France.

Song on the CD: "Butt Steak"

About the song: "Politically incorrect Rock-a-Billy song about food. New Yorkers loved it, thanks to the Hound show on WFMU. The rest of the lunatic fringe crowd heard it on Dr. Demento."

Song file location on CD-ROM: rock_pop\butt_steak\mp3

Artist history: "Released two E.P.s in the early 1980s, while riding the Neo-Psychedelic garage Punk craze. Cut first album in 1987. Reformed band in Kansas City in 1991 with guitarist Mike Costelow. Got some attention and got signed in France. The liked us and Jerry Lewis."

About the MP3 experience: "Love it!"

Other MP3 bands they recommend: Anybody from Kansas City

The Joey Skidmore Band info on the Web: www.midi.byweb.com

Special note from Rod Underhill: "My mom was from Kansas City so this band has got to be fantastic. I wonder if they knew my mom? Nah…"

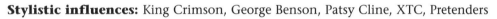

Melanie Sparks

➤ Melanie Sparks—Guitars, vocals

➤ Dexter Whittaker—Bass

➤ Jesus Nieves—Drums and percussion

Albums available:

➤ *Mabel's Beauty Shop & Chainsaw Repair*

➤ *Guess What's In (My Shorts)*

Live performances: Eastern Seaboard of USA

Stylistic influences: King Crimson, George Benson, Patsy Cline, XTC, Pretenders

Song on the CD: "Believer"

About the song: "The song is about a hypertensive diatribe lambasting Southern Protestant proselytizing zealots. Either that or it's about a bunch of rednecks."

Artist history: "Came from Alabama. No banjo, though. Been at this 'music thing' since 1996."

Song file location on CD-ROM: rock_pop\believer\mp3

About the MP3 experience: "So far, so good…with over 1,000 downloads there has been a lot of exposure."

Other MP3 bands they recommend: Halley DeVestern

Melanie Sparks info on the Web: http://i.am/melaniesparks/

Another Undiscovered Star

Melanie is one of the most impressive new talents that I've seen in a long time. If you have a chance, try to see one of her live shows.

The Torpedoes

➤ Brian Pool—Guitars

➤ Brandon Watson—Drums

➤ Jason Brown—Bass

Stylistic influences: Dick Dale, Junior Brown, The Ventures, AC/DC

Albums available:

➤ *Good for the Country*

➤ *Lucky You*

Live performances: USA

A Surf Music Testimonial

Incredible Surf music! *Everybody* loves Surf music! Cowabunga! Surf music is the only real music, the only music that truly matters. (Did I mention that I grew up in Manhattan Beach, California?)

251

The Torpedoes' logo.

Song on the CD: "Big Blue"

About the song: "'Big Blue' is one of those songs that can really grow on you. It has a straight ahead Country beat that makes your toe start to tap, outstanding guitar phrasing and complex composition. We called the song 'Big Sky' on our CD, though."

Song file location on CD-ROM: rock_pop\big_blue\mp3

Artist history: Founded in 1994 by guitarist Brian Pool in Sunnyvale, California. The band has paid its dues by playing countless local gigs around the San Francisco Bay Area and then hitting the road and touring around the USA. After adding drummer Brandon Watson in 1995, the Torpedoes recorded their first album. The Torpedoes have performed on several live radio and TV programs and their music can be heard on the Mindscapes million selling CD-ROM game: "Lego Island."

About the MP3 experience: "We have already been exposed to thousands of ears that otherwise would have gone unsaturated by The Torpedoes brand of instrumental Rock and Roll. Our first break in this format came from the nice folks at MP3.com and they continue to be important allies."

The Torpedoes info on the Web: www.thetorpedoes.com

Uncle $am Band

➤ Michael Bechtel
➤ Ken Wolfe

Stylistic influences: Wallflowers, Led Zeppelin, The Who, Pink Floyd, Bob Seger

Album available: *Love in a Blender*

Live performances: Pennsylvania

Song on the CD: "Love in a Blender"

About the song: "The song is about relationships."

Song file location on CD-ROM: rock_pop\love_in_a_blender\mp3

About the MP3 experience: "It makes for a more level playing field for independent artists versus the big leagues."

Uncle $am Band info on the Web: http://www.microserve.net/~usb

The Unknown

- ➤ Ken Blaze—Vocals
- ➤ Wayne Roscoe—Drums
- ➤ Chris Roscoe—Guitar
- ➤ Brian P. McCafferty—Bass, background vocals

Stylistic influences: "70s and 80s Punk and Pop"

Albums available:

- ➤ *Change*
- ➤ *Rocket Pop*
- ➤ *Still Unknown*
- ➤ *Seems So Live*

Song on the CD: "Self Control"

About the song: "The song is about a guy checking out another girl and betting busted by his girlfriend/wife. We've all gone through it...hey, we're all human, right?"

Song file location on CD-ROM: rock_pop\self_control\mp3

Artist history: "The Unknown has been playing its ultra-adrenalized Popcore in the Cleveland scene for nearly ten years. The band has gone through ten or so members, and its current lineup is now three years old. They have done two tours and numerous weekend trips supporting their four full-length albums. Along the way the Unknown has created its own Jiffi Pop Records to play and record their music."

About the MP3 experience: "MP3.com as well as other Internet commerce sites provide an opportunity that never existed before for people like us. I should have outgrown this music stuff a long time a go but the MP3 trip has been interesting and fun."

Other MP3 bands they recommend: Rod

Wacky Lemon Hello

➤ Lara Hughes—Vocals

➤ Julian Lee—Flute

➤ Ben Ortega—Drums

➤ Ron Weber—Bass

➤ Rick Wilkinson—Guitar

➤ Words and music by Lara Hughes

Stylistic influences: "Pretty eclectic, as a band. Eric Clapton. 70's Power Rock. Offspring. Police. Sheryl Crow. Beatles. Each new song tends to be radically different from those before it…"

Live performances: Pasadena, California, though rarely.

Song on the CD: "Trust"

Song file location on CD-ROM: rock_pop\trus\mp3

About the song: "A kind of bluesy track on the dilemma that occurs when you see the manipulation coming, but can't really do anything about it, because, well, such is the nature of manipulation."

Artist history: "Wacky Lemon Hello formed in its current incarnation in 1998. We are five errant Caltech grad students, postdocs, and staff, gathered together in a well-meaning but perhaps fruitless effort to deny the nerdiness that is out destiny."

World Music

The Internet can bring you information from all over the world, and music is no exception, as these tunes prove.

Ancient Future

➤ Matthew Montfort—Scalloped fretboard guitar

➤ Mindia Devi Klein—Flute

➤ Mike Yeaney—Lead vocals, back up vocals, rhythm guitar

➤ Phil Fong—Sarod, Irish harp, nylon string guitar

Stylistic influences: Matthew Montfort of Ancient Future claims to have coined the term "world fusion music" in 1978 to describe the band's blend of traditional world music and contemporary jazz and rock. The term has since become the standard term in the industry for describing this new eclectic music.

Ancient Future.

Album available: *Visions of a Peaceful Planet*

Live performances: "Anywhere that will pay the fee. The band is based in the San Francisco Bay Area."

Song on the CD: "Eternal Embrace"

About the song: "This song was recorded when all of the members of Ancient Future were in their early 20s. It was composed by Phil Fong and is published by Ancient Future Music (BMI). In March, 1999, it reached #1 on the mpulse.com Internet song chart."

Song file location on CD-ROM: world\eternal_embrace\mp3

About the MP3 experience: "The MP3 format is potentially a good promotional vehicle for new or unusual artists. It is a way that great music that otherwise might not get heard can have a chance at reaching an audience.'

"But it is a double edged sword. I worry that the MP3 craze is yet another way that music is being devalued in modern society: something very important is now free. There is no longer substantial government support for the arts. The major labels aren't big on supporting artistic development: in their pursuit of profit they often end up doing the equivalent of strip mining music, cashing in on trends and putting little back to seed the development of new music. That is left to smaller labels who don't have the financial ability to properly support the music, and often can't even pay the royalties they owe for records sold. And now people who might otherwise buy records can get more music than they can ever listen to for free.'

"Yet, there is some hope, for the Internet also provides the opportunity for music lovers to buy direct from artists, thereby actually directly supporting the music. But it will take raising the consciousness of the Internet community to make people aware of the dire condition of the arts in modern society and letting them know that finally they can do something about it. They can buy direct and support the arts after finding new music they like on the Internet.'

"My initial experience with free MP3 downloads of selected music from our records is that it has increased sales a very small amount at our Web site. However, the ratio of free downloads to sales of CDs is very low, about one sale per 150 downloads. Going over the message boards on MP3.com, rations of one sale per 2,000 downloads are very common, so our experience is better than most.'

"But right now the entire Internet is based on a 'gain market share at any cost' mentality. Web browsers are, after all, free. Amazon.com loses money selling books while putting local book stores out of business and its stock price stores.'

"Since there is no rush to buy stock in unusual music groups, I just ask that people consider the value of the arts and act accordingly—Matthew Montfort, bandleader, Ancient Future.'"

Other MP3 bands they recommend:

➤ Habib Khan

➤ Emam and Friends

Ancient Future info on the Web: `http://ancient-future.com`

Chupacabra

➤ Sunny Michelson—Lead vocals

➤ Jason Virunurm—Guitar, vocals

➤ Jason McDaniel—Bass

➤ Anthony Salvo—Violin, saxophone

➤ Brian Juan—Keyboards

➤ Dan Porras—Drums

➤ Cheryl Etu—Marimba

➤ Michael McKensie—Congas

Stylistic influences: Santana, the Allman Brothers, Poncho Sanchez

Album available: *Chupacabra*

Live performances: Colorado and the Western USA

Song on the CD: "Orbit"

About the song: "One of our first originals, written by guitarist Jason Virunurm."

Song file location on CD-ROM: world\orbit\mp3

About the MP3 experience: "MP3 is simple and great; the wave of the future!"

Chupacabra info on the Web: www.chupacabra.cc

Daniel Cox

Song on the CD: "Return of the Bossa Nova"

Song file location on CD-ROM: world\return_of_the_bossa_nova\mp3

Daniel Cox info on the Web: www.mp3-records.com

Another Solo Star!

Dan plays all the instruments on this song!

Dimitris

Dimitris is a new age composer, pianist, poet, performer, and medical doctor in Athens, Greece. He combines ancient and rare instruments with modern instruments, samplers and sounds from nature.

Album available: *Divine Dreams*

Live performances: Athens, Greece

Song on the CD: "Jazzen"

Song file location on CD-ROM: world\jazzen\mp3

About the MP3 experience: "A great way for sharing musical ideas."

Dimitris info on the Web: pentagon@newage-music.com

Kenny Dread

➤ Kenny Dread—Vocals

➤ Ramsey Gouda—Acoustic guitar

➤ Joel B—Vocals, mandolin

➤ Levi Chen—Gu zheng

➤ Deborah Buzil—Shaker

➤ Randall Throckmorton—Violin

Stylistic influences: Joni Mitchell, The Watersons, Van Morrison

Album available: *Powderhorn*

Live performances: Chicago, West of Ireland, South of France

Song on the CD: "Dublin"

About the song: "This one is based on a traditional song 'Handsome Molly.'"

Song file location on CD-ROM: world/dublin/mp3

Artist history: "Kenny Dread dropped out of music school as a young man and joined the Washington D.C. alternative scene. He recorded go-go anthem 'D.C. Groove' with Static Disrupters in 982 and toured the East Coast with Outrage until 1987. Outrage brought the funk to new-wave clubs like CBGB's and Danceteria and got great write-ups in *The New York Times*. During the 1980's Kenny toured with legendary vocalist H.R., lead singer of the Bad Brains, and appeared on four H.R. albums released by L.A. punk indie SST records.'

"The years spent playing bass and electric guitar with H.R. earned Kenny a stage name and confirmed the connection between charismatic music, spirituality, and travel. During this period Kenny also produced records for D. C. Punk and reggae groups and performed with reggae godfather Ras Michael and the Sons of Negus.'

"Kenny Dread stayed in London after H.R.'s 1989 European tour, recorded with X-Ray Spex singer Poly Styrene, and then formed the American expat Rock band The Immigrants in Aix-en-Provence, France.'

"This escapist fantasy provided much in the way of fine wines but little in terms of financial reward. An era of travel and study followed, including journeys to Morocco and Israel and extended visits to the West of Ireland, causing Kenny to develop his singing and songwriting in a more acoustic setting.'

"Based in Chicago since 1996, Kenny Dread recorded his solo CD *Powderhorn* in 1997.'"

About the MP3 experience: "Having my song featured on MP3.com on St. Patrick's Day, 1999, sent my downloads skyrocketing from 25 or so in a day to an average of 1,000 a day for the week it was featured. Old friends got in touch via MP3.com viewer email, a Japanese computer magazine wanted to include it on a Best of MP3 issue, and my confidence on the accessibility of my music received a serious adrenaline boost."

Kenny Dread info on the Web: www.yinyangrecords.com

Okapi Guitars

➤ Bernhard Huber—Vocals, various instruments

➤ John Laidler—Vocals, various instruments

Stylistic influences: Johnny Pacheco, Africando, Tito Puente

Albums available:

➤ *One Bad Man*

➤ *Sally Banana*

➤ *Choko Choko*

Live performances: Sydney, Australia

Song on the CD: "Okapi Guitars: Vamos (a la huelga!)"

About the song: "Tierra y libertad"

Song file location on CD-ROM: world\vamos\mp3

Artist history: "When the Okapi Guitar Band, a seven piece African pop/dance group based in Sydney, broke up in 1992, the two guitarists in the band hadn't had enough. After six years of playing live, they'd only scratched the surface of musical styles that claim more fans, worldwide, than anything heard on mainstream radio. Trouble is, those fans are mostly poor and live in the third world. But when music speaks to your heart, economics really don't matter.'

"So, they kept making the music: writing, arranging and recording, mixing the home studio lo-tech of Sydney into their shared hallucinations of Lagos and Harare.'

"Under the name Okapi Guitars, they have enthusiastically explored their passion for African music, independently releasing albums of the their original songs on a yearly basis.'"

Okapi Guitars info on the Web: http://www.zeta.org.au/~john/okapi.htm

Slainte

➤ Anthea Lawrence—Lead vocal

➤ Brynn Star—Background vocal and fiddle

➤ Kent Hooper—Whistles

➤ Bob McCaffery-Lent—Guitar and background vocals

➤ Jean Huskamp—Bouzouki

Rod Speaks

Celtic Stars!

Slainte is one of the most popular Celtic style bands on the Internet.

Stylistic influences: Dervish, Altan, Solas, the Bothy Band, Martin Hayes, Mick Moloney

Album available: *Slainte*

Live performances: Pacific Northwest

Song on the CD: "Star of the County Down"

259

Slainte.

About the song: "This is a traditional Irish ballad enriched by our fine singers and players."

Song file location on CD-ROM: world\star_of_the_county_down\mp3

Artist history: "Slainte, a Tacoma-based Irish band, began performing in the Summer of 1995. The nexus of the band coalesced from participants in a bluegrass and Irish jam session at the University of Puget Sound. The band's original name, 'Puget Sounds', reflected those origins; however, the band later changed its name to Slainte to emphasize its focus on traditional Irish music. The word *Slainte*, Gaelic for 'cheers,' or 'good health,' signifies the band's desire to play enjoyable, danceable, and spirited music for people whose love for the music transcends generation barriers. Slainte's performances are filled with the dance music of Ireland, including reels, jigs and slip jigs, polkas, slides, airs and waltzes. The band's fine singers also lend their voices to traditional and contemporary songs in the Irish idiom. Slainte has performed at Lakefolkfest, Northwest Folklife Festival, the St. Patrick's Day Dash, the Rob Roy Highland Ball, Wintergrass, and at many civic events."

About the MP3 experience: "The MP3.com experience, in particular, has been great for us. We've made contacts all over the world and are delighted at how enthusiastically our music is received. The financial benefit is less certain right now, but there is no doubt that getting one's music heard is worth a lot!"

Other MP3 bands they recommend: Anthea Lawrence

Slainte info on the Web: www.irishband.com

Oom

➤ Ian Osrin

➤ John Ackerman

➤ Bruce Mclaren-Lyle

Stylistic Influences: Reggae, South African Township pop

Album available: *Beats and Peaces*

Live performances: South Africa

Song on the CD: "Whito Kwaito"

About the song: "This is a bit of fun that we had mixing Ska with South African Township Pop."

Song file location on CD-ROM: world\whito_kwaito\mp3

Artist history: "Five years as a studio based two piece band with a variety of top South African artists as guests."

About the MP3 experience: "More publicity for an unknown band in one month than in five years of slogging."

Other MP3 bands they recommend:

➤ Babado

➤ Acoustic Kitchen

Oom info on the Web: www.digitalcupboard.co.za

Andrey Vinogradov

➤ Andrey Vinogradov—Composition, arrangement, keyboards

➤ Galina Lipina—Vocals

➤ Ivan Smirnov—Guitar

Stylistic influences: Mussorgsky, Rachmaninov, Sting, Jan Garbarek, Paco De Lucia

Album available: *Dryad's Songs*

Live performances: Moscow, Russia

Songs on the CD: "Again, White Campanulas," "Pearl Divers"

Rod Speaks

A True Genius

Mr. Vinogradov is one of the most talented composers that I have ever encountered. His songs are stunningly beautiful and truly unique. I hope that the entire world will one day come to discover this amazing talent.

Andrey Vinogradov.

Song file locations on CD-ROM: world\again_white_campanulas\mp3 and world\Pearl_divers\mp3

Artist history: "Andrey Vinogradov, a gifted composer and pianist from Moscow, Russia, born in 1959 in Ekaterinburg, graduated from the Moscow Gnessin Music College with a first in jazz and piano. He completed his education at the Gnessin Music Academy under Igor Brille studying composition and jazz piano. Later he joined a popular Russian jazz-rock group called Arsenal, founded by a well known saxophonist Alexie Kozlov and recorded two albums with the group.'

"In 1996, together with singer Galina Lipina, he released his CD entitled Dryad's Songs. It is a series of songs based on poems of Soloviov, Blok, Voloshin, Akhmatova and other Russian modernist poets. Andrey was particularly successful in mixing the chamber lyrics of Russian romances with the rhythms of jazz-rock and specific folklore melodies. Andrey's work is clearly highly influenced by the Russian classical heritage (Mussorgsky, Rachmaninov, and so on), but at the same time it cannot be classified as purely academic, because there are strong reminiscences of jazz in all of his songs.'"

Andrey Vinogradov info on the Web: `http://www.mp3.com/avinogradov`

Bonus Album!

Most CDs contain only a single album, but the one accompanying this book has a special bonus album in addition to the many MP3 files it contains.

Rod Underhill

The Author Rocks Out

Here's a special surprise for you! Presented for your pleasure, the complete Rock album: *Science Friction!* This album was initially released in MP3 form on the Internet and is presented here for the first time on disc.(Astute music fans will remember my good friend David Uosikkinen from his days with the wonderful band The Hooters.)

➤ Rod Underhill—Vocals, bass, guitars, and keyboards

➤ Joe Norwood—Guitars

➤ Miss Jan Schmidt—Vocals

➤ David Uosikkinen—Drums

➤ Glenn Taylor—Bass, keyboards, and drums

Stylistic influences: The Doors and other lesser bands

Album available: *Science Friction*

Live performances: San Diego, California

Songs on the CD:

➤ "Baby Come Back"

➤ "Driving LA After Midnight"

➤ "I'll Fade Away"

➤ "Judgement Day"

➤ "Science Friction Theme"

➤ "Shouldn't Be That Way"

➤ "The Norwood Stomp"

➤ "Another Planet"

➤ "Go to Sleep"

About the album: "I recorded this album over 1998-1999, recording most of the instruments myself. Glenn, Joe, David, and Jan helped out as needed. I wrote all the music."

Song file locations on CD-ROM: science\ (All the MP3s for this album are located on the CD-ROM in the folder Science.)

About the MP3 experience: "It tastes like ice cream."

Other MP3 bands they recommend:

➤ Cobain Morrisson

➤ Beyond Blue

➤ Red Delicious

The Least You Need to Know

➤ A wide variety of musicians are using MP3s on the Internet to promote their music.

➤ They are reaching new fans from all over the world.

➤ You are now ready to join the MP3 movement!

Afterword: The Future of MP3

The digital compressed audio revolution is raging even as you read this page. And it truly is a battle; the music manufacturing industry is fighting hard to put a rein on it, even as individual record companies and artists are plotting ways to make money in the compressed digital world.

Predicting the future even in the best of situations is a chancy situation. After all, if we lived in the 21st century that the science fiction writers predicted 50 years ago, we wouldn't have digital music, but we would all have flying cars in our garages.

So we can't pinpoint the future, but with a little thought, we can focus on some important and likely points.

1. The Digital Music May Not Be MP3

The revolution is compressed digital music. MP3 just happens to be the popular format. Assuming that it's going to continue to reign is kind of like someone assuming in 1910 that because a lot of people were buying Model T Fords, in the future everyone would own a Model T.

Many companies are working on competing standards, and not just minor little companies, either. IBM, Microsoft, and Lucent Technologies are all pitching their own audio compression schemes because there is big money to be had in developing the scheme that becomes popular. All these new schemes include systems to copy-protect the files so that record companies would be able to sell you compressed music that would work on your player, but would not work on someone else's player.

Compression schemes are also competing on quality and getting the same quality audio into less space or better quality sound out of the same space. Although there is only so much compression can improve, every little bit helps.

Big Companies Won't Give It Away

There is one quality to look for that the big-company standards won't offer: free access to the standard. One of the irritants about MP3 is that someone holds a patent on it and aims to collect money from everyone making encoders. This license fee adds substantial costs to many MP3 efforts. A quality compression standard that was free for all to use would likely be embraced by many. If such a thing is likely to arise, it will probably come either from academia or from a professional consortium...and even then, it will have to compete in the marketplace of concepts with formats that have financial backing behind them.

Still, all this doesn't mean that MP3 will be wiped out. Some of the attempts at new formats are really just improved versions of MP3. These use the basics of MP3 compression, but add copy-protection information or added compression features. Compare that with the way that home video tape has evolved. VHS tape has been around for decades now, and at the beginning, it didn't have the best video quality, and it didn't have copy protection. Now there is Super-VHS, and copy protection schemes, but the players will still play the same old VHS tapes recorded in the 1970s. Back then, there weren't tapes that would store up to nine hours, or little VHS-C tapes for handheld camcorders, but these features have been integrated into VHS, rather than eliminating it.

2. The Web Appears to Be Taking Over

Currently, the Internet is something that everyone is talking about and many people have access to. In fact, if you live in some communities, it is easy to assume that everyone has Internet access. Alas, that is not yet the case, particularly in our poorer communities.

However, it may well be true in the days to come. The Web, phone, and TV seem to be converging into what will end up being a single data tube that will be able to receive and send all sorts of signals. If that happens, that will change the way we access many things that are essentially data, music included.

3. Hardware Becomes Cheaper

It's hardly a new observation that what was impossible yesterday is available today, and cheap tomorrow. The first digital watches cost many hundreds of dollars; now you can find them for five bucks. The price of a portable CD player is well less than one tenth of what the first ones cost. In the last 20 years, the price of computer memory per byte has dropped over 99.99 percent. And it's faster, more compact, and more reliable to boot.

The price of compressed music hardware is likely to drop harshly, and the capability is likely to swell. A $200 portable player that carries a half-hour's worth of music is going to be seen by many people as an expensive novelty item. A $40 player that has 80 hours of music, on the other hand, can be the main device in your mobile sound arsenal. (And hey, wouldn't it be cool if you could just plug that player into a special interface in your car dashboard, and easily take those same songs on the road?)

4. Physical Music Media May Die

Once the big music owners see that everyone is hooked to the Internet and are likely to be able to play compressed music, there is a lot of incentive to sell everything via download, rather than having you buy CDs and compress them yourself. If they sell you the compressed file, they can make sure that the copy protection is in place so that you can't go around sharing the file with others. Better still, they are spared the cost of actually having to manufacture the CD, and they keep from having to share the cost with the CD stores.

For the customer, it saves the trip to the CD store. It's particularly good if your tastes go beyond the currently popular recordings. Even a good record store is only going to carry a fraction of what's still in print, which is itself a small portion of everything that has been in print. Online, however, everything is available, and there's little reason for anything to ever go "out of print."

Don't expect this to happen without a fight. There are too many dollars tied up in selling you physical CDs. All those CD store chains aren't going to give up without a struggle; expect them to try both to win you over and to erect legal blockage to this move toward all-electronic music distribution. They won't be the only ones facing this sort of concern because video rental stores are likely to face similar problems with Internet distribution of movies. Even the record labels are likely to keep in the fight because switching the customers to downloadable music means they no longer have control over distribution. It's just about as easy to find a small music label's Web site as that of a big label.

5. No Storage Needed at Home

If you have a CD collection, you know that the longer you have it, the more space it takes up. It's easy to expect that your home stereo MP3 player will need an ever-increasing amount of storage space—bigger and bigger hard disks to be filled with downloads over that ultra-high-speed Internet connection (even though the disk itself takes up little physical space). Just the opposite may be true—if the MP3 player is hooked up at a reasonably high speed, you really don't need to store the music at all!

Instead, every time you want to hear a song, it could be sent at lightning speed over the 'Net. This would not only keep the cost and complexity of your player down, it would also make it easier for the music owner to make sure that you aren't copying the tune. The music company might charge you a very small amount for each time you play a song, or it might keep track of which tunes you've paid for and are allowed to play.

6. Subscribe to Music

Once you're set up to download each song as you listen to it at home, the entire model for how you pay for music may change. Consider the way you pay for basic cable: a fixed monthly charge, no matter how much or how little you watch, no matter which of the basic cable channels you choose to enjoy. In the downloadable music equivalent, for some per-month price (say, $10), you could listen to any song you want, whenever you want, on your home stereo. No need to "own" any music, since you can always hear it. Some central tracking company would see how often people listened to each song, and split the artists' portion of the money appropriately. Sound strange? It's actually a lot like the way that radio stations pay for music. You may even be able to reduce your monthly fee if you let advertisers throw in occasional ads.

Of course, you could still play your own playlists, but this would also open the new job of *playlist jockey*. Some big band fan could program up good big band selections. Doctor Demento could offer a good mix of novelty and comedy recordings 24 hours per day. Chuck D. could offer a special program of his favorite old school tunes. Some hip college kid could offer up playlists of the newest unknown bands in whatever the currently popular genre is. When you choose to listen to someone's playlist, they'd get some small cut of your subscription fee.

7. Digital Music May Take to the Air

There are already various forms of digital broadcast going on. Soon, TV broadcasting will be switching over to HDTV, with digital compressed video and audio. Once people are listening to portable devices that have both decompression and radio tuning already built in, it won't be much of a change for the players to start decoding radio signals.

What would be gained from this? On one hand, it could be used to improve the audio quality of radio, putting a high-quality compressed signal in the same bandwidth that an analog radio system used to take up. On the other hand, several lower-quality signals could be compressed onto the same channel, allowing a wider range of listening options.

8. Music Will Still Be Music

All of this won't change the fact that it's not the technology that brings us joy. Little bundles of electronics may make the sound sharper, but they're still doing the same basic job as the old Edison cylinders: allowing us to enjoy the beauty created by talented musicians creatively exercising their craft. In the end, it's all about people, not machines.

Glossary

AAC   An audio compression system that gives better compression rates than MP3; short for *Advanced Audio Coding*.

analog   Used to refer to sound that has not been turned into numbers. An analog sound wave can be infinitely variable, as opposed to digitized sound, which is limited to discrete values.

ASFS   An encoded compressed music file format supported by Virtuosa Gold.

Audio Home Recording Act   A U.S. law passed in 1992 that increased home music copying freedom while placing restrictions on audio players and taxes on players and recording media.

auxiliary   Refers to a socket on your sound card that you can connect other audio playing devices to; also called *line in*.

bit rate   The amount of data used to hold a given length of music; measured in *kilobits per second* or *Kbps*.

CBR   Short for *constant bit rate*, this term describes MP3 files where each second of the music is compressed to the same size.

CDA   Refers to the uncompressed encoding method used to store audio on a standard CD; short for *Compact Disc Audio*.

CDDB   An online database of CD album information.

CD-R   Drives and media that let you make your own CD-ROMs and audio CDs with your computer; short for *compact disc-recordable*.

CD-RW   Drives and reusable media that let you store data in a CD-like format; short for *compact disc-rewritable*. Although CD-RW media cannot be read by normal CD players or CD-ROM drives, most CD-RW drives can also write to CD-R media, which does not have that limitation.

codec   Any system to store data in less space; short for *compressor/decompressor*.

compress   To store a set of data using less space while retaining necessary information.

constant bit rate   See *CBR*.

copyright   Legal right to control the reproduction of writing, music, photos, artwork, or film.

DAE   The ability of a CD-ROM drive to transfer the digital audio information from an audio CD to the computer; short for *Digital Audio Extraction*.

decode   To convert an encoded audio file into uncompressed, unencoded digital audio information.

decompress   To convert a compressed audio file into an uncompressed one.

digital audio   A recording of sound stored as a series of numbers.

Digital Audio Extraction   See *DAE*.

digitize   To convert analog audio into digital audio by repeatedly measuring (also called *sampling*) the sound wave.

docking station   A holder used to store a portable MP3 player. This holder is connected to the PC, and is used to transfer data to the player from the PC. Some holders are also used to recharge the player's batteries.

encode   To convert data into a specific file format.

encrypted   Refers to data files that are stored so that they cannot be properly read without a password or key of some sort. This process is used to create audio files that will run on your player but not on anyone else's.

fair use   A legal concept describing certain legitimate cases for reproducing copyrighted material without a license.

flash memory   Computer memory that does not lose stored data when the power is turned off.

hardware   Physical portions of computer equipment, as separated from *software*, which includes programs, files, and so on.

Harry Fox Agency   A recording rights service that you can contact to secure permission to cover a song.

ID3   A format for including informational tags in an MP3 file, allowing many players to display information about the song.

Internet radio   Streaming digital audio transmissions over the Internet that can be listened to by anyone with the compatible receiving program.

ISO   Short for *International Standards Organization*, a group that sets standards for various engineering and design concerns.

jack   A connector that receives another connector into it. Also called a *socket*.

Kbps   Short for *kilobits per second*, a measurement of the amount of data it takes to make a second of music in an MP3 file.

kilobit   1,024 bits. A *bit* is the smallest unit of computer data storage.

line in   Refers to a socket on your sound card that you can connect other audio playing devices to; also called *auxiliary*.

lossless   Refers to compression methods in which the compressed file could be decompressed into an exact replica of the original uncompressed file. Also refers to reproduction methods in which the copy is an exact match of the original.

lossy   Refers to compression methods in which the compressed file cannot be decompressed into an exact replica of the original uncompressed file. Also refers to reproduction methods in which the copy is not an exact match of the original.

mechanical license   A form of permission granted allowing you to cover a given song and release it on record, tape, or CD.

mic in   The socket on a sound card designed to have a microphone connected to it.

microdrive   A form of a very small hard drive that can be used in place of flash memory in some instances.

MIDI   Short for *Musical Instrument Digital Interface*, this refers to a standard for connecting electronic instruments and computers. Also refers to a file format used to store the computer equivalent of sheet music, with a list of which notes are being played and what instruments are playing them.

miniplug   The sort of plug used on the end of headphones for portable tape or CD players.

MP3   Short for *MPEG-1 Layer III*, this term refers to a standard of audio compression originally designed for inclusion with compressed video.

MP4   A term that has been used to refer to various audio compression schemes that are deemed to be better than MP3, including AAC among others.

MPEG   Short for the *Moving Pictures Expert Group*, a committee within the ISO that designs standard related to digitized video. Their various standards are labeled MPEG-1, MPEG-2, and so on.

MPMan   A series of portable MP3 players manufactured by Saehan and released in North America by Eiger Labs.

MusicMatch Jukebox   A Windows-based MP3 player, encoder, and manager that can also deal with CDs, WAV files, and other digital audio formats.

patch   A small program used to change or update another program.

player   A device or program that decodes and plays digital audio files.

playlist   A file with a list of songs for a player to play or select from.

plug   A connector that gets inserted into a socket.

plug-in   A small program that another program can run, adding functions to the larger program.

public domain   A legal term referring to works that are not covered by copyright (either due to age, to not having their copyright maintained, or to having material deliberately put into the public domain by its creator) and thus can be copied or used freely.

RCA plug   A standard style of connector usually used for connecting audio and video components.

RealAudio   A popular standard for streaming audio.

RIAA   The *Recording Industry Association of America*, a group that acts as advocate for the interests of a number of CD and cassette publishers.

Rio   A popular portable MP3 player made by Diamond Multimedia.

rip   To copy the digital audio information from an audio CD onto a computer.

sample   This term refers to a single digital measurement of a sound wave, with a series of samples being used to make digital audio recording. The term is also used to refer to segments of existing recorded works being included in a new work, as is often done with dance and hip-hop music.

SanDisc   A compact brand of flash memory storage.

SDMI   Short for *Secure Digital Music Initiative*, an attempt to create a digital audio file format that will be acceptable to the recording industry by alleviating their concerns about uncontrolled digital copying and reuse.

shareware   Programs that are distributed at no charge by the publisher, but with the expectation that the user will try them and then pay for them if they find the program is of use.

Shoutcast   A popular streaming audio solution supported by Winamp, often used for Internet radio stations.

skin   A file or group of files that creates an alternative look for a program without really changing its function.

SmartMedia   A popular standard for flash memory cards, used by MP3 players, digital cameras, and other portable devices.

socket   A connector that one inserts another connector into; also called a *jack*.

software   The programs and information that a computer uses. This is in contrast to *hardware*, which are the more physical portions of a computer. For example, a CD-ROM is hardware, but the data stored on the CD-ROM is software.

Sonique   A program used for playing MP3s and other digital audio.

sound card   An internal computer device used to turn computer data into output for speakers, and to digitize audio from outside the computer.

streaming audio   Digitized sound that you listen to at roughly the same time as it is being sent over the Internet.

tag   A piece of descriptive text embedded into an MP3 system.

tethered system   A hardware MP3 playing device designed to remain connected to your computer.

theme   An alternative design for a program's appearance, similar to a *skin*.

Usenet   A system of online message boards available through the Internet.

variable bit rate   A system of MP3 encoding that does not record every segment of the music at the same bit rate.

VBR   See *variable bit rate*.

Virtuosa Gold   A player/encoder program for MP3s and other digital audio formats.

WAV   A format for uncompressed digital audio files.

Winamp   A popular player program for MP3s and other digital audio formats.

Index

D

281

X-Z

Read This Before Opening the Software

Licensing Agreement

CD–ROM Installation Instructions

If you have AutoPlay turned on, your computer will automatically run the CD-ROM interface. If AutoPlay is turned off, follow these directions:

1. Insert the CD-ROM into your CD-ROM drive.
2. From the Windows desktop, double-click the **My Computer** icon.
3. Double-click the icon representing your CD-ROM drive.
4. Double-click the icon titled **START.EXE** to run the interface.